Kendal On Hudson Library

Please Return

Beads & String

Marnie Reed Crowell

Ann Chwatsky

Beads & String

a Maine island pilgrimage

by Marnie Reed Crowell

with photographs by Ann Flewelling

BEADS & STRING: a Maine island pilgrimage
Copyright © 2008 by Threehalf Press
PO Box 97, Sunset, Maine 04683

Written by Marnie Reed Crowell; photography by Ann Flewelling
Designed by Ann Flewelling with Marnie Reed Crowell

Other photo credits: *March Eiders,* Leslie Clapp; *April Salamander Hunters,* Ken Crowell; *February Barred Island in Snow,* Marnie Reed Crowell.

All rights reserved. Printed in the United States of America. No part of this book may be used or reproduced in any manner whatsoever without written permission except in the case of brief quotations embodied in critical articles and reviews.

www.threehalfpress.com

Library of Congress Control Number: 2008922564
ISBN 978-0-98-2177-1-1

There was a real possibility that we would lose the stories of the generous people to whom we owe the ring of Deer Isle conserved lands open to the public.

To them this book is dedicated.

My husband Ken and I knew all the donors or their children, so I set out to record these inspiring stories. Every one save Emily Muir, whose death inspired the project, read the manuscript and provided insights into their motivations.

Proceeds from the sale of this book will go to Island Heritage Trust, but the real profit will be that the stories may be available in years to come to inspire future generations to comparable deeds of generosity and idealism.

Marnie Reed Crowell
Sunset, Maine
2008

| CONTENTS |

March —— TENNIS PRESERVE —— | 03 |
Woodcock
Elvers

April —— SETTLEMENT QUARRY —— | 23 |
April Flurry
Vernal Congress

May —— ISLANDS —— | 43 |
Butterfly Collection

June —— SHORE ACRES —— | 61 |
Secrets

July —— MARINERS MEMORIAL PARK —— | 89 |
Spotted Sandpiper

August —— BEACHES —— | 113 |
Summer

September	PINE HILL	| 133 |

Lee

October	HOLT MILL POND	| 151 |

Fall Weave

November	SCOTT'S LANDING	| 169 |

Sky Poet
Thanksgiving, Deer Isle

December	HERITAGE, MAN-MADE	| 193 |

Burnt Cove Church, Felsted,
Heritage House, Opera House, Sellers House
Captain Al Shepard/Pace House,
Squire Ignatius Haskell House/Pilgrim's Inn

Recipes

January	CROCKETT COVE WOODS	| 221 |

January Dusk

February	BARRED ISLAND PRESERVE	| 249 |

Profound Cold

AFTERWORD	| 279 |

March —— TENNIS PRESERVE

It feels as if the whole weight of winter has been aiming at this moment, and like a comet, it has passed us by. Day by day the spring sun gets stronger but every night the mud refreezes. I sit parked in my car, in the midst of a sea of mud, spring melt beginning, waiting for Ann. I'm buoyed by hope, the hope I always have when embarking on a new creative project. I anticipate that Ann will be someone to whom I can introduce the joys of this Island and someone with whom I can share my pleasure at this special place. The sunshine warms me. I feel it's a fairly sure bet that we will find eider ducks here on the lee side of the Island in their spectacular courting aggregations.

Eider duck spring congregations are one of the wonders of the natural world, and the trip to see them is well worth the effort. When we get a fine day and the sun is out as it is now, the local fishermen all across the Island are outdoors with their boats which have been spending the winter stored on stilt props in their front yards. Sign of Spring.

This morning the shore cliffs and boulder faces are gleaming with melt water from the land. Fortunately the process has so far been gradual. Quick, heavy runoffs mean there will be no adequate recharge of the water table—and our wells will go dry. The fresh waters seeping into the sea are almost as much a spring sign as are the maple sap runs over on the mainland. The invisible but vital nutrients mean microorganisms are spring blooming in the sea.

Years ago, when I first realized that I was going to spend the major part of my life here on the Island, I decided to walk its entire perimeter. I figured that given all the coves and points, this would take some time, but it would give me a privileged insight into the island. Coastal properties are now increasingly in the hands of new owners, owners "from away," owners who value their privacy and no longer honor traditional rules of access. But Maine law states that the area between the tides is open to the people of the State of Maine. More specifically, the law states that there shall be public access below mean high water, for fishing, fowling, and navigation. I figured as a biologist I could claim the first, and as a bird watcher I ought to be able to claim the second.

Recent court findings have made me doubt my rights, however. How about navigation? Could I claim that? Some friends of mine are working on kayaking around the whole perimeter. My first time out in a kayak here, I was rolled by a wave. Over I went, life jacket, helmet and all, into the cold water. I don't have quite the sense of balance I used to. I fell while ice skating in the moonlight one January evening and cracked my skull. Hence the helmet, which I was not wearing on the night of my skating and subsequent helicopter ride to the hospital. Now I do about as well as anyone else at not falling, but I am no good at catching myself once I start to go over. So, better not get too ambitious about kayaking.

I've summered here forty seasons and lived here year round for ten. Eventually I realized that Deer Isle is not a single island; it is a cluster of islands close enough to be linked by causeways for landlubbers. I tremble to think of the total mileage of the combined perimeters but that total is a non-issue. I might think it a good idea to challenge less-generous interpretations of the law by outlaw forays, but scrambling around on slippery, seaweed-covered intertidal rocks is out of the question. One more serious tumble would surely be my last.

Today feels like a poem day. I was in college when I first learned that those vertical rows of characters floating on the Asian paintings I admired were actually poems. Gary Snyder, Jack Kerouac and Alan Watts were in on the secret and D. T. Suzuki's translations of Japanese works on Zen and the arts were suddenly becoming widely available. Haiku became popular in elementary grades during the years my sons were in school but not yet where we lived. I had to wait some years to meet these little poems.

Haiku were raised to an art form, not just a party drinking game, by a 17th century Japanese poetry master named Basho. A student of Zen, he made a trek around his island, Japan, visiting a string of shrines, temples, special places. As he traveled, Basho composed lines of poetry in his head. These subsequently became powerful miniatures that established haiku as an art form. Basho also carried his brush and ink stone with him and recorded his impressions in paintings.

All my adult life I have been an ardent admirer of the work of T'ang and Sung dynasty Chinese literati, whose delicate and lyrical works combine poetry, painting, and calligraphy in equal parts. Transplanting Chinese arts to Japan—tea, calligraphy characters, Taoism integrated into Ch'an to become Zen—this fascinates me. I love the gorgeously detailed paintings of Chinese Bird and Flower tradition no less than the stark, highly abstracted black-ink paintings and calligraphy of the Zen masters.

When I discovered surimono, the woodcuts commissioned in the 1800's by Japanese poets' clubs as New Year's gifts, I knew that I too wanted to work with visual images side by side with poem words. I was charmed by the additional idea that a picture might merely allude to content while not precisely illustrating it.

And then I met Ann, a photographer, first through her photographs which were on exhibit at our local bank. Here is someone who pictures the world the way I do, I said to myself. I began to ask around, and Frederica Marshall, the local *sumi-e* teacher, knew who that photographer was. In fact, the photographer was currently studying with Frederica, finding that Asian ink brush painting was instructive for the making of photographs.

Ann was familiar with my writing. In short order we could see that a partnership might be possible. Collaboration would give us the opportunity to explore the rich connections between verbal and visual image-making. I plucked up my courage and proposed to this stranger that we two might metaphorically follow in the footsteps of Japanese artists and writers and go together on a journey, both recording our impressions. In this tradition, Basho and his friend Sora set out in March of 1689 on a pilgrimage to Japanese shrines. Similarly we might set out to explore a dozen of the Island's special places, the natural areas open to the public. We agreed, Ann and I, that we would make our journey over the coming year and record it with the tools at our disposal.

It is my notion that Basho would have loved to live today with word processing computers, liquid crystal projectors, digital cameras, page layout software, and hypertext-linked web pages. Both Ann and I take photographs and we both write, just as Basho and Sora both wielded their brushes. We have agreed, however, that we especially like the flavor of my words with her pictures. So far, it seems that Ann is much more comfortable with computer technicalities than I, and she is patient, even enthusiastic, about my constant exclamations on the natural world around us. We seem to be not yin and yang, but quite a workable pair.

This pilgrimage project feels just about the right size. We figure it ought to take us just about a year. That's long enough to get to know each other, to learn each other's style of working, and short enough to commit to.

Ann arrives and unloads her camera gear. Together we head down the trail of the Tennis Preserve picking our way carefully from dry patch to dry patch, avoiding both mud and ice. Our pilgrimage begins!

This morning large rafts of eiders were reported off the bar in Sunshine. The nearest neighbor says she always sees them there in the thousands about the time of the vernal equinox. That would be a couple of days ago. Long-tailed ducks are still here and yodeling in the bay out in front of our house. Earlier, when ice sheets sealed all the coves on the lee side of the Island, sizeable rafts of eiders were off our bold shore on the west side, but they were so far offshore that I couldn't hear the mysterious "wildebeest" sounds Ann and I are hearing now.

Whak, wak, wak, wak. Aahooaghaa, aaunh, oounh. Wak, wak, wak.

Now that they can get to their favorite mussel-covered flats, the eiders are congregating once again on the shallow east side coves. What are they doing in their displaying and vocalizing? They flap and splash and rear back as if they are jazz trumpeters. How they bend those notes! What a wonder of the world is any large aggregation of animals! I am particularly fond of winter eider groups as so often I see them bobbing unconcernedly on steely cold grey Atlantic waters. Perhaps best of all is when a blizzard of snowflakes hisses down into the roily waters. So? The eiders take it in their perfectly-adapted stride, as they always have.

Brad Allen of Maine's Inland Fisheries & Wildlife Department says we winter most of the birds from the St. Lawrence, New Brunswick, Nova Scotia and Newfoundland. Molting birds here in August have been banded, so we can tell that what we have here in the winter is one big metapopulation of the birds from the provinces as well as our own local crop. About half of our local birds have headed south for the winter, to Long Island, to the Cape, etc. I wonder what proportion of our human population has headed south as well?

Under the surface of the sea, the first of the anadromous fish are returning to make their way upstream to breed. In the small creeks are the smelts, "a good munch" according to an eel fisherman I once met in the cove here by the Tennis Preserve. Eels, too, are making their way back from the Sargasso Sea. The small transparent form of eels known as "glass eels" turn dark when they encounter the fresh water. Then, they are known as elvers. No one has set the elaborate netting traps for elvers here for several years and Maine is thinking of declaring eels an endangered species.

The melt today makes things messy, the lane into the Tennis Preserve a challenging combination of old snow, overnight ice glaze, and mud. The mid-morning sun is noticeably gaining its spring strength and we are almost warm. Cozy in the miracle of polyester fleece, we find it lovely to stand at the water's edge and look and listen. Who needs summer for a day at the shore? Summer means crowds. Who needs crowds? Well, the eiders certainly do.

All winter the black-and-white birds that came down from the arctic have been displaying to one another, but now they seem to be reaching a frenzy of head bobbing, ducking head and shoulders under water, and surfacing with a splash. The eiders improve on this with their own specialty: they flap their wings and virtually stand up on the water—all with considerable fuss.

Each species of our winter ducks—the goldeneyes, the graceful long-tails (known as old squaws in former politically insensitive days), the cute little buffleheads, the scraggly mergansers—each has a bobbing routine with hooting, tooting, yodeling calls, but perhaps the eider's grunting gabbling is most mysterious of all.

If we do not soon move on, Ann will have filled yet another memory card with images of eiders. There is no shortage of subjects before her. As we step carefully over the roots along the shoreside trail, I tell Ann about adventures this past summer with Tom, our youngest son, and his family at this preserve. The Tennis Preserve is one of the earliest pieces of conserved land here on the Island, gift of Dr. Edgar M. Tennis and his daughter Mimi Asbornsen. Coincidentally Tom knows Mimi. She and her husband Matt have their winter home near Chatham, New York, where Matt is a retired physician, and Tom is Senior Project Manager for the Columbia County land trust to which the Asbornsens are making a gift of land.

Begun in 1986, the Columbia Land Conservancy is one of the nation's oldest and most successful land trusts. One of its strong supporters from the start was Peggy Rockefeller at her winter home in the Hudson River Valley. Easements which the Rockefellers originally gave to American Farmland Trust have, in part, been transferred to the Columbia Land Conservancy.

The story goes that Peggy Rockefeller was discussing the pressures facing the lands of Penobscot Bay, where she and her friend Tom Cabot both owned summer homes. Both agreed that even their prosperous families could not just buy all the properties worthy of being conserved. And even if they could afford to, they had the wisdom to know that the proper way to proceed would be to provide for local control and oversight of the resources. Maine Coast Heritage Trust was one of the results of their foresighted efforts. The American public has greatly benefited from the open space and conservation interests of Peggy and David Rockefeller—and not only in New York and Maine.

"It's admirable that the Rockefellers left natural areas as their legacy," Ann comments.

"The interesting thing about the Tennis Preserve—and for that matter, several others preserves around here—is that the gifts were made by folks who were decidedly Not Rockefellers," I say, musing.

"Did you know Dr. Tennis?"

"No, we never met, but we did meet Mimi and Matt and their daughters years ago when we went on a nature walk together. Mimi has spent nearly all of the summers of her life on Deer Isle, although the years from 1983-2000 tied Mimi pretty closely to the Asbornsen's farm in Columbia County. Milking Sweetie Pie the family cow, tending the chickens, freezing the peas, taking lambs to market—Matt figures they managed to grow some 80% of the family's food on their subsistence farm."

"You can't keep the farm out of some people," says Ann with a knowing smile.

"Yes, Mimi is ardent about her love of agriculture," I reply. "She once told me that she chose Wellesley College because of the farm-like open spaces of the campus. Graduate school in biology at the University of Pennsylvania is where she met Matt, who was in medical school preparing to become an internist.

"Mimi is energetic and attractive in the spare, lean way of a wren," I say, "but she might scold me for saying that. She's very practical and down to earth. You can easily picture her loving her farm and woods here, settling into precious summer days. Mimi and her husband are very generous about sharing both the land and the lore they have gathered about this place they so love. They're both eloquent and gentle.

"Last summer I turned the tables on them and went on a nature walk they gave. Matt carried along a photoboard with pictures he had copied from the historical society. He had all the facts and figures. In 1944, Mimi's father, Dr. Tennis, bought the Toothaker Farm, a property which dates back to the 1798 Proprietor's Map. Matt pointed out that many of the properties are shown with access only by sea, because the map predates roads on the Island. The farmhouse, when Dr. Tennis bought it, had no electricity and no indoor plumbing, but it did have a deep anchorage just off shore. It would make a wonderful summer retreat."

"Where was Dr. Tennis from?"

"He grew up in rural Virginia on the Chesapeake, the son of an oysterman-turned feed and grain store owner-turned local bank president. He wanted more than anything else to get back on the water. The shores of the Chesapeake were increasingly becoming built up, with real estate priced out of his reach, so he headed to the second largest bay on the eastern seaboard, Penobscot Bay.

"Dr. Tennis purchased the Davis Farm for back taxes in 1947, and a few years later he bought the adjoining Pickering woodlot. I've had fun reading about the first settlers to come to the Island. John Pickering arrived in the new country just twelve years after the Mayflower."

We come to a small clearing where the path forks. In the center of the old field is a cellar hole. Ann photographs the winter-worn weeds.

"I once had a photography instructor who was of the opinion that there is nothing to photograph in Maine after November," Ann remarks. "According to him, after frost, it's all just compost."

"Nice compost." I can see that Ann is capturing the lovely shadow line a withered vine casts curving over a lichened rock.

When she's ready to move on, Ann asks, "Where's the Asbornsen's house? Did we pass it on the road on the way in?"

"You can't see their cottage from the preserve trails. Over the years Dr. Tennis modernized the Toothaker farm house. His wife and daughter enjoyed spending their summers there, and they saw no need to build a new place. By the early 1960's the real estate boom had reached Deer Isle. Shore property was being sold by the foot. It was also the era when people began to subdivide for profit. Mimi says that with 163 acres and close to two miles of shoreline, Dr. Tennis realized that she would have a problem holding on to this beloved property. What to do? Mimi and Matt recalled all the pleasant roadside stops in state parks that the family had enjoyed over the years on the long trips to Maine. They suggested that Dr. Tennis give 100 acres to the State of Maine with deed restrictions. After much thought, in 1972 he did just that. In 1976 Mimi gave 30 more acres, including just over half a mile of shore land, all of which has been conserved with an easement to Island Heritage Trust."

We choose the left fork of the trail that runs along the shore. "Over time, Mimi and Matthew put in and maintained a system of trails on the eastern part of the property, what had been Toothaker and Pickering lots. By great good fortune, the Asbornsens counted among their Island friends their neighbor Ann Hooke, and Barbara Seeley and her husband, Ralph. Ralph had laid out miles of trails in the forests near State College, Pennsylvania, where they made their winter home. Barbara was the daughter of novelist Gerald Warner Brace, author of some of our country's early best sellers set on a fictional version of the Island.

"Barbara's great-grandfather, Charles Loring Brace, had been a chum of Frederick Law Olmsted, and college roommate of Frederick's brother John. All three had toured the British Isles together and come home with a heightened sense of the value of open space for the common man. Young Olmsted went on to design New York's Central Park. At the end of their lives, it was Brace who invited the Olmsteds to come see for themselves what a wonderful island this was."

"Someone puts a lot of work into maintaining these trails."

On the former Davis property Barbara and Ralph not only laid out a northwestern Tennis Preserve trail, they spearheaded the effort to form a Walking Trails Group to oversee and maintain the trails. Then Ann Hooke lent Matt and Mimi her enthusiasm and energy to lay out a southwestern trail. Ann went on to become president of Island Heritage Trust, and Ralph was eventually nationally recognized for his hundreds of miles of volunteer trail work in Pennsylvania. But sadly, the Walking Trails group is no more. One by one they all grew too old or passed away.

Carrying on her father's tradition, Mimi has given land and conservation easements to Island Heritage Trust. Unfortunately for the state of Maine, its coffers have not kept up with its enthusiasm. The only ranger presence for the Tennis Preserve has been the once-a-year visits of the man assigned to the Holbrook Island Preserve over in Brooksville, some twenty miles away. The effort of this good man has so far been adequate, since the Asbornsens and their allies, now joined by Island Heritage Trust, have tirelessly looked after the Preserve.

One can see the wisdom of designating a second conservation entity to oversee things, to ensure that the terms of a gift are met in perpetuity. Who could have foreseen the rise of local land trusts, the diminishing of state resources, and their changing roles as custodian for our communally-used lands? At present, Island Heritage Trust manages the Tennis Preserve. The Trust didn't even exist when the original gift was made. Only gradually has the land trust movement come to its current prominence. Over the years The Nature Conservancy has changed its role, gradually shifting from acquiring local preserves to concentrating on large holdings of bioregional significance. Nearly everybody now recognizes that a local land trust fulfills a unique and vital role. Ann knows a thing or two about land trusts herself, having served on the board of a local land trust during her years in the Appalachian mountain loveliness of Georgia.

The preserve trail loops around the point. At one place on the shore of the Asbornsen property, though not near the public trails, there is a shell midden. Not only the ducks but the Etchemins, the early Native Americans, precursors of modern Wabenaki, Penobscots and Passamaquoddys, had sense enough to spend several thousand winters on the lee side of the Deer Isle island group.

I cannot show Ann precisely where the midden lies, but archeologists could. They excavated here in recent summers and safely covered up the areas again, protecting them from the thoughtless predations of pot hunters. Such information is worth more than the humble remains pot hunters usually turn up.

"The field school they had here a couple of summers ago found the area pretty much dug over, but they did turn up an interesting coin called a jeton. Jetons aren't really currency but they were used in Europe for counting goods. Jetons were subsequently used by the French trading with the Indians. The jeton they found here had a hole drilled through it. Maybe someone wore it as a decoration."

"Bling!"

"Precisely!"

We take a short spur trail threading through spruces and yellow birch old enough to give the effect of a graceful canopy and come upon a small fenced graveyard, carpeted with the sere remains of lily of the valley. The blooms should be quite lovely in few months. To me the lichens on the stones look elegant, but maybe you have to be a botanist to love them. Several stones have attractive carvings: a gaff rigged sloop under sail, a lily, a weeping willow, and clasped hands.

I point out the the name Capt. John Toothaker on a stone at the far right in the front row. "Matt Asbornesen told me that the Toothaker family had changed their name from Whitaker and fled from England due to religious persecution. According to family tradition, Elijah Toothaker, the Deer Isle pioneer who came to this farm may be buried here without a stone. He was great-great-great grandson to John and Mary Toothaker who were accused in the 1692 Salem witch trials. What we humans inflict on one another in the name of intolerance! May they all rest in peace, wherever they are."

A memorial stone tells us Capt. William S. Toothaker died in defense of his country near Richmond in 1865, at age 37. Matt has told me that then-Private Toothaker died of so-called swamp fever, which is usually malaria. He died just days before the war ended. I can't decide whether I think it's an irony or somehow fitting that this Island fisherman who'd spent so many hours crewing on fishing schooners died on board a troop transport ship on the James River and he's buried in Virginia. By virtue of having been mentioned in Ken Burns's PBS program *The Civil War*, this man now has the additional distinction of representing the 99 Deer Isle men who went off to that war, especially the ten or so killed or wounded in the strife. In summer months his stone here is marked with our one nation's flag.

The breeze from the sea sighs in the tree tops. I suggest that we follow the path back to the clearing. "Some day," I say over my shoulder to Ann, "I wonder if my grandchildren and others will read my words and know that there have always been idealistic fools who spend their lives for others, for future possibility."

"The struggle to keep a livable planet in the face of human population numbers may be every bit as wrenching as The War Between the States," Ann suggests.

We circle out the Davis Cove shore loop to what was once the Davis Farm. Nothing remains but a few apple trees in the clearing, some bare lilac bushes, and stones that show where the house and barn once stood. Ann finds much to photograph.

"The photographs Matt copied from the historical society show the farm in its glory days. Matt has made it a personal quest to trace the story of twenty-three-year-old Roswell Perry Davis coming in 1873 from Carmel, Maine to establish himself here. Roswell's father invented such things as overshot mill wheels, pill box patterns, and wooden foot lasts for boot and shoemaking. How's that for Yankee ingenuity? In short order the son set his own resourceful hand to building a wharf here."

Ann and I tramp down to the shore where we find a rusted iron ring still protruding from the granite blocks. "Here you could tie up a small coasting schooner and wait for the tide to return."

As we retrace our way through the brush, I describe a photo Matt has, dated 1905, showing the field well-trimmed, the house well-kept, and nine children posed out front. Sadly, the third son, John, who ended up with the farm, also ended up making a reputation for himself as the laziest man folks ever met.

"Mimi said that John was so lazy that when a wheel fell off his wagon, he never repaired it; he walked. Two farmhouses in succession fell down around him. His wife finally left him, although Mimi says she heard she loyally continued to keep him in occasional soups and stews which she cooked and brought him."

Dr. Tennis had permitted John to remain at the farm even after the purchase. The physician in Matt Asbornsen speculates that an illness of this unfortunate man whom he only knew from brief greetings may not have been recognized. A neighbor told Matt of going as a boy with his father to visit John Davis. The two men got drunk on moonshine and passed out. Although diagnosis from the distance of time is always speculative, it's not unlikely that an overdose of bad moonshine, with potential for the harmful byproducts of improper distillation, may have doomed 'lazy' John to dementia or who knows what."

A single dark butterfly calls our attention. It is a Mourning Cloak. Like bears, these dark ones hibernate and come out when the spring sun shines. I look in vain for another of the first butterflies of the year to appear, the Compton's Tortoiseshell. I often see one at the swamp where alders line the road to my house. For me, the humble alders often offer a welcome first sign of spring. I can't see their nitrogen-fixing capabilities; I don't see any signs of returning life in their bare branches; but I know to pause by alders in the spring sunshine.

"This field looks like a perfect spot for woodcock," I say. "They should be coming back any day now. I'm told Dr.Tennis had no use for alders. They were hard to hunt through, and he liked to hunt woodcock. He tried to make sure the wet swales didn't grow up with alder, although it got harder and harder to find anyone to mow the fields as the years passed."

I point out to Ann the handsome spruce trees that ring the field. "Dr. Tennis and his local friend Peter Eaton planted those groves of red spruce which he got as seedlings from the state. Spruces are at least an appropriate species. I remember when the state Conservation Department in New York was encouraging us to plant autumn olive and Tatartian honeysuckle for wildlife food and cover on our farm. Now we are encouraged to pull them out as invasives."

Ann gently smiles, ever the non-judgmental clinical psychologist that she is in her other life. "Red spruce do grow well on the Island, don't they."

Red spruce is far and away the dominant species here; not an invasive, but an example of changing patterns in vegetation. "The Asbornsens say that their farmhouse was once a beacon for sailors making their way back to Inner Harbor. The old photographs show the surrounding hillsides almost completely cleared."

Old fields are growing back to spruce forest now that hay is not much in demand. Current shorelands zoning restrictions favor leaving a dense screen of vegetation, not just because it's currently the fashion to hide the houses, but also to help control potentially harmful runoff to the sea that feeds us. In time, when Mimi and Matt's two daughters, Karin and Birgit, are grown and followed by the next generation, the landscape will once again have changed.

We complain about reading that oatmeal will cure your cholesterol problems and whatever ails you; and then that it will not. Of course the truth lies somewhere in between. Dr. Tennis and Dr. Asbornsen would be the first to agree that what seems like good medical practice changes as our knowledge evolves. This is no less true for nurturing the body of what many like to call Gaia, planet Earth, than for our individual bodies. We humans can only do the best we can, trying what we think are good environmental practices.

We bless Dr. Tennis and the Asbornsens for the gift of the preserve.

Evening, 6 PM, and the moon is full and glowing like a pearl behind a cloud cover. It's a sweet early spring evening. We heard the first junco trilling its spring song this noon. Song sparrows were staking out the lilac bush territory at the old farm site on the Tennis Preserve, and the mourning doves are cooing. In spite of everyone grouching about how late spring is, and how much snow we have, the birds quietly stick to their spring schedules. Eagles have been reported in what appear to be mating-related aerial acrobatics at the most unlikely spots around town.

Eagles are still so unusual here that we tend to think of them as wilderness birds. We don't quite know what to make of the tumble over the Post Office, by the school or over at the bank. Giving up DDT, embarking on enthusiastic stewardship—and having the right habitats—have combined to make Deer Isle more or less the jewel in the crown of the state's efforts at eagle restoration. Our town has one of the highest numbers of nesting pairs in the state. Two adult bald eagles have recently been seen standing on the nest at Barred Island. We have been seeing both the white-headed adults and various permutations of brown immature eagles all winter, and now it looks like they are getting ready to have another go. Hooray.

6:05 PM, and the first "bzeep" of the woodcock greets us. He is what Ann, growing up amid the potato fields of Aroostook County, knows as the timberdoodle. I'm just a little envious of this old field. Where I live, tucked in the spruces, we do not see woodcock. I miss them from the part of my life which was spent on an old dairy farm in far upstate New York.

Ann makes her home just over the Deer Isle-Sedgwick bridge, fronting the Bagaduce River. Around her house lie plenty of fields and open country. She gets more timberdoodles—and more snow—than we do. I find it quite remarkable that the effect of the sea can be so dramatic. Just a few miles inland on "the continent" it's enough colder that they get snow when we get rain.

Looking over the dirty snow and brown and barren grass, I confess it's hard to wait for snowdrops when you know that in Boston, even outside Portland, snowdrops are already in bloom. I know I might still see the dark blue sesame seed-like swarms of collembolans, the spring tails, on the snow if I go into the shaded woods cross country skiing again. If we get a few warm days, instead, I might see a few intrepid spiders.

It's not the same.

Going Overboard

Snow flakes fall arrow straight to earth.
Lobster boats that wintered
under blue wraps in the snug tide zone
of defiant Christmas lights now turtle
ponderously back to sea
down potholed roads
lined with dripping birches
in celebration of last snow.

Elvers

I see him walking on the clam flats by the great butterfly bat wing nets.
What is it about his jeans, cap, and rubber boots that signal islander just as surely
as he reads me woman-from-away before we even speak?

What are you catching?
Eels,
he calls over his shoulder and keeps on slogging.
It seems inappropriate to continue hollering on the early morning air
so I stand on a rock
and wait.
He's not going to hurry his pace. I'm not going to retreat.
We wait for each other to finish our business.

I eye the rigging:
four huge gray butterflies or bats, take your choice depending on how macabre your taste, or whether you know the symbol for bat wings on Ming pottery. Dead panels, like a drowned embrace, drape full slack across the mud to hang when the tide comes back suspended from plastic pipe strung like soda straws on pot warp lines bright orange, perhaps from one great spool strung out across the cove here to bamboo, there to aluminum tent pole guyed all in turn by more orange warp and weighted at the ends by granite.

The mans slogs slowly from rock to rock
adjusting the muddy weights with some private precision
righting and pressing the poles to his own satisfaction.
At the confluence of each wingspread a wooden box,
not all that different froma shoe box except
that at each hinder end he's hung a bag like pantyhose.

Carefully he does not glance my way,
carefully he inspects this masonite center of mysteries,
reties its knots and makes his way closer to where I stand.
If he's reluctant he's damned if he'll show it and he says to me
Elvers, glass eels you might call 'em. Send 'em to the Orient.
I want to tell him of the ancient lucky symbol but I say instead
Do you ever eat them?
Nope.

Do you go smelting too?
Why yes, he says,
and quickly calculating what else I need to understand
 he manages not to sound condescending as he tells me
you can't go smelting at the same time you have these traps out.
Generously he adds
I go to a nice creek up the cove for smelts.
I like to go for smelts, myself. Fry up a good munch.
Have 'em for breakfast, or whatever meal comes next.

I recognize he's telling me something about the order of his life
so I ask, Do you check these traps every tide?
Yep.
Did you just get some?
No, I'm readjusting them now.
He says without my asking, The elvers only run at night. You ought to come down
here then. It's a sight to see, all the lights.

I ask what time the tide is high tonight.
Two-thirty he thinks. He's not lobstering just now.
Elvers make a nice way to fill in.

He can make a couple hundred a night.
But don't quit your day job? I say surprised
 when he does not banter
but says instead
I get kind of tired,
but it's nice down here at night. I hope we don't bother them
up at the house. You from the house?
No, I'm not.

Well, You want to come see.
Just a statement he makes, and I thank him and say
I will come some time,
hating that it sounds so much like empty courtesy.
A pause, sheerer than bat wings
hangs in the air as I calculate back and say,
You saw the comet here, then?

He straightens up, hands dripping from the fresh water sluice
of the little creek pushing back the sea. Perhaps
because he's been skirting so near the beauty of what keeps him here,
unmasked delight ambushes his face.
He throws his arms north to the heavens
in a wide gesture full of the wildness of it all.

Right up there it was, he says.
He meets my gaze and we grin together, cosmic islanders.

I'll come some night, I say.
Me and the wife, he mumbles, just to be sure there was no misunderstanding,
We'll see ya.

April —— SETTLEMENT QUARRY —— 2

This morning the honking of geese serenaded me before I was quite awake, and then the trilling of juncos. Fox sparrows, looking huge and ruddy, scratched energetically under the feeder in that distinctive two-footed gesture of theirs. Ann says she heard geese this morning as she was gearing up to come over for our expedition. The evening of the very day I e-mailed her about encountering the woodcock, one stopped her on her road. E-mails from friends all over the peninsula have reported robins in the lawn, juncos in the spruces, and geese in the pewter skies. It is emotionally confusing to think of that great race up the continent, so welcome from our point of view, perhaps desperate from the birds' eye view.

Just now the town roads have a new traffic. This is the season when most fishermen put their boats back in the water; going overboard they call it. Boat names also often exhibit a similar black humor. And this is mud season on dirt roads. I am very fond of unpaved roads. They are kinder on our environment than pavement, which reflects heat and increases toxic run off, to name a couple of the more obvious ecological reasons. However, just now, it is hard to cheer for mud.

The unpaved road up to the quarry in Oceanville is a well-built exception. It cannot be called mud, not really. It is granite, the specific form geologists call Stonington Granite and the countertop trade more generally refers to as Deer Isle Granite. The road from the head of the quarry face was built for the trucks that worked the Settlement Quarry. These days the granite quarried here goes off-island in huge blocks sent to Rhode Island or Canada to be cut. The hulks of cutting sheds here now stand empty. Stonington, at the height of the quarrying operations, had a population about twice the size of what it has today.

I remember when Mary McGuire served as speaker at the dedication of the Settlement Quarry Preserve, a most satisfying moment for her. Mary McGuire, dainty little woman now just short of her hundredth birthday, perky in her US Navy veteran's cap, has long been a fixture at the Island Memorial Day observances. In World War II she served in Naval Intelligence. With a BA from University of Maine and a PhD from Columbia, and years on the faculty at Chatham College in Pittsburgh, this retired Stonington schoolteacher is typical of the kind of Islander who is intelligent, well-read, and strong in support of local causes.

Mary's father Frank McGuire moved to Deer Isle in 1903 to manage the cutting shed at the quarry. It's hard to picture, but at the turn of the century the state of Maine had some 55 granite quarries in operation. Stonington was "home" to perhaps 2,000 men who worked in the quarries on Crotch Island, Green Island, Moose Island, St. Helena, and Devil Island. The Marsh Settlement quarry eventually became known as Settlement Quarry. Some of the larger buildings around town at one time were rooming houses boarding some of these workers. I've even heard that some workers lodged themselves by camping under nearby granite ledges, not such a different story from today's service industry workers trying to make do with camp ground accommodations.

In 1922 Frank McGuire and his brothers James and Thomas purchased Crotch Island, and later the Settlement Quarry. The names of Mary's brothers Francis (Nick), Thomas, and Robert are memorialized on granite benches overlooking the quarry. Like any risky and dangerous extractive process, the quarry has had a colorful history, with both triumphs and heartbreak, boom and bust. The benches symbolize our past put in perspective, the granite industry, literally and figuratively, underlying much of our history.

Once you learn the look of "our" Deer Isle granite, it's an interesting challenge to see where you can spot it. It is found in such cities as Boston and Philadelphia and New York, in the Manhattan Bridge piers, the Triboro Bridge, George Washington Bridge, the "Deer Isle Pink" in Grand Central Terminal in New York, Rockefeller Center skating rink, the Museum of Fine Arts in Boston, and Bancroft Hall at the US Naval Academy. Seams of granite that were prone to fracture in undesirable ways were blamed for the demise of this Settlement quarry. Granite from Crotch Island was landed here and packaged for shipment by truck to the cemetery in Arlington as part of the John F. Kennedy Memorial.

Granite blocks now ride in roped and lonely grandeur atop flat bed trucks booming down our roads. I try not to be following too closely when they make their way over the arching bridge off island. They make the bridge shudder. The granite blocks, the size of small tool sheds, have been quarried these days out at Crotch Island and landed at the wharf here at the foot of the Oceanville quarry for transfer to the trucks that carry the granite away to be polished and fashioned into granite counter tops.

We no longer pave our cities' roads with granite paving blocks. We make our buildings with cement and steel and concrete. Economic considerations today even allow us to ship granite quarried and cut in China for decorating our gardens. Environmentally obscene, but far from the only way in which economic forces work at cross purposes with environmental health.

Besides the horrifying number of schooners filled with paving blocks that, in the days of windjammer shipping, used to get caught in storms and sunk, granite also had other ways of killing men. I knew a few old quarry workers here who slowly died of silicosis, granite dust in their lungs. They were the lucky ones. Others died faster, none more dramatically than the unfortunate victims of blasting and crushing accidents. The preserve here is a lovely place, but it is also a monument to these workers. Perhaps it is not such a coincidence after all that local pronunciation rhymes 'quarry' with 'worry.'

The dynamite storage ruins we encounter near the quarry face are not only historically interesting, they look as if they might be a specially-commissioned art work. A bit farther on, the sunny seat where we like to bring winter picnics is essentially a large crevice in the granite, around two sides of which has been wedged a bench. The granite walls act like a reflector oven. A large granite block in the center functions as picnic table.

The view here from the head of the quarry is splendid. Swans Island and the blue of Duck Harbor Mountain on Isle au Haut decorate the horizon. The ducks that gave their name are the eiders. When the birds were flightless in molt they were herded into the cove there. The duck drives provided welcome food for most frugal Yankee diets.

We enjoy the picture sign here that labels all the islands spread before us. It is quite a challenge to match all of them, stacked and hiding one another as they are.

Ann is much taken with the light on the blocks of granite and the traces of drilled cores for blasting. We can see where the granite cracked in layers parallel to the surface as if breathing a huge sigh of relief when the overlying rock had been gradually eroded and glacially scoured away. These horizontal joint sets were used by quarrymen. In addition to the natural sheeting joints themselves, we see where superheated water forced a mineral soup into cracks in what was a paroxysm of intrusions. Bands of color resulted where the minerals slowly cooled.

Here at the quarry there are beautiful bands of fine-grained pink stuff a label tells us is called aplite. We recall such pink and also white quartz in jagged lines in the salmon pink granite of the cove at the Tennis Preserve that Asbornsens tell us is aptly called The Oven. The granite itself is an interesting pudding, a mixture that boiled up from deep within, some 360 million years ago. By definition, granite is this mixture. The recipe is 1 cup of pink feldspar, 1 cup white feldspar, and 1 cup gray quartz. Mix in tiny flecks of black mica called biotite, like currants in a pudding. Cool. Melt the finest granite grains and squirt this aplite sauce into any cracks remaining after the pudding has set.

You can "read" what amounts to instructions for how long to cook the pudding, and at what temperature. The minerals of this molten magma crystallize out at different melting points. During a long uninterrupted cooling period, the feldspars may "grow" large. Since the granite was at one time five or ten miles down, one can also make inferences about how deep the crystals were: the deeper the cooler; the cooler the larger the crystals of feldspar. The pink and the white shapes may suggest anything from roses to gull droppings; the black bits look like cockroaches, or whatever else your fancy dictates. Very Taoist.

We cross a bare stretch of granite with a line of cairns gently steering us to avoid trampling the fragile vegetation. Even without being a botanist, you get the feeling that this is not unlike a mountain top. The tiny plants here bake in summer, freeze in winter, and get scoured by the winds. I suppose the breeze is even salty here.

This place is so reminiscent of a Greek amphitheater that the drama and dance folks are delighted. They have already had a very successful dance performance here and last summer an Opera House Arts group including Pilobolus dancers helped stage another performance with lots of local participation, a sort of dress rehearsal for what they're calling *Quarryography*. I love it that the Pilobolus Dance Company takes its name from a mold, an organism which has the ability to "sling-shot" its black spores toward sunlight at amazing velocity. The professional dancers in Quarryography are wonderfully athletic. Their lean bodies look lovely against the rough stones.

They use a back hoe in their ballet. Rick Weed has a big excavator that hauls up a giant puppet made of cable. He really gets into working the big machine with the dancers. There were such things as backhoe rodeos, and Rick has been in the one for Maine.

Ann takes a last long look at the open quarry basin with its great benches and blocks before we leave it to head into the woods. "Some night I'd like to see the stars from here, " she muses.

"There ought to be very few lights to interfere," I say. "Awfully dark for photographs I would think," I tease. "It's a wonder nobody ever broke their neck here in the era when this was a teen party spot."

I consider the human dramas for which this place has provided the stage setting. What an opera these stones could sing. The establishment of Settlement Quarry as a preserve open to the public is a tale akin to both grand opera and melodrama. Just as there was no agreement among the owners and workers at the granite quarries, among the ship captains and their crews, between the hotel owners and landlords and the town's tradesmen and the farmers about what the future of Stonington ought to be, so too in our time, there was little agreement in 1996 over what the fate of the Settlement quarry lands ought to be.

The Trust for Public Lands, a national non-profit organization, worked with the land trust to purchase the Quarry property. In addition to a few lots for residential and commercial enterprises, a two-acre public deep water boat launching ramp on Webb Cove was offered to the town with the state Bureau of Parks and Recreation agreeing to pay most of the purchase price.

The town voted it down. The corporate world retirees had their agenda; the young fleece-clad recreation enthusiasts in their kayaks had their ideas; the fishermen in Stonington had their own ideas about making sea access available to folks from off-Island. Not enough attention was paid to soliciting opinions from all or apprising everyone in town of the nature of the proposed transactions. No matter how well-intentioned the project, suspicions of self-interest and misinformation swirled in higher and higher tides and threatened to engulf all.

I know from attending national land trust gatherings that ferreting out the stories behind preserves and conservation easements across the country is apt to yield decidedly mixed conclusions. Greed, ignorance, short-sightedness, power struggles: we hear it all. Parents who do not trust their children, siblings who will do anything to keep family land out the hands of one another, divorce settlements turned nasty. Because what I know of our friends here does not much match that profile, I must use Ann as a sounding board to keep my descriptions of folks here realistic. As a trained clinical psychologist she offers another perspective on family dynamics. We both, however, have faith in people and in our ability to learn from our mistakes.

We make our way down the trail winding through the lower reaches of the quarry. Only traces remain of the cables, winches, derricks, cranes, coal-fired boilers and even a railway that once worked here. It must have been an impressive sight in its heyday. Ann asks me to explain just what is the difference between so-called Stonington granite and Deer Isle granite. Oh, my.

"Ann," I laugh, "if it's hard for people who don't come from this Island to understand why a twelve by twelve rock needs two town governments, just let me tell you about the geology here. Perhaps I should say t'was ever thus."

According to Roger Hooke, a geologist who retired to the Island, there are three facies, or varieties, of granite recognized here. All three are called Stoningon granite or Deer Isle granite, depending on which geologist is talking. They are all called Deer Isle Granite in marketing, too.

Roger would probably basically agree with my "pudding" analogy, but he would want to talk more about the "oven" in which it was cooked, the magma chamber. The Settlement Quarry and Crotch Island facies formed near the middle and top of the magma chamber, respectively. They are finer grained and have more white feldspar. Some of the pink feldspar grains rimmed with white feldspar reflect circulation of the grains in the magma chamber. The bright salmon-color pink feldspar grains that are found at Oak Point—once called the Oak Point facies of Deer Isle granite—those are thought to have accumulated at the bottom of the magma chamber.

"Darker crumbs at the bottom, light custard in the middle, whipped cream on top. Picture some of the Island's famous Grape Nuts puddings, the ones flipped with the crumbs on the bottom."

Ann looks a bit puzzled. I tease her that she lives in Sedgwick, across the Reach, where perhaps Grape Nuts pudding for the past fifty years hasn't been as popular as it is here on the Island.

"The granite from Sedgwick is all grays, none of the pinks. When you find gray granite cobbles on the beach, you can be pretty sure they are from over the bridge. All the granite is thought to have intruded into the volcaniclastic Castine and the Ellsworth schists that make up Little Deer and the northern part of the town of Deer Isle."

Ann smiles. "Deer Isle rocks! The Castine Volcanics and the Ellsworth Schists vs. the Deer Isle and Stonington Granites. Sounds like the state basketball championship tournaments."

"The Continental Collision Classic!"

Ann was born and raised in Maine, so she knows about basketball. However, one would only have to experience a single winter here to be aware of the high school basketball mania that grips the entire state each year.

Ellsworth schist makes up the northwestern third of Deer Isle. These rocks are metamorphosed sediments, various shades of greenish gray. They were once layers of sediments at the bottom of what geologists call the Iapetus Sea. They usually show wonderfully interesting folds, often with sparkles of platy micas gleaming in the layers.

Allen Myers, husband of our island Congregational minister, is himself an ordained minister as well as a geologist specializing in oceanography. He calls himself a "geologian." He gives a wonderful walk for Island Heritage Trust at the Tennis Preserve in which he most graphically describes the formation of the Ellsworth schists when the Iapetus sea floor laid down the sediments that were then squeezed and thrown up when the continental plates collided. Picture a ring of volcanoes squirting up at the edge of all this action. Then for a hundred million years there was no ocean here. Until the Triassic.

I relish the drama, in a speeded-up version that I can barely comprehend, of all those hydrothermal vents sizzling around us. Allen described continental glaciers as moving like cold honey poured onto a table somewhere west of Hudson Bay. As they oozed down to the coast here, the bottom was shuffling along with the movement of the plates. The preexisting ancient valley of the Penobscot River was flushed. The soil was removed, as well as the layer of rotten rock, scraping right down to bedrock in some places. In these rock deposits of the Ellsworth schists of Deer Isle, the town, men hoped to find copper and silver to mine from what are probably the remnants of the vents. And there's even a rare marble bed on the northern part of Deer Isle, metamorphosed limestone.

"The oldest rocks are in Deer Isle."

"Not Stonington?"

"Doesn't that sound as if it's some sort of social comment? The sense of rivalry between the two towns is very strong. People our age remember when there were two high schools, two basketball teams. And formerly, the sea captains mostly lived in Deer Isle, the quarrymen in Stonington. The sea captains shipped out every spring for a good part of a year or maybe even more. They were sort of emigrants. The quarry workers were mostly immigrants, Swedes, Scots, Irish, and Italians. The newest Stonington immigrants now are the ones who have money. They come from Texas, the South, England, wherever."

"And they too are changing the character of the place."

"You bet. These incoming artists and the Summer People and the tourists are certainly culturally distinct, identifiable by their accent and their clothing. The Island is still ethnically pretty homogenous, white, but we are getting a bit more diverse." As we pick our way along the quarry trail, I can't resist adding, "Stonington had a sort of outlaw reputation. In fact, the whole Island does."

Ann says, "Would-be newcomers can find that intimidating."

I laugh. "Yes, and perhaps some of us who live here don't try very hard to discourage that image. We've got enough people here. The other day we watched John Steed, the Opera House manager, and a crew filming a documentary about our so-called 'burners' who make those tire tracks on the roads. They're like graffiti artists. They lay rubber by standing on the brake and flooring the accelerator at the same time. A big puff of blue smoke, a noisy squeal. Interesting marks, a real calligraphy, and a bit of a class statement. I'm not sure how they know they are not going to meet someone coming the other way."

"It is worth your life to tackle the Island roads, the way the pickup trucks tear around," comments Ann.

"It has been like that ever since we've been here. The new Stonington now is really trying actively to steer its destiny. Working town, fishing community, or row of seasonal art galleries, boarded up and empty all winter. What combination do we want? It will be interesting to see what forces shape the Island next. Whatever comes, it will probably affect the whole Island. What started as territorial rivalry, differences based on how far you could walk or ride or sleigh, or where you fished, those distinctions are now irrelevant in the face of the current round of changes."

"The glacier scours all," Ann says, stopping to photograph a particularly handsome pattern in the rocks. She asks from behind the lens, "Can you tell the various rocks by looks?"

I laugh. "Well, Allen kept asking me on that walk to identify different kinds of lichen on the Tennis trail. I finally had to tell him that not only did many not have common names, but also you might well not tell the species just by looking. One does the analysis under a microscope and by chemical tests. Or one fakes it. He says it's the same for telling the rocks apart with accuracy. He calls the urge to give some answer of authority the 'male answer syndrome' or the 'science teacher syndrome.'"

We laugh.

"But there is some basic sorting you can do by eye. There are only at most a half dozen types of bedrock exposed here, depending on how you count them. There are the grey-and-pink granites and the salmon-pink Oak Point ones. All that is greyish green and dark is not Ellsworth schist, but that's a good first guess, particularly if the rock is clearly foliated, wavy, wrinkled, folded. The big boulder in the middle of the Tennis Oven cove is interesting because you can see that it has had pebbles tossed into it. Then in the collision of the continents the layers were subjected to stress—folded, squeezed, pulled—and the pebbles were squashed, smeared, deformed. It's called a pudding stone, and you probably can tell those by looking.

"Another recognizable look is the very distinctive, flinty, greenish rock speckled with white felsite from which many Indian arrowheads and tools were made. Artifacts in the middens here on the island are made from rock of Mt. Kineo in the Moosehead Lake region. That would have been brought here either as the raw stuff transported by the glacier, or in trade. It weathers to a grayish white, but it's still a distinct specked look.

"Roger is quite keen on what the family of serpentine rocks up at Pine Hill tells us. Darker grey coarse grained rocks with soapy green veinlets might be Pine Hill peridotites with serpentine, and the blacker green ones may be Torrey Pond Serpentinite from North Deer between Torrey Pond and Eggemoggin Reach. I can't tell the two but geochemists can." The Torrey Pond rock is a black, medium-grained intrusive igneous rock, rich in iron and manganese, originally formed as a basalt at a spreading center on the sea floor. While still part of the sea floor, the hot fluids circulating through the original basalt altered much of it to serpentine. The white veins are probably asbestos, a fibrous form of serpentine.

"Most of the Little Deer bedrock is Castine Volcanics. They can look just like the Ellsworth schists, but not as wavy. They're metamorphosed ash, tuff, and agglomerate—pebbles or even larger, spit out of volcanoes. Those volcanoes! Here! Five hundred million years ago. And then those granites intruded."

"And now it's PFAs!" chuckles Ann.

"So PFA doesn't really stand for Persons From Away; it's Petros From Away?" I say, detouring off the road back to the parking lot a short way to point out glacial polish and scratches to Ann. "Roger's main interest is glacial geology. Glacial till, which is a mixture of clay, silt, sand and gravel, covers much of the bedrock of Deer Isle. It was left by the ice sheet that advanced over Deer Isle about 30,000 years ago and lingered here for 14,000 years. The ice was about a mile thick over Deer Isle. Roger says that as ice moves across a landscape, it entrains rocks. Don't you just love that word, *entrains*? Like a sandpaper block, it grinds the entrained rocks against the underlying bedrock, leaving parallel scratches on the bedrock that reflect the direction of ice flow. See?"

The marks, like giant bear claw scratches, are quite evident on the granite.

"I love to look at the big boulders—what we used to call erratics, the ones which do not match most of our rocks here—and the smaller cobble stones on the beach, and guess where they came from. What I find really interesting about trying to read the beach rocks is that not only has the sea done its share of shaping, but rocks trapped in the moving glacial ice were themselves scratched in the process. Because these rocks could rotate, the scratches on them go in different directions. All this scratching and grinding produced a lot of fine sediment, and that's the matrix of the till."

"I enjoy looking at the boulder fields along the highway as I drive from Blue Hill to here," Ann declares. "I like to try to picture lakes and moraines and ice sheets."

We, Ann and I, are both of an age when geology was not much taught—at least not to women and not in small schools—and most of what we thought we knew has been reinterpreted since the 1970s, when plate tectonics theories began to be accepted. You can almost guarantee that whatever you read in older books, even those by so clear and fine a writer as John McPhee, is now being reinterpreted. It's all quite confusing, so geology interpretive walks here are always very popular.

"Well-drillers and town planners are both making use of all the geological mapping that Roger and his students and colleagues have been doing," I add. "I kid Roger that he loves to study not only what big sheets of ice do, but he's entranced by any big yellow earth mover."

"The boys and the toys," observes Ann. A former potter herself, she asks, "Aren't there some good clay deposits here too, gift of the glaciers?"

"Yes, the Presumpscot formation, marine clays deposited as the ice retreated from Deer Isle. The weight of all that glacier depressed Earth's crust below sea level. When the ice margin stood at Eggemoggin Reach, Deer Isle was under nearly 200 feet of water. The Presumpscot is composed of large quantities of silt and clay—rock flour—reduced by the grinding beneath the glacier. Then these fine particles were flushed out into the sea. The waves pick them up; the tides carry them back in, and in quiet coves they settle out. When the clay settles, it tends to stay put. Locally the clay contains fossil shells, with some species in it now found only in colder waters further north and off Iceland. The Presumpscot is normally light gray, but where it is exposed at the surface it has oxidized to pale yellow brown."

On all the walks I've been on, the conversation always gets around to global warming. Allen confesses that his wife Alice gets annoyed with him for his calm perspective on cycles of warm and cold, an attitude quite characteristic of all the geologists I know. We are most assuredly in another interglacial period, a temporary warming between colder periods. He concedes that for humans, to greatly accelerate the rate of changes is not a pleasant prospect. For Alice, and for me as biologist, such near-resignation is disconcerting. They think in terms of three hundred million or six hundred million years ago. All those zeros! We think in terms of this year's crop of bird nestlings, or the future of our own grandchildren, and theirs.

Oh, well. April is a challenging month here. It's a tease. One day we seem to have sweet sunny weather as nice as what the radio tells us is south of us, and the next day we seem plunged cruelly back into winter. Being near that great heat sink of ocean works to our disadvantage at this season. April is not Deer Isle's finest hour. Everyone seems to have flowers but us.

We walk down the old quarry road in companionable silence. Only a chickadee calls from time to time. It's the birds that have to be our consolation now. Perhaps it is just that the skies have been relatively quiet for the winter months that makes them seem so grand. Well, that's not fair to those wonderful winter ducks, most of whom are leaving us these days.

Winter ducks are the best-kept secret of the Island, the one feature I did not expect when I changed my status from a seasonal inhabitant to full-fledged year-rounder. Clearly the richness of the winter waterfowl scene is a private treasure the Islanders keep for themselves. Now that we are always nonchalantly scanning the skies for spring arrivals, I feel positively disloyal about it. I lie in bed each morning listening intently for some new bird song.

Mad April brings out the best and the worst in us.

Tonight is warm, raining like the tropics. We have been waiting for a night like this to go out and observe a normally hidden world. At 8 PM, just as it is getting fully dark, we rendezvous. Our expedition this time requires our spouses, Ken and Charlie. Calling all hands to hold umbrellas and flashlights! We head once again to Oceanville, following the main road to Settlement Quarry. We drive slowly, car windows cracked so we can hear those tiny frogs called spring peepers. At a swamp we pull over and listen. This is the marsh of the old Marsh Settlement. The occasional quacks that sound like ducks are wood frogs. The peepers sound more like they're screaming than singing. Really deafening.

Where the road twists through the woods, the pavement is thick with strange shapes, almost like angle worms. Quite an unfamiliar silhouette in the headlights. There! Is that a salamander? Or a willow leaf, a green bean, or a cigar? One rears up its head and looks around like a very miniature dinosaur, black with yellow polka dots. We observe that when a salamander lowers its head, it is about to scoot, arrow-like, forward. Scoot? There is no hint of speed about these little creatures.

Ann and I hop out of the car and walk quietly toward a group of them. Hesitantly I pick up a salamander; it seems to barely notice me. It feels silken smooth, strangely cool on my hand. What shall I do with it? Spotted salamanders are headed both ways across the road. Does that mean some have mated and are returning to the forest, while others are headed out to the pool? Do the car headlights confuse them? Or are they just not in a hurry?

Just then a car comes hissing by on the wet pavement. Horror! Yes, our headlights do reveal several now-squashed forms that so recently were salamanders. This is a conundrum. We are parked safely off the road so we do not alarm the passing traffic. If we were going to go out on the road to move the 'manders on their Big Night, we should certainly have reflective vests and some warning system of flaggers up the road. Goodness, this could get complicated.

I put the salamander safely in the grass at the road edge, but there is no way we could make a difference here; the numbers are simply too great. While the salamander did not feel slimy like a fish, it may not be good to handle them. If you handle a live fish, you risk destroying its protective anti-bacterial slime coat. Certainly after you have touched one salamander you could be in a position to transmit disease from one animal to the next. Maybe it's better not to touch them. But it's certainly not a good idea to let them get squashed. They will not move, even when gently nudged with a stick. So, reluctantly, we leave them alone. Maybe another year we can organize a guard crossing patrol.

We sit quietly for a time in the rainy night, watching to see what the salamanders will do. At the side of the road, blotchy spathes of emerging skunk cabbage stand like miniature hooded figures in vigil. Do salamanders time their Big Night Out by the calendar date or by temperature or other factors? Do they all have some sort of built-in rain gauge? In my garden the crocuses have withered and the daffodils have just fully opened. Red maples are in bloom and wrens are back singing in the woods.

One after another the salamanders put their heads down and start to move like so many pencils, gliding forward, propelled by some unseen, mysterious force. I suppose it is their wide eyes that make salamanders look so unthreatening, gentle, trusting—and as I am being anthropomorphic—none too smart. Since salamanders may move quite a distance from the woody forest duff where they spend most of their life to the vernal pool where they breed, we may be looking at what amounts to the entire salamander population of the Settlement Quarry Preserve.

Ann manages to figure out what she needs to know about getting photos without drowning her camera or getting too much light. To get just the right angle she stretches out on the rainy pavement.

"Charlie, please move the light. Over here. OVER TO THE RIGHT. Oh, it's my own headlamp. Sorry."

Ken walks back to the car to douse the headlights, leaving on the warning flashers. Out of the dark we hear him rather loudly, "Damn!" What did he do, bump into the side view mirror? Then comes a mournful "Oh damn, damn, damn. I stepped right on it."

We inspect a pool at the roadside with our flashlights and see what the text books call "a congress," referring to the sex life of salamanders. We can just get our umbrellas wedged in over the overhanging bare alder branches. The umbrella drips runoff onto Ann's back, but not her camera, so she is happy, except that it's awfully hard to figure out what to do about the reflection of the flash on the water.

The males and the bigger ones that we think are the females are slithering over one another. From time to time one or another of the group dashes up to the surface, moving through the water with a very serpentine writhing to pop its head up. It appears to take a gulp of air, or maybe they are just taking a look around. They look like that faked photograph of Nessie, the Loch Ness Monster.

According to the textbooks, the female takes a sperm packet and puts it into the pouch of her cloaca. The large salamander we watch hanging onto a submerged twig seems be a female extruding a mass of eggs. They form a globe about the size of a golf ball, a globe made up of pea-sized spheres, each with a spot of life in them. She had better lay a lot since the traffic back on the road is squashing a fair number of salamanders.

Strictly speaking the vernal pools that make the ideal habitat for these nurseries are so shallow that they dry up more quickly than predators could mature in them. That leaves out fish and bullfrog tadpoles too since they need two full years to mature. I hope no misguided soul decides to bring bullfrogs to the Island.

Curious, we drive miles of wet country road. Sure enough, everywhere there is a low spot with alders or a pool on one side and forest on the other, there are "herds" of salamanders, swarming like migrating wildebeests in the Serengeti. The roads are popping like so much popcorn with salamanders and frogs of various species. What a night!

Vernal Congress

8:30 PM, April 26
I'm standing in the rain
watching
        Ambystoma maculatum congress,
as they say with irony or discretion.

I suppose I
could time
        the intervals
at which a snaky head breaks
water to gasp a breath of air,

or measure
        the temperature
of the clear pool with its litter
of winter-worn leaves,

or hypothesize on the gender
        of the large, heavy brown ones,
the shiny blacker lean ones.

 or calculate
        how many dozen it takes
to make the seething softballs here.

Voyeur, scientist,
figuring words
        to tell about the nudgings,
            writhings
    —you're not invited to the secret rite.

        Just watch.

The only sound in the wet dark
is the gentle plash of rain,
drops dimpling and geysering above
the domino stars of the salamander backs.

The creatures float and sink:
a languor utterly without guile,
a twirl and twine unarmored, enamored.

My flashlight's gleam writhes too
with a steam of my mammal breath.
Light glances over the dark pool
through shrubbery hung with lichened lace,
onto naked dripping spruce trunks.

Wraith wavering with my breathing—
the shimmer that is them, oblivious
to my light—
I could no more bring myself to stamp my foot
than reach a hand into their world:
Touch the magic mirror and the image vanishes.

They have disappeared, the dinosaur dancers,
wee folk gone by dawn, Cinderellas
of a Brigadoon that comes when
the maples haze red with bloom
and the hermit thrush comes back to sing,
yesterday and tomorrow.

April Flurry

    We're ready
    to take the maple buckets down
    when in some great pillow fight
    big flakes of sugar snow
    whirl over us
    in April madness.

I heard robins in the yard,
behind the bank,
at the Post Office and the dump:
robins robins hawks
song sparrows
robins robins redwings.
Yesterday they all came back.

    We hurl our expectations
    immoderately
    toward spring
    and laugh away
    the cold and grey.

Mark Island Light
44° 08' N 68° 42' W

May   ISLANDS   3

May comes with such a rush, and haltingly. One can keep track of and savor every detail as it arrives. It's like stringing beads, these impressions that make up a northern spring. Beads and string—that is what it takes to make a necklace. Deer Isle is a gem surrounded with a ring of more than a hundred islands, beads of an archipelago scattered across the ocean. The preserves on Deer Isle, too, make a necklace in much the same way Frederick Law Olmsted conceived of his parks. Ann and I are planning a trip around the whole of Deer Isle this month. Our first stop will be Barred Island, gift of Frederick Law Olmsted's grand-niece Carolyn, the first of the beads we plan to thread on our string of prose and poetry and photos.

However, we keep having to push back the date. My brother, Walt Reed, takes tourists out in his lobster boat to see the islands. Already he is booked for almost every nice day of the summer, and some that will undoubtedly turn out to be not so nice. He has so far been out a time or two this new season, but it's been a challenge. Ann and I fear cutting into his regular business when we go out with him. We cannot book very far ahead. How would you know what the light conditions will be on such and such a day? So we are getting impatient and uneasy.

For the entire first half of the month it seems it has been cold and grey and wet, one northeaster after another. In spite of that, there is a certain clockwork about it: the seals have been slapping the water with their flippers in a ritual we can hear far over the water. Eagles are brooding their fuzzy grey chicks, two to a nest. Our phone has been ringing with people calling to say how flabbergasted they are with the beauty of two male scarlet tanagers, an oriole, and an indigo bunting. Some even report that they have been buzzed by the first hummingbirds, so they want the formula for sugar and water for feeders.

When we first came here for summer research all those forty years ago, it always took me some time to get used to the fact that the whole western wall of my existence seethed in liquid unsettledness: the bay and its waves. Now of course, mountains seem to me so sedentary after the sea that I wonder how people stand that. It is that same odd but fleeting sensation of something to get used to that sweeps over me often these last few days. Tiny shadows dance in the periphery of my vision—new leaves—and warblers, waves of them, tiny birds flitting through the branches that so recently were bare twigs.

In spite of the grey days, we have flowers! We do not have a great parade of wildflowers blooming, an impressive succession of what botanists call the spring ephemerals. Our spruces never let up shading for a moment so there is not much of that brief shade-free moment of opportunity here. Still, we know where to find a few violets; the red maple trees oblige, and the shadbush is starting to come out. Shadbush, Island pear, shadblow, serviceberry, or as my uncle in North Carolina says, "sarvice," is our equivalent of the cherries in Japan, where I understand there are some eighteen principal kinds of cherries, and the whole nation goes wild over them for a few weeks in spring. There are traditional cherry blossom dances, cherry blossom viewing picnics, festivals, and even cherry blossom ice cream. Maine has seven species of *Amelanchier*, but they hybridize freely, showing many subtle variations. Some trees look positively fluffy with blooms, while others have slender long petals that give their trees a languorous elegance.

Now I look at shadbush blossoms with a new appreciation, and yesterday I received yet another layer of meaning. The crows had been scolding up a storm so I looked out, and there in the mizzling rain, sitting on the barely blooming shadbush, was one very wet hawk. Amid the delicately red leaves and snow of petals lashing in the wind, a broad-winged hawk teetered and held out one wing and then another. It turned around on the branch and either the wind whipped it or the bird fanned its tail, shaking off rain or struggling for balance. As a biologist I know I am not supposed to attribute human characteristics to birds, but this bird certainly looked both fierce and angry. I could well see why the Japanese samurai loved to invite rivals over and seat them in full view of a scroll painting of a militant threatening hawk or eagle. A sort of warning, "See this? Watch out for me."

The bedraggled hawk seemed to glare from its perch on the branch tossing like all the unseen nests swaying in the cold storm, "Nature is not always neat and nice, you know."

This morning dawned bright and clear and crisp. Birch branches with their fans of still-furled new leaves glitter with rain drops, an image which never fails to remind me of Indra's net. I am most fond of the idea of a Net of Being thrown over the palace of the god, a net in which every knot is decorated with a jewel that reflects all the others. Everything is connected to everything else and reflects all else. Science and religions are opposites? Not according to this awed biologist with the eye of an artist and heart of a poet. I am quite sure today will be what I call the Day of New Leaves. By mid-day the birch leaves will have opened in their green fashion not totally unlike the way a butterfly emerging from its chrysalis unfolds its wings. I always know I am not running my life properly if I am too busy to observe this brief happening or too preoccupied even to notice when this special day comes.

What we humans have been grumbling about as bad weather seems to have deterred even horseshoe crabs over at Ann's on the Bagaduce. They were expected to come ashore and breed at the recent full moon. However, that came and passed with only a horseshoe crab or two seen. In all the years I have walked the shoreline, I have only once seen the empty carapace of one small horseshoe crab here on Deer Isle. I think that's because the Island lacks the warm, protected, shallow bays that the young hatchlings require to grow fast enough. Ultimately it is too cold here. Too cold for them—and for the bulk of the human population. I have often thought of a bumper sticker announcing, "I'd rather be cold than crowded." I am a hermit at heart.

Ann and I are looking forward to many jaunts out to the island archipelago spangling Penobscot Bay, but we have in mind a whole-island, day-long circumnavigation before the tourist season proper starts. Any delay makes us nervous. Imagine what this season delay means to those who earn their whole year's income in the next short months! It's been so stormy the past weeks that fishermen could not get out to fish for bait; the lobstermen who had some bait have not been able to get out to haul their traps even if they had found a break during which to set them. The owner of the island's only garden nursery is fretting that another week or two of cold wet weather will put him entirely out of business.

My brother planned to put his boat, a lobster boat that was deemed too small for the fisherman who wanted to move up to a bigger one, into the water on Mother's Day. Walt did accomplish his launching on time, and a few other boats have been out setting their lobster traps, but not many. There seems to be general agreement that it is still pretty cold.

When Ann and I cannot stand the wait any longer, we opt to go out in our boat, a 17-footer we call *Whisper* because her motor is relatively silent. Whisper is fiberglass but designed like an old fashioned picnic launch: black hull, spare lines, teak trim—the type designed to take small parties of Victorian "rusticators" out to nearby islands for their outings. We cannot hope to make it all the way around the island on such a windy day as it is today in such a small boat as ours. We will have to content ourselves with a short excursion along the shore. The wind is out of the north so we will explore only as much of Sunset's shore as seems comfortable.

We meet Ann at the dock dressed warmly. On either side of the float are two empty lobster boats, their UHF marine radios left on full blast. We hear the joy at being once more free on the sea in the voices of the men out there as they converse with one another.

"I thought I'd put my traps out where we were discussing the other day, you know? Between the two shoals? But there was somebody's traps there already."

"Well, it don't really matter where you put 'em. They ain't really moving yet."

"Right," and neither man sounds very disappointed. After all, it's a fine day, with the sun out at last.

Lobstering around here is still a closed club with strict territorial rules. Walter made a big point of taking the pot hauler off his little lobster boat when he decided to go into the tourist-hauling business. The fishermen were glad when he bought the boat from a fisherman. They were happy to see another boat removed from the competing fleet. They welcome Walt and love to make a show of holding up their catch so Walt's passengers can oooh and ah at both the authentic "salts" and their catch. Although various fishermen have assured Walt that he could easily take out a recreational license for a few demo traps, they follow that in the next paragraph with woeful tales of so-and-so whose traps were cut.

Across the nearly empty harbor we see Diane and Robert pulling out. They have been out setting his traps the past few days. His family is the one who have almost single-handedly kept the lovely little Burnt Cove church in decent repair. The steeple serves as beacon to all who sail here. Diane, Bob's wife, has been pressed into service as Bob's helper while they await a grandson graduating high school. He is to spend his summer as sternman, lobstering to make enough money for his college tuition.

I learned all this when I went to borrow a couple of fish boxes the other day. These large plastic crates are the measure that our local nursery uses to dole out mulch. The only alternative is to buy it by the truck load. That pretty much sums us up here on the Island now. If you are one of the new persons from away who are into estate gardening, you buy a truck-load.

Or you grow local, and then chances are you fish or know someone who does.

We motor out of the harbor and head into the wind. Barred Island lies just off our bow. The state wildlife department flew over two weeks ago and reported that there are active nests on Mark, Barred, and Carney Islands now, all Island Heritage Trust properties.

The bald eagles have been sitting on the nest here at Barred for the past month. Last year they successfully raised one chick. The year before that a single chick fledged but lost its life in a tangle of spruce. Reading the keel mark and foot tracks on the sandy bar that gives the island its name, it appeared that the inexperienced bird was flushed by a kayaker late one afternoon. When the eaglet was discovered hanging by one leg, it was too late to save it. How the Island mourned the loss!

The other day I e-mailed Ann my *May Day* haiku. She replied with this version:

Alone with the hermit thrush
and scent of arbutus trailing
with Mayday Mayday in its wake.

Responding to that distress call is of course what we are doing, getting some precious bits of the landscape here conserved, accorded at least whatever protection our civilization can offer by laws. Some of our conserved islands are open to the public; many do not permit public access. The islands under protective easement are not marked on any map as preserves, but many islands do enjoy that invisible protection of a conservation easement. For a variety of reasons the owners, the donors, have chosen a relative anonymity for their good deeds. Although you could go root out the list of conservation easements held by a trust, land trusts across the country traditionally honor a preference for a low profile and they do not publish this information unless the donor instructs that it be shared.

The bay sparkles. Our boat bounces over the waves with what almost feels like enthusiasm. Those empty lobster boats at the dock know what I mean. Eagerly we scan the skies and island tree tops as we head out of the cove and cross the mouths of Crockett Cove and Goose Cove.

Aha! Both eagle parents are sitting conspicuously perched on limbs near the nest on Barred Island. Shouldn't one of you be off getting food for those chicks? One of the birds shifts and makes an uneasy cry. We move off promptly. There are federal regulations about how close one may come to an eagle, but the state biologists are careful to be vague. Whatever the eagles say is too close for comfort, that is too close. Scram.

As we make our way around the island I ponder the invisible web stringing together the scatter of largely uninhabited islands off the coast here. Boat tours in New York State's Thousand Islands at the junction of Lake Ontario and the St. Lawrence River take visitors through the myriad islands and islets to gawk at the houses large and small covering the islands almost from one shore to the other. Since the heyday of Bar Harbor and that of the Thousand Islands as playgrounds of the very wealthy coincided, I am not sure what combination of factors spared us that overdevelopment here.

Do the eagles have some sense for preserved land? They could not possibly know that Barred Island is part of the Barred Island Preserve, gift of Carolyn Olmsted. Until the subsequent gift of George Pavloff, former Goose Cove Lodge owner, Barred Island would only have been accessible to humans by boat. In high summer season we would scarcely be able to thread our way through the abundance of lobster pots set in the waters here. Today we are cold, but not crowded. Yet. Apparently the eagles appreciate the low density of humans here too. Every dawn they can be seen patrolling this shore. Undeveloped islands serve as resting places for the eagles of all ages that spend parts of the year here. The scatter of islands centered around Barred Island has been designated as being of national significance for wildlife. It shows.

Walt says his clients love to be taken along this stretch of shore to admire the grand homes that look out on the sunsets that give this area its name. Usually they pass right by the modest home tucked away among spruces. That one is where I live. My brother never mentions it.

The first cottages we see after Barred Island are the small ones belonging to the grandchildren of naturalist Dr. Ralph Waldron, who started Goose Cove Lodge. Next is a large, new, shingle "cottage" echoing the lines of Felsted, home designed for Frederick Law Olmsted, creator of New York City's Central Park. Felsted itself is a bit further along the shore, but this home is a prelude. The owners of this home, June and Bill Lenoci, spend the cold part of the year in Asheville, North Carolina, where Olmsted did what was to prove almost the last landscape design commission of his life, the grounds for the Biltmore estate of George W. Vanderbilt. The Lenocis have donated a conservation easement that compliments the Barred Island Preserve. Everybody wins. The town gets increased taxes from the large home. The scenic and historic and wildlife values are conserved, and the marine resource potential of the area is safe-guarded from polluting runoff resulting from any intense development.

If you stand on the preserve's boulder knoll overlooking Barred, most of what you see—somewhat inelegantly known in the planning world as "viewshed"—has some form of conservation protection. This is quite remarkable, given that islands are increasingly taking on the mystique of diamonds, a lovely and scarce commodity which confers status by its expensive price tag.

Off our bow a group of porpoises surfaces, the first we've seen this season. Sign of spring! We look to see if any has the little shadow of a calf snuggled in by their side, but it's very hard to see in the brief instant the porpoise comes up to the surface, blows out in that distinctive "chuff" exhalation of theirs, and silently submerges. They may continue on their way invisibly—or they may circle around, either checking us out or surrounding some small school of fish. These mysterious mammals so like fish are incredibly ballet-like in that graceful curve as they break the surface. Their dorsal fin echoes the lines as they slip away under the sea, sometimes leaving the faintest echo of a calm or slick to mark where they were. That is about all Ann manages to capture with her camera.

"Once when we were sailing with our son Tom, we encountered a Minke whale out here," I tell Ann. I tell her about Edith Quinn, the dear woman who grew up out on the islands here. "I met Edith when she was in her eighties; we sang in the Sunday choir. During the war Edith looked out and saw a submarine rising. Initially her husband did not believe her, of course. A submarine? And I think I had trouble getting Ken and Tom to turn and look at the whale!"

A red nun marks Sellers Rock. Twice a day, the rock looks like a submarine surfacing or submerging. When I first learned the name of this ledge, I worried that it might have taken its name from some disaster at sea. Even marked by the Coast Guard, it is a hazard. When I discovered that the map of the first settlers of the Deer Isle showed a Charles Sellers marked just here, I felt reassured. His farm is shown running from Crockett's Cove to the south to Small's Cove on the north. That is just about the extent of what Fredrick Olmsted purchased for his estate. In the Olmsteds' time the ledge or reef was marked by a spar. The shore along here is now protected by conservation easement but you can still see the iron rods drilled into the shore, traces of a development the financially-strapped Olmsted firm had planned here before they lost title.

I point a house out to Ann that is nearly invisible in the trees. It is the home we've built over the years. Next comes the prominent white house built in about 1910, known for years as the Reed Cottage, no relation to me. "You can see the house from the top of Mount Battie, 18 miles across the bay. The house stood empty for the first years we were here, before being renovated by some folks from Texas. And then it was purchased by our current neighbors, Ken and Cherie Mason. Ken is a retired Quaker Oats president and Cherie's a voice actress who uses her dramatic personality on behalf of animal welfare. If you are making your way down the dead end road by land, atop the Texas-style ranch gate you now see a carved wood fox in honor of Cherie's children's book about our fox."

We throttle *Whisper* down to an idle to enjoy looking at Felsted, Frederick Law Olmsted's home tucked into the curve of the beach. Clearly Frederick Olmsted not only had an eye for landscape, he had first pick. Well, not quite, but he was among the early Victorians to choose to build summer homes here. Interestingly, the locals refer to the stone foundation on the shore back at Barred just where the sand bar leads to the island as the "salt house." They are referring to the storage place for the salt of fish drying racks that once were set out on this shore. Summer people refer to it as the Olmsteds' changing house for the bathing picnics on the beach. Both are probably true.

As I give Ann the story of the people of this neck of the woods, I smile, noticing that once again I launch into a family tree. How very Island! How very necessary when the odds are so high that everyone is related to everyone else and you had better know it and be appropriately tactful!

"Frederick married his brother's widow, Mary, and adopted his brother John's children. Carolyn Olmsted and her astronomer sister Margaret spent all their childhood summers here and eventually inherited The Binnacle, the farm next door to Felsted. Frederick Law Olmsted, senior, designer of New York's Central Park was often referred to as FLO Sr, not to be confused with FLO Jr."

Ann rolls her eyes.

"The Olmsteds had come to Deer Isle at the suggestion of their friend Charles Loring Brace, who summered on Dunham's Point. Remember my telling you at the Tennis Preserve that my friend Barbara Brace Seeley had done the trail work? Her grandfather, this Brace whose name is associated with the Children's Aid Society and the orphan trains taking city youth west for vacation in the late 1800's, was, with Olmsted, a champion of the ordinary man."

I make a mental note to look up for Ann what Olmsted himself wrote about the purpose of his public parks. ("It is an open-air gathering for the purpose of easy, friendly, unceremonious greetings, for the enjoyment of change of scene, of cheerful and exhilarating sights and sounds and of various good cheer, to which the people of a town, of all classes, harmoniously resort on equal terms, as to a common property."— *Maine Olmsted Alliance for Parks and Landscapes Journal*, Autumn, 1998)

"After Olmsted's death, Felsted, which had been completed in 1896, was sold out of the family. For a time it became a bustling hotel. When that enterprise failed, Bill Pashley purchased the grand Shingle Style cottage designed by William R. Emerson, and restored it by removing the hotel additions. Pashley family members eventually moved here year round. Young David Pashley was for some years a student assistant to Ken in his island mouse population research."

We motor slowly around the point of land, noting that the shoreside cliffs get somewhat steeper.

"Margaret Olmsted bought Barred Island back and she and her sister inherited The Binnacle. Carolyn—Carol to the family—was somewhat shy and reclusive, remaining in the shadow of her older sister as long as she lived. Margaret had died by the time we came to the neighborhood, but we enjoyed Carolyn's peppery, pixie-like humor. It matched her always informally-cropped hairdo. When she moved here to take up permanent residence, she figured as just one more eccentric whose privacy was to be respected and whose doings would be recounted with amusement and affection. Her love of the Island, its people, and her fierce protection of every flower and twig in her purview were legendary. In 1976 Carolyn gave Barred Island to The Nature Conservancy 'for the enjoyment of the people of Deer Isle'. I love it that that is what it says right in the deed."

Ken guides the boat as close in to the shore as he can. He tells Ann, "If the tide is right you can spot the overhang that is known as Captain Kidd's cave. According to the Olmsted sisters, a Chicago lawyer wrote the story for his literary club, and subsequently it was widely syndicated."

Ken points out that one side of the cove, the north side of Small's Cove, is clearly lined with gray shores; the south side marks the beginning of the pink granite. Across the cove stretches a bar that may have spelled the doom of the British warship *Bona Ventura* in the War of 1812. Stranded, with only a few cannon shots fired, she became the prize of the American privateer Paul Jones. Somewhere in the extensively remodeled Binnacle may still be some of the timbers salvaged from the British warship that were used to build the farmhouse. A neighbor is proud of the rusty cannonball that'd landed in his meadow. Clammers in the cove occasionally turn up not just Indian relics but cannon balls. Time marches on.

The tide has turned, and so do we. The wind is making it too choppy for Ann to photograph even so picturesque a shore as this. Ken suggests we may find smoother sailing in the lee of the islands on the Stonington side of Burnt Cove. We might go check the Mark Island eagles' nest. Ann and I need no coaxing.

Just past the mouth of the cove lies Fort Island, a small low island. It took years of finagling, but we have finally secured all of it for the Maine Coast Heritage Trust. The island was once a base for duck hunters. Even today there is a period in the late fall when it sounds like World War II with all the shooting in the waters around here.

Back in the '70s someone had written a book, a journal, about building a house on an equally small island off the other side of Deer Isle. Since there was no legal reason why not, Fort Island seemed destined for the same adventure. The owner approached Ken, knowing how Ken loved the islands. He sold what turned out to be only three-quarters share of the island to us "so no one else would be tempted" as he put it. It took years to get the owner of the other quarter to agree to transfer his interest to the trust, but Maine Coast Heritage Trust now holds the deed to the whole of the little island.

Other islands in this triangle have been equally fortunate. Ken had discussed conservation easements with the owners of Second Island back when his research was in full swing. He was in contact with most of the island owners back then for permission to study the mouse populations on their islands. The easement on Second Island was one of the first in this region. It has taken some years for people to understand that "conserved" is not a jam, and "easement" does not necessarily mean a power line right of way. Under a specially crafted agreement, families retain ownership and perhaps some other rights (including paying the taxes), but give or sell the development rights to a conservation organization. Conservation easements have proved to be a wonderful tool. Ask any eagle.

I point out a young seal off our starboard bow. But much too quickly for Ann's camera, the seal dives in a fast slurp. We are surprised that it is so spooked.

Once past Fort and Second, we come in range of the automatic fog horn sounding from Mark Island. The story of the preservation of the lighthouse here is one dear to us. Mark was the principal focus of Ken's research. By the time we had arrived in Stonington the light keeper's house had burned to the ground. The square white stone tower remained, with its light and horn's functions automated. The Coast Guard visited just a couple of times a year to service the equipment.

I'll never forget the day before the final day to register with the Maine Lights program to apply for one of the lighthouses from the Maine Lights program. This program was a stroke of genius. It had become clear that the Coast Guard simply did not have enough money to tend to upkeep of lighthouses. The mechanism for transferring lights

to private hands for preservation was too cumbersome since each effort required an act of Congress. The bright idea to keep the old fashioned lights burning was to perform the equivalent of a group marriage ceremony or a group citizenship ceremony. All of the lights along the Maine coast would be transferred in a one-time only ceremony, a process considerably abetted by then-senator George Mitchell. Any lights remaining with no sponsor would then be turned off and replaced by automated navigation buoys.

I had telephoned the Stonington selectmen to ask who was intending to go to the session on how to fill out the application and to offer our help at filling out the background questions. Beyond doubt Ken and I had spent more time on that island than any one else, Coast Guard included, since the lighthouse had burned. The Maine Lights group was taking no chances. Here were the questions and here were the answers, how to fill in the blanks.

I was told essentially, "Oh, we decided our plate was full. We just could not take that on, even though it's a great idea." What a frantic afternoon of phone calls. The Island Heritage Trust—the only qualified 501c3, not-for-profit, bona fide conservation group here, quickly empowered us to go over to the Rockland meeting and make application.

I tell Ann about the lighthouse as we motor up to it. The view of the lighthouse is one that is familiar to many and much loved in this state. In the Portland Museum of Art hangs a painting by John Marin who painted here for a couple of summers before moving farther downeast to Addison. Marin's daughter-in-law tells the story of taking her brand new sailboat from Boothbay to Addison one summer. Just as they left North Haven behind, a fog bank from the open ocean closed in around them. Her partner fretted even after the fog cleared briefly and Norma Marin exclaimed, "We are okay now. I know where we are."

"Don't you have to consult a chart to figure out which light we are seeing?"

"Oh, no. This looks just like the painting. We are right by the Thoroughfare into Stonington," came the gleeful and relieved reply.

The image is perhaps one of Marin's more realistic paintings. The Museum offers note cards and fridge magnets of the image, surely the mark of popularity achieved.

"When the lighthouse was officially transferred to local control, we threw a huge party in the high school gymnasium to celebrate. Too bad you weren't here yet," I tell Ann. "It was a snowy evening, a blizzard in fact, but it was the right event at the right time. Many people associated with fishing were nearly at the end of their savings. It was only March so there were some lean times ahead. This was an excuse to party and swap tales of how the little light on the island at the entrance to Stonington's sea lanes had saved their life or that of someone they knew. Others told how they used the foghorn's sound to tell them what sort of weather we were about to have. In fog and certain winds the sound carries surprisingly far. The tone of affection in their voices reminds me of how people talk about the particular pitches of church bells in the mountain villages of Northern Italy."

We are floating well within range of the automatic fog horn. Ken takes care not to let us drift too close.

"I used to be the official steward for Mark Island. The Coast Guard continued to service the navigation instruments, so my role was chiefly as liaison and watch dog. Once my brother launched himself into the business of guiding tourists out to see the light, he was the logical steward."

I muse about how often it is People From Away who volunteer in many significant ways in their newly-adopted communities. Odd as it may seem, my brother in his other life was an insect toxicologist. Walter's profile gives insight into who is taking care of many of Maine's special places these days. As soon as possible on moving here from away, Dr. Reed shed his academic title, and acquired new ones: Registered Maine Guide, Master Mariner, Maine Island Trail Association Monitor Skipper, board member Penobscot East Research Center, and Island Heritage Trust Steward for Mark Island Light. In his spare time he is an EMT for the island's ambulance corps, and now acts as their Assistant Chief. He has never been happier in his life.

Walt's brother-in-law, my husband, ecology professor Dr. Kenneth Crowell, recently president of Island Heritage Trust, had studied the globe and chosen to come here in the early 1960's to study the populations of mice on the islands in the archipelago off Stonington. I tell Ann about Ken's mouse studies. "It took some years to convince the lobstermen that Ken, this fellow who kept the same hours they did, was actually trapping mice, not poaching their lobsters. People would jokingly ask me if I had a favorite recipe for cooking mice. One of the girls who cleaned and closed the cabin we had rented for the first seasons discovered one year that Ken had forgotten a tray of frozen mouse specimens in the refrigerator's ice cube compartment. We had almost quelled the rumors when the movie *Never Cry Wolf* came to the screen. In it, the actor playing author Farley Mowat lifts a mouse by the tail and eats it. Oh ho, so we WERE eating the mice."

Ann laughs. Kens shifts the boat into gear again.

"Over the years many islanders have come to see that Ken's devotion to the islands perhaps matches theirs. We were approached by a number of local people whose family and economic situations prompted deep concerns over the future of their islands. Working with the The Nature Conservancy, Maine Coast Heritage Trust, and the Island Heritage Trust, we have been able to help a number of people devise arrangements that have suited the family members while preserving the character of our islands by means of various fee title transfers, conservation easements, and other mechanisms."

There is no sign of any eagles at or near the new nest on the edge of Mark. Could the recent stormy weather have been too much for them? While heading south was a good idea, there are still large swells to be reckoned with. Two eagles swoop over from nearby Scraggy Island to brawl over Mark. Rolling and feinting, talon to talon they interact. We have seen as many as six eagles of various ages sitting on the trees or on the rocks at the tide's edge on Scraggy. Perhaps there is a nest there? We circle that island slowly, riding the swells, inspecting. Ann finds she is getting a lot of photos of eagles sitting in tree tops without their heads.

A group of crows comes over and dives at the eagle sitting in the tallest spruce there. The eagle ducks and screams, a most exciting noise that seems not to daunt the crows in the least. Scraggy Island used to be the only heron rookery in this part of Penobscot Bay. When we were able to acquire it, we put a conservation easement on it for the great blue herons. Alas, within years there were no more herons, only eagles here. Well, not precisely alas, but what we expected. The eider ducks that nest at the perimeter of Scraggy under the overhanging spruce branches may still be there in spite of the eagles. We see no signs of interaction today as a group of adult eiders swims by while several eagles watch. We have watched eagles diving at ducklings in the summer, a sight that is hard to witness with equanimity.

A sharp crack rents the air. We look around and then at each other in bewilderment. Smack! There is that sound again. Not far off we see an adult seal lying at the surface, somewhat on its side. With a flipper it demonstrates once again how the noise is made. We do not see another seal. It seems a bit late for this to be a courtship antic. The smacking noise we heard was probably a mother seal sending an alarm signal to her pup. Very effective! We never saw the pup. Not long ago the seal population was low, but now they enjoy relative abundance.

We are happy with our excursion and turn our bow toward home. I hope Ann got some good photographs and that she managed to keep her camera dry. She gets pretty intense when she is lining up a shot. If she had a problem she would not know it until she goes to download. I look forward to tomorrow morning's e-mail when she will have sent me the pick of today's crop.

Why is it, though, that I feel vaguely disappointed? It was sensible to stop beating north up the bay and loop back to the south. Why wasn't that enough? So, we were not able to get going on our round-the Island trip. What is so special about that? I want to go because I want to see the Island whole, from a new perspective. It would be not unlike seeing the island from an airplane. You see relationships that otherwise are not obvious. I want to share that with Ann. It is very interesting to see what catches her eye.

Surprisingly few Islanders have ever been all the way around Deer Isle by water. Is that because lobstermen don't want to venture out of their territory? Lobstermen are famous, or notorious, for observing territorial holdings. And then, no one could blame them for not wanting to go tooting around the Island on a day they were not fishing. That would be a busman's holiday. But even Island landsmen did not venture into other parts of the Island. "The newcomers—especially the birdwatchers—seem to go everywhere," one old friend told me with wonder in his voice.

Here we are faced with the ocean moderating the arrival of spring. Since everyone on the mainland has apple blossoms, shouldn't we at least get a good boat ride in exchange for our watery surround? Visiting the islands that make up and ring Deer Isle: that's a really grand necklace of beads, and we want to string it!

Butterfly Collection

Spring Whites

Petal blossom snow
drifts down
the May morning
save the one
fluttering upward,
day moth sprite.

New England Economics

Paint-bare clapboards
silvered by time
and winter,
but by the door
a lilac wealth
and the languid dazzle
of a yellow Swallowtail.

June — SHORE ACRES — 4

June is the foggiest month of the year in Maine they say. Who is they? Anyone who ever chartered a yacht here and spent their days waiting for the fog to clear. Ann and I have been trying to schedule a trip with Walt but the weather has made it a challenge. Today however Walt reports that from his house across the Island on Mountainville (elevation 200 feet above sea level) he can already see Marshall Island. The fog bank now lies out to the south of Stonington, so we will give it a try.

Round the Island at last. For years and years the tradition here of the Deer Isle Yacht Club was a one or two day race around the Island every August. Strictly speaking the yacht club has no club house; it is only a pier and float and some three generations of sailors in everything from small turn of the century one-design boats, to modern fiberglass racer-cruisers. A family affair, the Round the Island Race now has been supplanted or subsumed by the high-power, high-tech racing yacht circuit.

As ground crew managing logistics, car transport, etc., I never got to make the circuit. For reasons I cannot quite explain—even to myself—I somehow feel it important to circumnavigate the island in one go, to gain new insights, to put the island—linked islands really—in proper perspective. Ann and I have been making our pilgrimages around the Island not by analogy with a wagon wheel's rim, but by trips from the hub of my home, out along its spokes. This means that we can organize ourselves according to the vagaries of the weather and the pleasures of the season. Today, however, we will travel the rim.

"Here's a map. Well, perhaps it is a chart since it is nautical. You could almost use it to navigate, Walt."

Walt grins and offers his hand to me, and to Ann, as we step aboard the *Gael*, Walter's lobster boat, and head off on our adventure.

Running my finger down the map to its left corner, I show Ann where Burnt Cove is. "Here we are, and we will head up the western side of the Island, farther than our last trip I hope!"

At the mouth of the cove are several dories with a large circle of net seining between them. Nearby is anchored a small bait boat. Perhaps something in the lobster fishermen's future is looking up. But what is that grey head out there in the middle? A seal? Another? And another? How did they get in? Slither over the top? I'll bet that someone will not be happy about going to all the trouble to set the seine to feed the seals. Ann is delighted at how the line of floats suspending the nets speaks to her of our theme, beads and string.

We speed on up along our shore, retracing our earlier short jaunt. Deep in Crockett Cove are homes designed by artist Emily Muir. Emily Lansingh came here to summer with her parents as a girl. When she married artist William Muir, the couple decided to make their home here. The Maine art scene had already drawn an early generation of such painters as Winslow Homer, and then came John Marin, Rockwell Kent, and Zorachs, and of course, eventually the Wyeth family. The Muirs knew and befriended and aided many of the artists who were enchanted by Maine for a half century.

Widowed fairly early, Emily was well known locally for her independence. An outspoken champion of the less privileged, Emily was convinced that beautiful housing could be built affordably (even if another characteristic was that the houses often leaked). She was committed to integrating the outdoors with interior living spaces. Leaking roofs were not what she had in mind; natural stone and native plant-lined foyers were more like what she aimed for. Emily really was an artist rather than an architect. She demonstrated here at Crockett Cove how homes could be integrated into the shore landscape unobtrusively. Ever the pioneer, she then donated the backlands to The Nature Conservancy as a preserve.

Just beyond Barred Island with its preserve and eagle nest, Olmsted's handsome Felsted nestles into the shoreline. The granite blocks of the foundation so exactly match the granite shore that it is impossible to say where nature ends and structure begins. Since Emily Muir loved to go around the bay in her succession of motorboats, I am sure she often admired this home, already famous in her day, and she took the lesson to heart.

We pass Small's Cove, where the pink granite shores are replaced with grey. Walter likes to tell his passengers about the War of 1812 naval skirmish here, when cannonballs ended up in nearby fields after locals and one of Her Majesty's ships encountered each other here.

The day is clearing nicely. The season is still early. There is only a single windjammer off in the distance and a single sloop. At the Deer Isle Yacht club, there is a scattered confetti of empty pink or white mooring balls, only two sail boats at anchor there. Dunham's Point just beyond the yacht club was for almost a century the island's prime address, catering mostly to the summering Southworth clan and their friends. Many summer "rusticators" are not yet on the Island, if the blind eyes of still-drawn old-fashioned white roller shades and empty flagpoles are any indication. Along the shore are the newer much larger, grander homes that are today's standard for shore property.

I am reminded that we always have to keep a weather eye out. We have tried in vain to sail this stretch when the wind shifted and the tide set us so we simply could not make headway. Other times a line squall or the wicked downdraft from late summer afternoon brewing thunderheads made things most interesting. We have been soaked by the chop from an east wind screaming across the narrow waist of the Island accompanying grey lines of what the weathermen call roll clouds. I am in awe of the first people who routinely, or at least regularly plied these same waters in birch bark canoes.

Still heading up the left side of the map, our first destination on this trip is Hardhead Island. We do not mean to land. It rises cliff-like out in the bay, looking like something from Scotland or a Canadian wildlife film. Bright orange lichens incongruously paint the dark heights. The treeless summit is bright with yellow mustard bloom and swaying green grasses. One face has been taken over by cormorants, locally known as shags. We can clearly see good-sized young in their nests.

But as we come around to the lee side of the island, it is the sound of other birds that most captivates. The air is filled with an almost twitter, though a slightly sharp and raucous variation: terns, common terns. Even after the Audubon Society was formed and plume hunters stopped gathering their feathers to decorate ladies' hats, common terns had become uncommon, driven to the brink of extinction by loss of habitat and the rise of the herring gull population. Thanks to humans and their dumps! Humans and their dogs and very presence disturb tern nesting sites. Our fairly casual waste disposal system not so many years back provided gulls with a banquet, and they were quick to take advantage and multiply. However, the state stepped in, ordered the dumps closed or covered, acquired a good many of the bay's sea bird nesting islands and closed them to the public during the nesting season.

Off the dark sheer face of the cliffs hurtle small black guillemots. They are no doubt nesting in the crevasses of the cliff face. Puffin-like, but needle-nosed rather than parrot-beaked, these small birds quite closely resemble their more famous near relatives. Slightly plump, and black with white oval wing patches, they are darlings.

The terns, streamlined as fighter jets, however, choose the grassy hilltop, open to the sky. As we float a respectful distance off shore, the terns appear with shiny small fish in their bills. They are feeding young. How exciting! Hardhead is now the principal remaining nesting place of the terns of Penobscot Bay.

Along one rocky shore just above the seething waves rests a small covey of dainty gulls. Are these the same dainty laughing gulls that rest galleon-like on the shallows at the Causeway between Little Deer and Deer Isle not far from here? Without going closer we cannot quite make out whether or not they have the spots on their bills that would mark them as herring gulls. We don't want to go close enough to make any of the nesting sea birds nervous and change their behavior. They have quite enough challenges, as it is, in this world. Both ring-bills and laughing gulls are seen much more commonly now than they were a few years back. The clattery harsh call of the laughing gulls is now one of the bay's distinctive signs of spring.

Handsome black-and-white male eiders are bobbing in the lee waves. Does that mean their hens are sitting on eggs somewhere up there on the heights? I hope so. We are not sure just who the brown ducks are, females unmated, females taking a break from nesting, or last year's females that hang around for a year and serve as baby-sitters? First year male eiders always confuse us with their unique half black/

half white plumage until we get used to being fooled by these strangers, "half-drakes" the locals call them.

Off to the east, like following a spoke of the wagon wheel into the center, lies the Causeway Beach and newly-protected Carney Island where eagles have chosen to nest this year. Ahead of us stretches Pickering Island, which has significant easement protection. An osprey peers at us from its shaggy tree top nest. The shore here is lovely contorted grey schist, the layers of which make the island look like an ancient Chinese landscape scroll painting. Since the fog has been drifting around in wisps the effect is most complete. Ann is so delighted she has already used up more than one memory card for her camera and we are not yet half way around.

Ken points out Bradbury Island where he came as boy when he was a camper at nearby Robin Hood Camp. The boys would sometimes be dragooned into coming out to the island to round up Sunday's dinner—the sheep that were pastured out here. Most of these islands were completely cut over, first for firewood and then for fuel to feed the Rockland lime kilns that made the plaster for the prosperous new homes springing up in the communities of this growing nation.

Spruce was also cut for pulp until the opening of the North Woods, then western forests, and next the southern timber industry made island lumbering uneconomical. Left to their own devices these islands regrew the coat of spruce we see today.

On nearby Crow Island the eagles have once again chosen to nest. A number of islands in this neighborhood have some form of protection, being either fully owned by The Nature Conservancy or protected by conservation easements. The Nature Conservancy properties largely represent the era of the sixties when they were virtually the only conservation game in town. Among the farsighted individuals who determined back then to leave the part of the bay they loved safe for the future was the beloved children's book author and illustrator, Robert McCloskey. McCloskey would put his little family in their rowboat and set out from here for Bucks Harbor for groceries, an impressive row.

People now go to nearby Bucks Harbor to see Condon's Garage which appears in his books. Because of intervening islands you cannot quite see the Scott Island home where McCloskey lived with his wife and daughters Sal and Jane. From the mainland, your best chance to get the feel of the scene is to go to the Causeway at the Little Deer end. Island Heritage Trust now owns a convenient overlook from which you can see the island panorama that clearly inspired McCloskey's watercolors, a veritable page from *Time of Wonder*. From out here we too can see long views of the hills off to the west and to the east, Blue Hill, which is quite recognizable as the bear's hill in *Blueberries For Sal*. Sal still owns the house here. At the western end of the island the barn-shaped structure that Bob McCloskey used as his studio still stands. Both his daughters still live in the region and are well recognized for their contributions to environmental preservation.

I often think Maine scenery looks pretty much the same year round, but I see today that is not quite so. The islands show their hardwood in a lovely and subtle birch brocade, shot through here and there with the silver of new poplar leaves. How welcoming these islands must look to the tiny traveling warblers that make their way from Central America up the coast to Maine and beyond each spring.

Off there in the greenery lies the distinctive humped shape of Pine Hill on Little Deer. Before the summer is over, this will be the island's newest preserve open to the public, thanks to the generosity of its current owners. Ann and I will go to photograph the special plants that grow there, associated with the special minerals of the place.

The charming setting of what was once Pumpkin Island lighthouse comes next into view as we round the top of the map. Now a private home, this marks the apex of the Deer Isle/ Little Deer group. It also marked the halfway mark in the old Round the Island race. Many a time I came here to watch the passing boats. Often I watched a few Dark Harbor Twelves or Seventeens sail by. These elegant little wooden boats were designed at the turn of the last century for a one-design class out on Islesboro just off to the west. McCloskey often included paintings of his daughters at the helm of their lovely Dark Harbor.

Our family is fortunate enough to own one of the last of the Twelves, so named for its length at the waterline. It is my favorite boat to sail, both for its elegant lines and the sweet old-fashioned creaking noises its gaffed rig makes, wooden hoops braceleting the mast.

As we round the corner, heading down the right margin of the map, down the lane of water called the Reach, we see the soaring tracery of the Deer Isle - Sedgwick bridge. Opened in 1939, it is reputed to be highly arched so as to make sure the masts of the New York Yacht Club could clear its span.

Walter points out the fins on the green can that marks the turn here. They are designed to reflect radar so the marker is very obvious. Prudent kayakers around here have similar gadgets mounted to their low-slung craft. The lobstermen dread what might happen in the fog in these waters becoming so heavily visited by paddling kayak neophytes.

From here, a sailing vessel stands a good chance of making the run out to the ocean on a reach, that is, with the wind coming at right angles to the centerline of the vessel. Hence the name Eggemoggin Reach, or simply The Reach. Ann looks as if she is enjoying herself. No matter what the waves are doing she leans far enough over the rail to make the captain nervous. She is very pretty and reserved in a dainty way. But put her behind her camera and she reminds me of a happy family dog leaning out the window of the car, ears flying in the wind, tongue hanging out of a huge grin. Smell that good bay air; feel the wind in your face!

We head UNDER the bridge. Somehow I had not realized that I never knew what the underside of the bridge I travel so often looks like. Even from this perspective, its clean lines soar. What an artist David Steinman, designer of the bridge, was.

"I've heard that a small plane has successfully flown under the bridge," I say. "Maybe even more than one."

Ann says, "Now that's the stuff of local legend."

Walt adds, "And it's probably true."

As we head past the gap between Little Deer Isle and the main part of Deer Isle, I tell Ann about the early settlements here by the native peoples who were known as Etchemin. This was a good place to construct fishing weirs by jamming brushy poles into a stockade formation in the mud of the clam flats. "Eggemoggin" means Place of the Great Fish Weirs. We can spot the piles of rubble that mark what was once a ferry boat landing. In fact there were two wharves along here, Scott's Landing and Ferry Landing.

All the shore property along the Reach is privately held. The only possible public access will be an ambitious project being undertaken by Maine Coast Heritage Trust with the Island Heritage Trust. If indeed they are successful in raising the needed funds, the Island will have a place for its retired sea men to come and watch the boat traffic, the sailing races, the schooners under full sail, the satisfying views of the water, the bridge, and the distant scenery.

On this side of the Island, the spokes leading into the heart of the island are long. Sheltered coves host most of our winter ducks, and shell middens near the shores tell us that the First People knew where the pantry was fullest.

"Hold out the palm of your left hand," I instruct Ann. "Do you see how it resembles the map of Deer Isle? We began at your wrist on the left side. Burnt Cove. We sailed up the bold shore of Sunset, the fleshy base of your thumb, along the western edge of Deer Isle. Your outstretched thumb is Little Deer. Then the crotch of your thumb is the Reach, sliding down along your index finger, out to sea. All your other fingers represent the parallel grooves of islets and inlets, the east side of Deer Isle and the scatter of islands off Stonington."

Peering deep into the recesses as we head down the Reach, we pass Poplar Point and spot the Reach Beach at Gray's Cove nestled between silvery new-leaved poplars and Oak Point. Artist and basket maker Elizabeth Compton made a gift of the beach to Island Heritage Trust. At one of the trust's Walks-and-Talks outings I met a scientist who studies marine worms. He made digging in the mud so much fun that we all were motivated to go to the hardware store and buy our own version of the nifty little spade he used to show us the amazing variety of worms that hide in the sand. I look forward to revisiting the worms later this summer.

I can see why Oak Point got its name. We have no comparable stands of oak over on our western harsh and rugged side. Over here they see the sun rise over Mount Desert. Walter has to concentrate and use his chart plotter to pick our way through the submerged ledges here. He is willing to take us in toward Fish Creek just far enough to glimpse Shore Acres Preserve over at the mouth of Greenlaw Cove.

We want to get an idea of the clam flats in behind Campbell Island where mussel growing licenses are being requested. This island has just been sold to the Chewonki Foundation by the Island Institute as part of the Institute's recent move to divest itself of real estate. The protective covenants travel with the deed. Some limited overnight camping will still be allowed, and large scale development will not. The rocks that await the unwary probably offer their own form of protection from overuse.

We drop anchor to take time for lunch. The sun feels welcome. Summer certainly takes its time getting started at the ocean's edge. With a little help from the captain, I can just spot the plain white, handsome but modest farm house that belongs to Judy Hill, the friend who donated her property to the Trust to become Shore Acres Preserve. Judy said they called it that because that's what it said on an old sign they found in the barn. I happen to know it's also the name for one of the very grand Shingle Style Bar Harbor cottages on Mount Desert, designed by William Emerson, who was also the architect for Olmsted's Felsted. I bet someone here had a sense of humor, Judy.

How glad I am to have Walter at the helm over here. Charts are all well and good, but so is local knowledge. This is his side of the island. I am quite unfamiliar with the territory over here. We can see Walter's house tucked into the trees on the height of Mountainville. Much of the hillside and several of the islands are protected by conservation easement, thanks to Walter and his neighbors.

The bold shore of the Tennis Preserve looks handsome from out here. We strain to pick out the small notch of the Ovens cove, the pink beach we enjoyed in winter. I am sure both Ann and I are thinking about the thousands of eiders, now dispersed, and their mysterious sounds. No eiders today, and, I note, no docks. One of the surprises of the trip has been the burgeoning number of docks sending out their tentacles and floats along the coast. I completely understand the desire for having one's access to the sea fashioned in this way that accommodates our considerable tides. The difference between high tide and low tide averages some ten feet here. Nevertheless, I don't enjoy seeing what look like long aluminum ladders sprouting like freakish facial hairs on the face of an aging beauty. Tennis Preserve deserves a medal for what it does NOT do. Its wild shore has a remarkable unspoiled appeal.

The whole sheltered aspect of the coves over here gives me a real feeling for why this area is so attractive in winter to visiting arctic ducks. Almost every south-facing cove over here has shell middens eroding out of the banks. As I look around us at the beautiful edge of land and sea, I think that this territory must have been a wonderful place to live if you were an Indian, a First Nation person, as the Canadians like to say so accurately. The way I put it makes Ann laugh: "Indians here four thousand years ago must have thought they were in Fat City!" *fat* being quite a crucial element for survival.

We will have to make our way out around the long neck of Sunshine to peer into the next coves, Long Cove, Southeast Harbor, and the waters off Oceanville. I am fascinated to experience how different it seems over here. I had thought the Reach felt lake-like, impressed by the fact that you see the other side of it. Once we left Oak Point behind us, we are far enough south to begin to sense that the ocean is just "out there."

The tip of Sunshine has long been home to a skilled lobstering community, most of whom are named Heanssler. In addition to the fleet of fishing boats whose names I mostly do not recognize, the nearby islands sport structures quite prominently. Never having been over here, I am surprised at all the buildings on the islands. Nothing like the Thousand Islands or some parts of Washington State mind you, but nevertheless I am surprised at the number of flag poles, outbuildings, and even what looks like a tennis court.

The subtle forms of a cluster of buildings peeking out from shore are Haystack Mountain School of Crafts. What a major influence on the Island that enterprise has been. Taking its name from a former incarnation inland, Haystack not only offers employment for a significant number of local people, it offers them courses here in the winter at a time and at a price they can afford: free. Many of the newer settlers of the past decades are Haystack alumns, former faculty or students.

We opt not to follow the coves all the way in to Mariners Memorial Park created by the Evergreen Garden Club at the head of Long Cove, or to thread into Inner Harbor as far as the bridge into Holt Mill Pond and its Stonington town-owned salt marsh preserve. In years gone by these sheltered waters provided safe anchorage for a huge fleet of vessels carrying salt and mackerel in the salt fish trade.

Walt's favorite island is Little Sheep just ahead of us. This little island is owned by the State of Maine. It is truly cute. Maine Island Trail Association manages it. Walt is not only a skipper monitor for them, he is a constant salesman. "If you even look at Maine islands, you should belong to MITA!" he says. There are two kayaks pulled up on the shore and by the looks of the tent, some hardy soul is already camping there. We wave.

The shape of a sperm whale carved in pink granite opposite a green can navigational marker tells me—even before Walter does—that this must be Whaleback Ledge. I have seen many of the vistas over here out the windows of homes I have visited for parties, for Hospice volunteer work, and for Christmas Bird Counts, but this trip is such a gift! The weather has to be cooperative and many other aspects have to coalesce, but my oh my, what an interesting perspective from the water!

Speaking of perspective, from here one can look over the intervening islands and see the towering cranes of the granite quarry on Crotch Island that marks the western entrance to the Thoroughfare. At this end we can see the cut rock faces of the old quarry at Oceanville, now known as Settlement Quarry, which has become a popular preserve.

We scan Eastern Mark for signs of great blue herons. There is now a colony of about thirty nests there, perhaps including some of the very birds that used to nest on Scraggy, the island next to Mark Island Light, over at the west end of the Thoroughfare glittering in front of us.

Since sailing ships of old used this passage as the shortcut sea lane into Stonington, it became known as The Thoroughfare. Mark Island Light marked the western end of the Thoroughfare: Eastern Mark Island, with no light, marked the eastern end. Confusing perhaps, if you don't live here where they call the bay east of Vinalhaven and North Haven but on the west coast of Deer Isle, the Eastern Bay. It all depends on your point of view.

On the shore nearby we can no longer see Emily Muir's house. The property was purchased after her death by new owners who had other plans for the house site, 'grandfathered' as it was, located tantalizingly close to the water view. The rambling house that Emily and her family built was soon demolished, ironic fate for an architect's home, even if it wasn't exactly a masterpiece. The replacement house should afford a beautiful view of Russ Island, which Emily eventually gave to Island Institute. Wreck Island off in the southern distance also passed through Emily's hands to The Nature Conservancy to become a protected jewel in the Stonington archipelago. The islands have since been transferred to the Island Heritage Trust for local, hands-on care, and Philip Conkling, president of Island Institute, has his hands full with the success that he and his dear friend, the eminent photographer Peter Ralston, have made of Island Institute.

The afternoon breeze has picked up, and the day sparkles as we head into the Thoroughfare, across the bottom of our map, along the shipping lane that for two centuries has served as the principal main street of Stonington. We have to make a choice whether to follow the Thoroughfare up to the doorsteps of the town, or circle farther out toward Merchant's Row, the sea lane that functioned as a ring road, a bypass, in the days of commerce by sail. This offers a fairly rock-less route around the islands, but we have come in search of a fairly intimate acquaintance with the islands.

We take a bit of a side trip to inspect the float of the mussel farming operation. This one cultures mussels on long suspended ropes. Humans like the rope-cultured mussels because they are tasty, and furthermore, they usually don't have the pearls that wild ones coping with sand are apt to have. Eider ducks love the rope-cultured mussels because they have thinner shells than the wild ones. Eiders eat mussels whole and crush the shell in their gizzard. The mussels here are protected from eider depredation by what looks like a green plastic snow-fence, a mesh fastened to the perimeter of the float. We are most amused to see an additional force on protection duty—a scarecrow. I am not sure that is the proper term even though this is a farm at sea. The effigy in question is not a man in overalls, but a very folk art-looking wooden eagle. Brightly painted, it is not intended to keep away crows, but eiders.

"Not really a scare-eagle but a scare-eider?" I suggest.

"Eider way you want to look at it," comes the word from behind the camera.

The deep blue shape of Isle au Haut frames the view in the background for the islands out here. Maine seems to do big business in vanity license plates. One plate I saw recently offered the local pronunciation for this name said to have been bestowed by Samuel Champlain, that illustrious French Person From Far Away who visited here in 1604: IleOhHo

Walter usually sees large flocks of eiders out here. The area is recognized as a favored and highly significant eider molting grounds. Duck Mountain and Duck Harbor on Isle au Haut take their name from the earlier practice of herding flightless molting eiders into the cove where they were clubbed to death. Sea ducks formed an often very significant survival fare for humans, first the Indians, and later the Europeans. Harlequin ducks are found in the area, particularly off Spoon Island. These gloriously handsome ducks are occasionally seen inshore during the winter storms. Just this winter they were reported in Sheep Thief Gulch. That name does not appear on the charts, but the other names here—Humpkins Ledge, Hell's Half Acre, Grog, and Devil, might also be trying to tell us something.

Out to the southeast is Saddleback Island, recently purchased by Maine Coast Heritage Trust. Indians lived there even to recent memory. When we first came here, we met Penobscots coming in their pickup trucks from Indian Island up by Orono to enjoy the shore and gather sweet grass. Only the vehicle has changed much over the millennia.

Gooseberry Island just beyond McGlathery is protected by an easement held by Acadia. Like Isle au Haut, which is part of Acadia National Park, that represents protection, but Mainers have a deep mistrust of anything federal. I do not know whether that was part of Margaret Hundley's thinking when she chose The Nature Conservancy to take care of islands she no doubt regarded primarily as bird habitat. Ken used to go birding with Margaret. She was, with Ralph Odell, essentially the area's ornithology authority. She willed her islands Round and Millet to TNC, which were recently transferred to IHT in the Conservancy's policy of concentrating on large, ecologically significant parcels and leaving the smaller properties to the more appropriate local custody.

I realize that most of the protected islands in this stunning archipelago have one thing in common: they were all owned at one time by naturalist Persons From Away. I think this reflects the need of the local people for the money to be realized from such sales. While none of the buyers were wealthy, they must have seemed relatively or at least sufficiently affluent to make them targets of sales offers. Since by local tradition one went where one wanted, probably not much more than the right to pay real estate taxes was considered as given up. The subsequent transfer to conservation organizations has proved an excellent way to make sure one's descendents will always have the right to enjoy the islands. Many of the islands are open to the public, and all contribute significantly to a healthy marine environment, not to mention the charm of unspoiled beauty. What a scattering of gems, this island archipelago!

We can really sense the open sea as the boat, comfortable and seaworthy as it is, turns its teeth into the wind. It's cold! Glimpses of Stonington from the water have the charm of a needlepoint sampler. Gratefully we head for the protected waters of the Thoroughfare. I can scarcely imagine lobstering here under sail in a small boat, but that's what men here did. Allen Fifield, our first friend in Burnt Cove, used to tell me stories of his days fishing as he fashioned netting, that is, he knit bait bags and trap heads. Allen was a salty character and taught Ken the decidedly salty name the fishermen had for the pair of huge boulders on the western end of Crotch Island. As if the name Crotch isn't rude enough, the fishermen use a rather Shakespearean epithet, Old Man's Arse, for describing the two huge pink granite boulders nestled cheek to cheek against each other on the shore. Their huge size (big as buildings) and their contours and crack must be unmistakable glimpsed even briefly through fog. I'm sure Walter never points them out on his tours, and equally certain that many of his customers do notice and do privately nickname these distinctive rocks.

As we marvel at the cranes and piles of abandoned granite blocks strewn about on Crotch Island, Walt tells us that each block of the granite being quarried these days weighs thirty-five thousand pounds. Small wonder the bridge trembles when the trucks carrying the huge granite blocks pass over. The granite counter top market has been a main force in reviving the industry. Walt should know. When he first moved to the island, he started a very successful small business in Deer Isle granite gift items.

We check for seals resting on the ledges by Mark—just two—and smile at the sound of the fog horn as we pass, not because it's a lovely sound—it is not—but because it is familiar. We know we're almost home.

The lovely spire of Burnt Cove Church at the head of the cove makes the message official, completing the picture no less forcefully than a red Chinese seal completes and compliments a scroll painting. Since Emily now lies buried in the churchyard there, it occurs to me that I have been here long enough to have buried a significant number of friends and acquaintances. I am conscious of how the local accent has changed, the particular sounds that have all but disappeared. As Ann and I document our responses to the physical loveliness, I find myself again and again trying to give her some idea of the people I have known, the donors who founded the preserves, or their children who were often no less important in the process. It's a story that is recent, contemporary and on-going, a dynamic hypertext, beads on a string.

Not only are the natural areas jewels, but the people connected with the lands were gems, generous to the core in ways large and small. Emily Muir was the one who loaned us her building crew to build our house. She gave me a sketch she had made as girl, a drawing of Mark Island Lighthouse from the steamboat. Carolyn Olmsted bought my first painting, an eider duckling, and saw to it that eventually I got the painting back.

I'm to meet with Judy Hill next week. Her parents sold us our first sailboat at a ridiculously modest price: our first living room couch cost more. Judy's father had designed and built the boat, and her mother sewed the sails on her treadle machine. Judy and her sister learned to sail in that sturdy craft, as did our sons and then our grandchildren.

Are we, Ken and I, almost the only ones left who personally knew these extraordinary ordinary folks who so generously endowed this island with land in trust for the future? The fact that Deer Isle is not Mount Desert, and our builders and benefactors are not the Rockefellers and their friends, is indeed an interesting story, one very likely to be overlooked. It feels important to tell the story for future generations to ponder.

Obviously, the cast of characters here is little more than a sample. One can no more accurately credit a single person with the preservation of land than give credit for the ocean to the final wave that breaks on the beach. Further, the possibilities for pilgrimage are many. On each of the many other ways to traverse the islands, in space and in time, the folks you would meet would be different. Necklaces, necklaces, necklaces.

I consider this a red letter day. Not only is it a day in June, not a rare day in June, because it is very, very foggy, but it is a day thronged with the deliciously ordinary.

Ann and I are heading over to Judy Hill's property on the Reach. As we get out of the car, I observe that one of my favorite species of moths has put in an appearance: spear-marked blacks—black-and-white winged, day-flying moths. I love this little creature with the silvery chevrons on its wings. In the first place, my affection may stem from the fact that it took me years to be aware THAT it was; then more years to learn WHAT it was. And then I had to cope with the humbling acknowledgment of my ignorance. This very common moth flies by day, not night as I had foolishly and lazily supposed.

Shadblow is quite gone. The other day three pink lady slipper orchids sprang up not far from my front door. Sadly, after a single night of splendor, one of the plants looked like a colander kelp, thanks to the multitude of holes scraped into the leaves by the slugs. Slugs had even decapitated a bloom which I then rescued, taking it indoors to live a bit longer in a vase. However, its survival may not be called living. It would not be destined to produce seed. That is the sad fate of much that we labor to save.

Across the island apple blossoms are blowing petals in the wind and humming with bees. There is still considerable doubt as to whether any bees were able to fly on the crucial days to see that the strawberries got pollinated in time for berries for Fourth of July.

Judy routinely leaves her car parked at the head of the lane leading to her shore when she feels it is too rutted for the clammers to take their pickups down it. This signal works amicably and she has never seen any sign of ill feeling about access. As a board member of Island Heritage Trust, Judy is one of those spearheading the trust's concern about maintaining traditional shore access for clammers.

The junipers and huge "wolf" pines with branches that once branched out to the sunshine in all directions at the head of the trail at Shore Acres Preserve can be read as a manifestation of the power of old field succession. Amid the juniper there are still mats of blueberries not yet shaded out by the encroaching woods.

The blueberry colors at this time of year are among my favorite, a combination of red and green for which there is no adequate name. To make matters even more interesting, ordinarily I hate magenta, but just this week the rhodora blossoms are out, decidedly magenta. I would not think the coppery-orange of red and green would partner well with magenta, but it's a combination I love.

At corners of blueberry fields in our area sit stacks of somewhat weather-worn bee hives. These rent-a-bees have been trucked in from the south, an invertebrate migrant labor pool. The hum of bees in a row of pin cherries is pleasant, but the hives inside the electric fence "compounds" up in the big commercial fields around Cherryfield I find frightening. As well I should. Signs clearly warn intruders of DANGER. The fence itself seems to promise Gulag-style voltage. The air is filled with bee traffic worthy of an Alfred Hitchcock film. The barrens there are kept absolutely a blueberry monoculture by aggressive herbicide use. To my eye it looks as if some diseases from another planet has taken over.

The Shore Acres woods certainly does not suffer from "mono," being environmentally exceptionally diverse. Our local retired forester loves to give nature walks here. Last year's maples and birches enrich the bark texture offerings. A parula warbler and a black-throated green sing off in the shaggy forest. How I love it but find it challenging that on Deer Isle the warblers come all at once like a final exam rather than lesson by lesson.

Shiny green leaves of goldthread that bloomed a month ago and star flowers and bunchberry's miniature dogwood blooms line the path. They glow like stars in the fog. March is when the sea here is at its coldest; September is the warmest month. The air over the sea is always warmer than the water. When there is sufficient humidity in the air we get fog. All the spring runoff we've had so far this year has sent cold melt water down to the sea. The great gyre that is the Gulf of Maine has really been churning with the power from the rivers and streams stirring it and keeping the water temperatures low and humidity high.

The engine that powers the Gulf of Maine is one of those complex natural systems that we are just beginning to understand, one that we expect to be impacted by the forces that drive global warming.

The Greenland glaciers melt. Being fresh water, they reach their greatest density just before freezing and, heavy, drop. The fall drives the deep ocean circulation for most of the world. What if we accelerate warming? Will the resulting melting disrupt the system? What if... what if...

Foggy air cocoons us, warm, quiet, utterly stilled. The hum of mosquitoes around our heads fairly roars. Droplets of water conduct the sound even better than dry air does, so we stop to listen for the Mark Island horn from across the island. Judy says she has often heard it. If anyone else were on the trail we would surely hear them. I am always amused at how far I can hear every word the lobstermen say to each other as they haul their pots off our shore—or how many intimate details I have heard of the lives of the kayakers who paddle by there apparently unaware of the phenomenon.

Ferns are at their most charming these days: the fiddleheads of most species have coyly unrolled most but not all of the way out to their full luxuriance. On our side of the island the north winds still patrol the bay and our ferns are noticeably behind these. The path through the woods on the Shore Acres Preserve, which Judy so generously donated, is still a bit squishy as Ann and I head down to the shore. The winter snow cover we had this year means that more mice were probably able to hide from predators such as foxes and snowy owls to survive in safety. That means we can expect more Lyme disease this year as the spirochete causing the disease passes from rodents to deer ticks to humans. So far there has not been much Lyme disease reported here.

Containers of every sort—old tires, cans and the like—will be brimming with the water of our long wet spring, just the sort of places *Aedes Canadensis canadensis*, the species of mosquito that carries West Nile disease, likes best. West Nile too has not been reported here. Both will no doubt soon make their appearance. Wet woods are not to that particular mosquito's liking, so we do not have to worry about them— just the other hungry ones—as we make our soupy way down the trail.

Unfortunately the blackflies are out in full force over at Ann's. Here on the Island we are not much plagued by blackflies. They require moving water to breed, and we have only a few small streams trickling out to the sea. There are drawbacks to living across the bridge on The Continent. In the Maine Woods, the situation is dire. They say there you have only two animals to fear—the bears and the blackflies, and usually the bears don't bite. Ann and I joke about this as we brush off mosquitoes that have already raised welts on my face and neck. I remind Ann that, like blackflies, it's only the females who bite. Adding insult to injury, studies show that the she-devils particularly love the taste of people who have gotten angry. Seems we give off different pheromones when we get mad. This morning at the grocery store I heard a man report that thanks to all the rain, the mosquitoes over at his place "would lift ya' hat right up."

A few weeks ago this trail was almost impassably wet, so instead of trekking here we joined the clammers at the Causeway Beach for a work session-cum-barbeque. Then the clammers were facing the painful closing of the flats—throughout the entire state—because of the fresh water run-off from all the rain. Not only does the change in salinity enable different populations of bacteria to bloom, but the floods bring down all manner of potentially toxic runoff so the flats must be closed.

As the clammers pointed out, it really hurts to have the flats closed just now. All this hard winter they saw flats frozen under sheets of ice so they could not get out to dig. Just when they might hope to recoup some, the runoff closed the flats. To make matters worse, red tide was making an earlier than usual appearance this year, riding the wind-driven cold currents into our area of the bay. The clammers were devoutly hoping that things would improve by the Fourth of July. Speculation abounds as to what astronomical heights the price of clams might reach by then but so far it does not look likely that flats will reopen in time.

The clammers in attendance that day would have come even if it had meant missing a working tide for them; that's how much they believe in the clam reseeding project. There was much joking about their being out on the "closed" flats with their clam hoes in hand, but they also had a special permit for the group in pocket. They fanned out under the direction of University of Maine Sea Grant's marine biologist Dana Morse, Marine Extension Associate with the Darling Marine Center. Continuing the three-year clam restoration project at this spot, they laid out a variety of test materials to encourage the settling of clam spat and protecting them from subsequent predation. These "clam tents" were expensive erosion control fabric that looked almost like bedsprings, or a white plastic "hardware" cloth to which floats were tied at intervals, or loops of PVC which turned sheets into min-Quonset huts.

In 1999 the Deer Isle-Stonington Shellfish Committee was able get an ordinance passed on the island limiting commercial clam licenses principally to island residents. Previously, off-island clammers had unscrupulously cleaned out several prime areas.

"They came in 14' aluminum boats and left with every single clam. Piled to the gunnels they were. Don't know who would buy those clams. Can't even eat the little ones, and nobody wants the tough old big ones."

"Those little clams are just so cute. Even after… well, more years than I would care to admit of digging I still think that," admitted one of the two sisters who dig. "Island clam buyers now will not purchase any clams from such diggers."

Classic Maine summer morning fog came and went and came in again, painting the scene with an unrealistic loveliness. Talk turned to recreational licenses and their holders. If you own a commercial license you are no longer eligible for a recreational license here—it's viewed as potentially just an excuse to get out and raid our flats. The genuine recreational clammers, however, are viewed with amused affection. "They don't know where to dig, or how to dig, so they just take a few token clams and head off to buy a good mess for dinner." I refrained from telling them about a relative of mine who once resorted to sneaking out to "plant" some clams in his cove so he could show his visiting grandson how to dig clams.

The clammers then added some detail to the perils of not knowing where to dig. "There are springs out there, where the fine clay just pools."

"Honey pots," laughed another.

"Regular sink holes. The clammers know where they are, but you step in one, and you could just sink, 4 feet, 8 feet, just gone."

I don't know whether the story was for my benefit or not. I have not yet confessed to Ann that one of the days when I volunteered to census the horseshoe crabs over at her house, circumstances forced me to go alone. I was checking out an area not in our plot and accidentally stepped into a hole, sinking to my waist. I was sufficiently stuck to feel apprehension, which makes me think the clammers do not exaggerate.

I had caused some amusement to the clammers when I found myself stuck in the mud on the day we were reseeding. I sank deep in the colloidal ooze thanks to the properties of its clay as we stood and talked.

"Just curl your toes and rock back and forth in your boots, dear," they urged. "Rock, baby, rock!" called Dot, the clam warden, from her safe perch atop a barnacled rock.

When I finally managed to come unglued, I nearly toppled, but one of the muddy men in hooded sweatshirt and big boots had reached out and gallantly saved me. "You got to just accept that some time you are going to wipe out," another consoled me. "Happens to anyone."

"I've been clamming here since I was four. My grandfather taught me," Chandler Eaton, a classically Yankee-looking fisherman who also happens to be a certified organic gardener said to me as we slopped along over the gooey mud. "We never took the tiny ones and always left the biggest ones as seeders. I always had all the clams I could dig in the spots we took care of that way."

Chan may have been initially skeptical of the "expert from away" (Walpole!) who had come for the day, but the informal manner of marine biologist Dana Morse quickly won over the clammers. This affable young man taught the clammers how to gather scientific census data.

"Take a coffee can and press it into the mud till it's full. Then empty the mud contents into a plastic bag and leave it by the test plot. Then we come along and gather up the sample, wash it in this screen sieve and count and measure all the little clams. Very high tech, right?"

"Just like pannin' for gold," laughed one clammer, and indeed it is. Such data are crucial both for environmental base line studies and the comparative reseeding tests, but even better, Dana also listened attentively to the men and women diggers with their extensive local knowledge. So far there has been little data gathered about the actual clam populations here or much of anywhere on the coast of Maine. On the Island alone the clam committee reckons that locally dug clams contribute to the economy here some $700,000 annually. Best we document this resource before it is threatened.

As the fog moved in and then receded that day, a pair of bald eagles came and went to feed their two chicks in the new nest established on the island across the way. To watch the eaglets, spotting scopes and even one astronomer's telescope were set up along the beach during the cook-out which marked the successful completion of the day.

As Dorothy Powell, the island's no-nonsense clam warden, sauntered over to take a look through the telescope, the clammers joked "Anybody out on the flats had better watch out. Dot can see you real good now."

Ann and I are still absorbing and processing the events of that clam reseeding day. As we wend our way through the regrowing timber stands at Shore Acres, we talk about the idea of managing for sustainability. We talk about how evolving situations and consequent changing ideas of management are coming about. All this happens within the working life of a single man. What a challenge.

Like the lobstermen, the clammers are quick to say that they value being their own boss. Unlike lobstermen, the clammers can go out early, work in the low tide, and return home by midmorning with a good day's pay. The best among them can make as much or more money than they would as some fisherman's sternman. Good clammers, like lobstermen, are tough, savvy, and strong as well as independent. After that stepping into waist-deep holes counting horseshoe crabs at Ann's, I am certainly convinced that local knowledge is a wonderful thing. I do often think about what is being lost as ways of living here change.

Beyond doubt, I am increasingly aware of the change in the character of the population here on the island. Both the kinds of people who live here and the kinds who visit are changing. My brother, I observe to Ann, never refers to his customers as "dudes." That, however, has long been the common term used here on the island for the paying customers of the windjammers that cruise these waters. Recently I was doing some reading about what was the only three-masted schooner in the tourist trade around here, the *Victory Chimes*. Inspired by the profitable trade that ranchers in the West were turning by becoming dude ranches, in 1954 a Maine syndicate bought the Chesapeake Bay windjammer named the *Edward and Maude*, refitted her and renamed her *Victory Chimes* to carry paying customers who wanted to experience the romantic notion they have of the sea.

There was quite a fuss here in the state when the design for the new twenty-five cent piece was first announced. The three-masted schooner on the quarter didn't look quite right, but the *Victory Chimes* is surely the image representing Maine.

We've started seeing windjammers once again on the bay, ever since Memorial Day. At about the same time, the tide of out-of-state auto license plates began to rise. Parking places in front of the post office will soon fall to record lows I suspect.

Judy and her sister, Elizabeth, went to high school on the Island. Their parents, Clark and Marjorie, thought about avoiding the rat race of urban life and taking up farming. Clark turned his interest in the Hill Brothers shoe company over to his brothers. Lib and Judy (who shared the name of Marjorie with her mother) were here attending the French Camp. Marjorie came home with photographs of possible Island places, and they chose the one that seemed most promising for farming. Clark declared that the old house and outbuildings didn't appear to have anything wrong with them that he probably could not fix. Marjorie agreed that was probably true, so they headed to Deer Isle. The family jokes that they were probably the first hippies. Not too far from the

truth. They quietly led a life of self-sufficiency not unlike that to which the Nearings over on Cape Rosier aspired and which they popularized in their writings.

Marjorie was beloved librarian at the town library for years. Clark not only made most of the tools he used, he made charming shadow boxes of ship models. From time to time these little craft gems turn up at Island house sales, treasures much sought after.

After getting her PhD in psychology from Boston

University, free spirit Judy taught a while at Harvard, and in Mexico, before heading off to Alaska, while Lib married and raised three children in New Hampshire. Judy serves both the Deer Isle-Stonington Historical Society and Island Heritage Trust as an indefatigable board member, and she maintains the family farm house in all its former braided-rug dignity. The handsome classic house and barn and outbuildings can be glimpsed from the trail edging the preserve and looking back from the shore outlook.

As the preserve trail leads up a rise of land to overlook the cove, the trees are ever more festooned with lichens making them look to Ann and me like trolls with mustaches. A grand fallen pine trunk lies in moss-covered majesty. It is what foresters call a nurse tree, quite mysterious. Mossy stilts standing around an empty space are the only clue that an older tree once lay there. The tree we are seeing was once just a sprout atop the one that has vanished. All looks very much like a storybook forest for Hansel and Gretel, gentle but not really fearsome. However, I suspect Judy's father would have had some words to say about the challenges of trying to wrest a living from this land.

The spear-marked blacks are not the only moths we scare up. Another tawny one may be a maple moth. There are plenty of red or swamp maples here, and poplar. I feel we are confirming our observations from the boat trip. Ground truthing, as it were.

Our way is now strewn with blue mussel shells and empty clam shells. We are approaching a prime flat, it seems. Crows and raccoons no doubt agree. When we step onto a sloping pink granite boulder at the shore's edge, we can look back at the bank and see fragments of old clam shells, a midden eroding out of the bank. Indians, too, knew a good shellfish spot when they found it.

Ann and I stand gazing out at the blue profile of Mount Desert Island and the Reach where we so recently sailed. We look across the narrow band of the remains of last year's growth of salt hay, sea lavender, and seaside goldenrod, remembering the aerial view photographs we have seen of the circles left by mussel draggers. That abundance of scattered mussel and clam shells we saw back on the path testifies that the otters, crows, raccoons, and maybe mink—as well as man—need to harvest here successfully. The clammer's boat pulled up and resting on the shore is merely waiting the next good tide. This is where the mussel farm application is pending. What would the addition of a mussel farm do to the water column here? Mussels are very efficient filter feeders. Would the operation affect clamming?

Local fishermen hate the idea of having areas of the sea closed to them. They distrust intensive farming activities, wondering how they can do anything but disrupt crucial natural patterns in the water column. The clam committee is following this development closely. They appreciate full well the concept of managing a habitat for increased but sustainable yields of food for our burgeoning world. But…

Secrets

High in the birch,
wee bird face yellow-green as
sun in spring-new leaves,
what are you doing there?

Beating your wings
like a hummingbird,
launching out
with maypole streamers—
birch tickertape,
bark confetti bits
drifting on the June breeze.

Ah, disappear into the
shadows of spruce,
beak full of bark
from which you'll weave
a tiny cup of hidden nest.

As you strip the birch,
your destiny you do unroll:
not sex, but parenthood
society's best kept secret.

Spotted Sandpiper

Just at the silver seam
between the sea and shore
the spotted sandpiper
teeters, speaks softly to itself
a poem it has by heart.

July — MARINERS PARK — 5

4:00 AM: the roads are fairly empty. The occasional pickup truck speeds along, somebody's sternman a bit late for work. Lobstermen see quite a different world here than the rest of our stay-abed population sees. I am quite sure that feeling of exclusive ownership is part of the allure of this tough profession. By 4:45 the stars have all faded. Two pickup trucks are already parked at the tide's edge, clammers working this tide for all it's worth, being one of the few areas in the state still open despite the run off and red tide issues.

A couple of thrushes are yelling across the meadow at each other, "creep" calls back and forth. For the past hour, male songbirds have been tuning up for the day with call conversations rather than the full songs that come later. Catbird has tuned up with an outpouring of sound.

The edge of the sky dome becomes lovely lavender-pink. Above is a band of pale yellow and then above, that baby blue dome overhead that for this brief time looks pure, innocent.

Hawkweed heads are tightly closed, screwed shut like eyes unwilling to look at the sun. Mosquitoes are out in good number, though not any blackflies yet.

I have come to regard the hill where I sit or stand on the granite bench as the center of a clock face. Birders all use this convention so they can easily tell a companion to look at "Four o'clock for the sparrow, another at six." Perhaps that clock idea is what has inspired me to consider Mariners Memorial Park around the temporal clock as well. This lovely little spot is open to the public from dawn to dusk. In early summer here, that means quite a few hours.

At "9 o'clock" on my spatial clock face, I hear a yellow-throat and the burr of an alder flycatcher, down in the alders, of course. The air is still. The tide clock shows a single channel remaining out in the middle of the clam flats. As I sweep the flats with binoculars I hear the clattering call of several terns. Knowing they probably nest out on Hardhead, the terns' last stronghold here, I am impressed. Of course, by air, the distance is not that great. I follow their flight, threading in companionable undulations, white sprites.

I walk through the dewy grass to the small hill where I laid out the white sheet last night to check for moths. A friend reports that once again her porch light has attracted a luna moth. It is as if this species is determined to be present for the Fourth of July North American Butterfly Association's annual butterfly count. Like the Audubon Christmas bird count, this is an effort to recruit amateurs to help gather data that some day may be important to a species' survival. So far I have not enough people on the Island who feel willing and able to count the eighty to a hundred species of butterflies we are at all likely to have in our range over the entire season.

The moth wouldn't technically qualify anyway, since it is not a butterfly, but oh so lovely the pale jade green color and its gracefully long-tailed wings that I feel specially blessed whenever I see one. What I have been seeing so far this season is an enchanting array of delicately marked brown-rust-grey-and-white small and medium-sized moths. Sure enough, they await my inspection on the sheet hidden somewhat discretely so no curious person will come investigate. I had considered getting permission to pitch a tent and leaving a light burning all night to attract a bumper crop of moths, but I decided against that.

In past years the little park was an attractive nuisance, the scene of out of control parties. The picnic grills were trashed; broken bottle glass was everywhere. When the picnic tables the Boy Scouts built were vandalized, that was the last straw. A committee of the dedicated Evergreen Garden Club members volunteered to "love this place" into safety and security. They put up new signs, planted garden flowers in the parking area turn around, mowed a walking path around the perimeter, and planted the hillside with naturalized daffodils given by grateful patients in honor of a much-loved physician, Dr. Thomas Garland, who was retiring. The civilizing campaign has worked quite well.

I'd hate to be responsible, even inadvertently or unjustly, for in any way causing visitors to think the day-use-only rules are not truly meant. I'll settle for making a beer syrup to paint on nearby tree trunks so I can come back early tomorrow and make a moth overnight count.

Off at the edge of the woods I hear a red squirrel chirring, and then the snort of a deer, and the sharp small sounds as it stamps away. Chickadees call fiercely to each other.

At "5 o'clock" a few white wisps of clouds above the tree line light up, perhaps half way up the sky dome. Off to the south and west, like a giant bathtub ring is the grey haze I have come to recognize as the ominous signal predicting that we may be due for a day of unhealthy ozone levels in the air, a smog inversion just when we finally have a lovely, warm old-fashioned summer day. That seems to be the new fashion.

A twitter overhead—and I see a lone tree swallow circling this meadow like a kestrel. To a blackfly I imagine the dainty bird bears all the hefty threat of a hawk.

5:00 AM: dawn itself, the actual rising of the sun, is coming. Radiating up from the ragged spruce tree line there is now a gorgeous glow. Because our house faces firmly west I rarely get the opportunity to observe dawns. I relish the details. I never get used to that "high energy" look.

6:00 AM: Seagulls, herring gulls, off in the cove are mewing. Sunlight now illuminates the far shores. Spruce trees stand out from the summer green of poplar and birch. Sunlight gleaming on the hull of the single lobster boat moored out in the channel is tourist-calendar lovely.

Not far from where I am, I now see the gauzy tent of a colony of tent caterpillars, none stirring outside as yet. They have quite denuded the top branches of the little cherry tree in which they have built.

Chainsaw whine comes across the cove waters. A nearby development has local residents quite upset at the density proposed. Our island is not well prepared for the onslaught of enterprising souls who are quite prepared to maximize their own profits to whatever degree they can get away with.

7:00 AM: butterflies are beginning to warm up. Azure blue fairies, small butterflies actually, start up as we walk. Summer Azures. Entomologists have now come to feel that Spring Azures are more properly divided into a species that feeds on blueberries, another that is devoted to chokecherries, with perhaps several more. Since their caterpillars emerge at different times and eat what is in bloom then, different azures do not interbreed. Isn't that a significant part of the accepted definition of species?

Ann somewhat gleefully points out that blackflies are now awaking, and that her property "over the bridge" is far from the only home they know. How, I wonder, did the Indians ever stand the insects? It must be the tiny stream that feeds the head of this cove, Long Cove, that provided them breeding habitat. Right adjacent to the stream is the spot known to this day as The Haulover. One could canoe from the big bay on the west, into what the early settlers designated as the Mill Pond, and at the end of that, one can carry a small boat cross the spit of land to use Long Cove to carry you all the way out to the Reach and Frenchman's Bay. Otters do it all the time. Ken saw a family of otters the other morning, crossing our little dirt road, an adult and two kits, on their way from the sea to the bog a short ways inland.

The catbird is still caroling exuberantly. An osprey circling above us gives its distinctive cry. The occasional chink of a clam hoe floats across the cove. On this shore a clammer leans against a boulder having a morning coffee and a snack. We wave to each other, and he resumes his arduous labor.

A car pulls up and out jumps a poodle. Out the driver's door comes the dog's master, and then a woman unfolds from the front seat. The couple wear binoculars. The air is suddenly accosted with the whine of a motor nearby, one of the new landscaper's "must-have gadgets" I would say from the obnoxious whine of it. I can read the birders' body language loud and clear. For the moment all bird song is drowned out. The man and woman seem to be saying to each other something like "Is this what we came on vacation for?"

Trying to get away from suburbia, but it follows them here. They shrug and head off to the woods path to follow their dog. I see no sign of a leash. Presumably they see no sign, at least not the one that informs guests of the park to keep their dogs on a lead at all times. How well I recall sitting at planning meetings of the garden club's park committee, discussing dog policies. It was considered quite generous to allow dogs at all. The state regulations for public places and insurance regulations are quite clear that dogs must be on leash at all times. We decided that this park is more like a domestic garden than even the suggestion of a wilderness area. Plants that behave themselves and animals that behave themselves are welcome here—and people who behave themselves, for that matter—all are welcome, native or not.

8:00 AM: the dew on the grasses is drying and the hawkweeds are opening where the sun hits directly. Nearby, oxeye daisies are offering bright yellow platforms to the new day. On one a small moth lies in an odd position. As Ann bends closer with her camera, I see that the little moth is in the deadly embrace of one of the flower spiders, what is called a goldenrod spider, a round, white and yellow quite lovely creature, if you can ignore the details of how it gets its breakfast.

Along the stems of the hawkweeds glisten spoonfuls of foamy spittle. Related to leafhoppers and treehoppers are the spittlebugs that make these spit globs. Perhaps the foam keeps the young spittle bug nymphs from drying out or perhaps it keeps them hidden from predators.

Spittlebugs are small, green, triangular and hump-backed, much like treehoppers. The Buffalo treehopper, which is found on apple trees, takes its name after the characteristic shape it shares with the American bison. The eggs of the Buffalo treehopper were laid under the bark of apples and other deciduous trees. Now these spring-hatched nymphs are in the grasses at the bases of the trees.

The treehoppers are just now starting to come of age, in mid-July; that is, the lucky ones who have managed so far to avoid predations, diseases, and being parasitized. It strikes me as somewhat remarkable, and humbling, that the insects themselves face a turn-around-is-fair-play situation. Just as humans may become ill if they are bitten by a mosquito that has previously fed on an intermediate host infected with a disease organism, so it is with the plant and insect world.

I find the many species of tiny treehoppers cute. Of the 2,500 species there are of treehoppers alone I claim to be able to differentiate none of them, lumping them as treehoppers or leafhoppers or spittlebugs, and feeling satisfied with even that naming. I am aware that when the treehoppers have fed on a previously affected plant, they carry the infecting organism, a phytoplasma, or various viruses on to hosts such as our domestic grains, beets, raspberries, garden flowers, and turf grasses. The unhappy results become apparent to us as leaf scorch, or the odd growths known as witches brooms or aster yellows. Infections may plague maples, grapes, elms, roses—and I called the 'hoppers cute. All in the eye of the beholder, as they say.

A car in the parking lot. It's the elderly gentleman with the two scottie dogs, more appropriately called Highland terriers? I would call them "magnet doggies" for the pair I had as a child. One black and one white, these small plastic figures were glued onto magnet bars. Their two ends repelled or attracted each other in most enchanting ways. Put one dog on top of a piece of cardboard and the other below for more magical effects. These little doggies are obviously well trained. I see them and their master out for their morning constitutional in various places around the island.

The garden club has had a path mowed around the perimeter of Mariners Park so that it is fairly easy walking for the somewhat challenged. If you walk clockwise and then turn around and repeat the walk in a counterclockwise fashion, you will have done exactly a mile. The view in one direction is spectacular, in the other, quite different and wonderful. We call it the Miracle Mile. It will do wonders for your health if you do it often. We marked off tenths of a mile so you could encourage yourself to do whatever multiple the doctor has ordered. I see that recently some fancy stakes have appeared including a web page address.

Part of the miracle of this mile is what it surrounds: a park. It is not a municipal entity, just the result of the foresight and dedication of generous-minded volunteers. Furthermore, these folks were dyed-in-the wool local Island volunteers, folks quite busy enough earning a living from the meager resources of a Maine island. In 1961 a group headed by Ethel Farrell and Captain Walter Scott chartered the Evergreen Garden Club. Ethel's son John still runs the Island's only photography shop and Islanders still engage him to photograph their weddings the old fashioned way. The Scott family was one of the Island's first European settlers to arrive. They've been serving the island as mariners—fishing, crewing yachts, manning the ferry, you name it, ever since.

The twenty-three acres of the old Morey Farm at the head of Long Cove would have made someone a very nice estate. The view was charming, daisies and black-eyed Susans spangled the meadow, and the blueberries were abundant. What more could any one ask? As a club project the garden club members decided that these twenty-three acres should be a park for the benefit of the whole community, not just those tucked away at the ends of lanes on summer estates. In 1962 they erected a granite memorial, which still stands by the water's edge to commemorate "all the men who have lost their lives at sea."

Perhaps it was the generous endowment of summer fog, but Island gardens used to be extraordinary in the days of home gardens, before it took two income earners working away from home. At any rate, these energetic and knowledgeable gardeners planted ornamental trees and shrubs along what they called Memory Lane. To be certain that this park does not get swallowed up in the race to progress or profit, the Evergreen Garden Club granted a conservation easement to be held in perpetuity by the Island Heritage Trust.

9:00 AM: the hawkweeds, both orange and yellow species, are now a-buzz with insect traffic. Most are the attractively-colored small wasps and flies that most of us are never aware of. I remember in Costa Rica being asked what species is the most significant carnivore, the predator in the rainforest. Most people answered "jaguar", but the correct answer referred to these inconspicuous wasps that parasitize other insects by laying eggs on them that hatch and dine on the victim's flesh. Nature is no less fierce here in this old Maine field we call Mariners Memorial Park.

Ann has a field day in the type of habitat that ecologists call old field succession. The light is perfect and the place is superb, even if to the untutored it might look like a shaggy old field. I see Ann bending near gleaming flower after flower with her macro lens. The tachinid flies that visit the flowers are not much to look at, but many of the small flower flies and wasps are quite attractively colored, with jewel-toned eyes or thorax. Now that I have learned to look more closely at the throning air around the drifts of blooming flowers smiling back at the summer sun,

I could sit for hours just watching the insect traffic. Many are marked with black and white or yellow stripes imitative of what we think of as the stinging wasps and hornets.

I say we think of them as the stingers, but in fact most do not sting unless we provoke them. Having lived amicably for years with various wasps and hornets banging themselves on the white clapboards of the old farm house which was my home I can speak to their tolerance.

I did have a quite justified run-in with a group of paper wasps who built here under a deck bench. They were really angry with me when I tried to banish them using a large mixing bowl and thin cookie sheet. The only ones of the bees and wasp family that I would not call benign-if-unbothered are the yellow jackets. They seem to have quite nasty tempers—and an unerring sense for picnics.

Among my favorites of the flower-visiting flies and wasps are what we call accurately hover flies. Here is one right before my eyes, defying gravity, wings a blur that puts even a hummingbird to shame. Quite a few insects are amazingly accurate little bee mimics. Some of the clear-winged moths I see later in the summer are such good copies of hummingbirds, I really have to look twice. All quite steal the show from flowers, at least if the human audience is entomologist, or daughter of same, as I am.

It's very anthropocentric of us to label as "pests" those organisms that eat what we were planning to eat, and label "beneficial" insects those that prey on the ones we call pests. There are so many, many kinds of organisms out here, that I feel quite humble in their presence. A good dose of humility is in order whenever we mere humans decide to meddle in this complex system. We really do not yet know what we are doing.

I hear the birders at the forest edge making that hissing noise they call "pishing." I guess they have not thought how disturbing that must be to a nesting bird. Well, yes, they do know it's disturbing. That is why they are doing it; to draw the bird out where they can see it. However, they probably think they are the only ones who ever visit this remote island outpost. Visitors to our island preserves are generally unaware of just how many of them there are these days. A steady stream of visitors tromps all the paths on every summer day and a good many of the other days, year round. Just take a look down at your feet and see the path wear and you will get an idea what we are dealing with.

10: 00 AM: a twitter and a tree swallow darts into nest box placed not far from the parking lot. Some year perhaps we will add additional nest boxes and the tree swallows might then leave the spares for bluebirds.

Making their leisurely way above the sea of daisies and hawkweeds and ripe grasses are several ringlets. These small butterflies are a gorgeous study in subtle colors. A close look with binoculars reveals delicate shades of buff, of rose, of lavender.

There is nothing subtle about the bright flash of orange that is a skipper; and then another flashes up. The two interact like a pair of pugilists. Feint, feint, feint; they rise higher and higher in the still, sunny morning air. I had just a glimpse of the biplane look of the wings of the first one before it took off. These look like paper airplanes with delta wings folded not quite firmly. Whether a skipper folds its wing sharply over its back or holds them out parallel with the ground or holds one set partway in between is one way we separate them for identification.

Back when we had all the rain, I spent quite a while with a field guide making charts to help me learn to identify damsel and dragonfly species through binoculars. So how is it that when a large, chunky grey dragon comes clattering over my hilltop, I still can't be sure which one? Another and another noticeably smaller-sized one comes by. Perhaps I am making progress because I know to look for general color, then color of abdomen (and whether or not the abdomen has a distinctive enlargement at the far end) and whether or not the wings have any distinctive markings, and then the markings on thorax…and the eyes, did I get the eye color? And if green, do they meet at the crown or are they quite separate….

11:00 AM: an SUV with an out-of-state license plate pulls up to the parking lot and disgorges four ladies in wide-brimmed hats. From the music of their chatter it seems they are obviously enjoying each other's company and the bright day. As they near my hill-top perch one sees my clipboard and calls out "Are you painting?"

"With words," I reply.

"Poetry or prose?"

"Some of each."

"Oh, good on you! We are trying to decide where we are going paint today."

And off they go down the path. An eagle soars overhead and they stop to watch. I hear the pitch of their conversation crescendo appropriately.

The bright yellow hawkweeds and buttercups glow with that same energy-field-look of this morning's sun. As I watch a black-throated green warbler work its way around one of the spruces at the edge of the bog, I delight in its golden "thumb print," the facial marking that bird books will tell you is its identifying field mark, actually a shade of chartreuse. Chartreuse? A totally inadequate description of the gleaming color set off in full contrast by the wee bird's jet black chin and bright dark eye. Warbler, hawkweed, buttercup; all seem to radiate a glory that is more than the human can apprehend.

12 noon: Ann and I retreat to the shade of the large oak tree. It's not too hot: it's just that the light is not good and the birds are quiet. Although the oak leaves are very new, a few still coppery, their pigments not quite masked with green chlorophyll, many leaves already show tiny dark spots, wrinkly puckers, and snipped away edges. I cannot resist looking for insect handiwork—knobs of galls or the curls made by leaf rollers—before I sit. Ann smiles. "I might have a good shot of the entomologist's daughter on her knees this morning, at worship in her own fashion," she announces.

The two of us enjoy a few more words about our surprise and delight that our combined words and photos somehow convey to a spiritually hungry audience something they find fulfilling. What is it I read in her images that wordlessly tells me they are Ann's and that she is deeply in awe of what she is photographing? How is it that a phrase or two suffices to let Ann know that she is reading words I have penned? What is it that the broad range of people who respond have in common?

Another car arrives and a young family piles out, heading for the shore. They never notice two figures in the tree shade. Our conversation veers to the Fourth of July influx of visitors. For a month now the Island has been in a spoken or unspoken frenzy of preparation for the season.

First we had the bird migrations; now it's people. Not only do we have a surge in summer people and casual tourists, but more and more plan to stay year round or at least make this their principal residence.

New this spring are *keep out* signs posted at the driveway entrance to the park and along its south boundary. Two new houses have appeared there. "Please respect our privacy" reads one new sign.

A twitter over the small bog that straddles the southern park perimeter draws our attention. A pair of tree swallows are chasing off a fluttering falcon. Small, it looks like a kestrel. A robin tut-tuts in the warm air. The swallows return again and again over the bog as if they too regard it a jewel to be protected.

I tell Ann about the small bog that she cannot see. The park committee considered putting a boardwalk into its heart so more people could see it. Even if we had been able to acquire the requisite wetlands permits, we finally decided the effect would have been too disruptive. Besides, the bog inhabitants deserved some privacy. As if to enforce this notion, the tiny wetland bog is bordered by poison ivy on one section.

A dense stand of wild azalea, spent blooms of once-magenta rhodora, circles another edge. This is one of the most spectacular stretches of this lovely flower I know of on the Island, but I wager few people know of it. Sensitive ferns, alders, and an interesting shrub called nine-bark form a hedge and moat. Out in the center of the bog, just beyond where you can see without wading, stand young tamaracks. The lacy green tops of these larches are starting to sway gently in a faint breath of afternoon breeze. Two goldfinches come zipping by, pause on these sentinel tree branches, and move on.

Bogs are characterized by specialized plants and insects which have adapted to the acid conditions. I expect the center, the invisible heart of this small bog, may already be blooming with the graceful pink slips of rose pogonia orchids, and soon arctic cotton grasses will wave their modest tufts of white. In spite of this common name, this bog plant is a sedge. Another of its common names is hare's tail— a perfect name for these fluffy little bunny tail puffs. In some places they call rose pogonia by the name of snakemouth, but not here! A month ago we might have found bog elfin butterflies in late afternoons. Where there are sphagnum mats we might find the small rosettes of sundews, sticky leaved plants which trap tiny insects.

The public attitude toward wetlands is still often one of contempt. Building plans may be thwarted. The pools are considered insect-breeding nuisances. Mosquitoes are not only annoying; we fear they are carrying diseases.

1:00 PM: the air traffic control of the flower flies and tiny bees in the hawkweeds and daisies on the hillside before us has never flagged. Glamorous yellow Tiger Swallowtails which appeared with blooms of the lilacs of the garden club's Memory Lane are fluttering through the dappled sunlight of the forest edge.

Over the short-mown grass ringlet butterflies float. The grass clippings dried in the sun give a strange buzz-cut look to the gentle field contours by the parking lot. The park committee decided it should have a policy of mowing only enough to keep succession from advancing. I cannot quite understand where our country's current mania for mowing comes from. We are destroying nests of bobolinks and meadowlarks in such numbers that we may lose these lovely singers from the planet. The man who volunteers to mow the paths here at the park loves to ride his mower. It is very difficult to restrain his zealous ministrations. Must be a guy thing.

For some years now I have been trying to recruit amateur butterfly fans for the NABA annual Fourth of July butterfly count and the Maine Lepidoptera almanac effort. I consider this park the butterfly capitol of the Island. Just while we rested in the shade, I saw an American (two-eyed) painted lady, the surprisingly orange flash of northern (pearl) crescents, what I like to call the mini-Monarchs, as well as a couple of cabbage whites, now the most common butterfly species in our nation, but introduced here by accident little more than a century ago. Associated only with blueberries are several species of tiny so-called micromoths. What happens to them as blueberry barrens become ever more intensely managed? What are we losing?

2:00 PM: As we venture out again into the sunlight, I inspect the turf for wild strawberries, the tiny little native gems, the sort my grandmother sent me out to pick in quantities sufficient to make jam. Europeans probably brought with them their own varieties and look what we have made of them now in California and elsewhere! Raspberry canes, too, probably came with those first Europeans, although the Native Americans knew a variety of rasps and blackberries and dewberries and the like to supplement their diets.

Honeybees in straw hives called skeps came aboard those early sailing ships bound for these shores. We have still today a number of native ground-nesting bees who serve us inconspicuously as pollinators. As the European honeybees increasingly succumb to virus or some other pestilence, we may come to appreciate the natives even more.

My lawn-mowing friend likes to expound on native vs. naturalized plants. In his mind, if it was born here it's a native. Plant, animal, or presumably, person. If it grows rampantly and is a nuisance—i.e., poison ivy, a native if there ever was one—it's an invasive alien. As the state makes an increasing effort to distribute lists of native and invasive plants, I wonder if he has moderated his views any.

Ann and I wander the field, and at her request, I point out the natives and the others. Yellow rattle has just come into bloom: alien. Like most gardeners, Ann is quite knowledgeable about plants but has only recently considered the question of origin. I, on the other hand, have always been fascinated by plant geography and by what I would call plant anthropology.

Perhaps most of the old field succession plants here are imports: Common mullein, common yarrow, red clover, the narrow-leaved vetch, which will soon be blooming in a lovely lavender-blue, Queen Ann's lace, ox-eye daisies, common tall buttercups, the short little stalks of butter-and-eggs: all aliens. The goldenrods, black-eyed Susans, fireweed, and butterfly weeds we can call our own, as well as the profusion of late summer asters.

The naturalists up at Acadia National Park have been having quite a time this spring with lupine. It seems that Mainers love their picturesque lupines along every roadside. There are lupine festivals, one here on the Island, and a popular children's story in which the main character, Miss Rumphius, is considered a beautifier, not a bio-terrorist, for strewing seeds on everyone else's property with gay abandon.

Botanists do not yet know what makes a plant an agreeable,

nicely tame garden plant or perhaps a lovely naturalizing plant such as daffodils, turn suddenly into a cancer-like invasive like kudzu, multiflora rose, oriental bittersweet, or some of the honeysuckles. Garden lupines seem to thrive on dusty roadsides but have not so far exhibited the greedy characteristics of that late-summer purple painter, loosestrife, which definitely has the reputation of squeezing out everything else where it would like to grow.

Park officials and knowledgeable botanists decided to banish the lupine from the park while they still could, having suffered much at the roots of purple loosestrife. Howls of protest resulted. The eradication has been at least temporarily halted for further study. I wouldn't be surprised if they're studying how to chop down the offending plants under cover of night.

I have friends who think they are doing butterflies a favor by strewing lupine seeds around. So far I have only seen bees—not to be sneezed at—at the lupine flowers that bloom and self sow so readily. I think people read about the situation near Albany, New York where endangered Karner Blue butterflies—relative of our Azures—depend for the survival on a diminutive species of native lupine. This grows on the sandy flats beneath the scrub pines which have been nearly swallowed up by shopping malls and superhighways just outside the city. Having seen the area, I wonder if the world's last Karner Blue will end up on some shopper's windshield.

The stand of lupine now setting seed on the knoll in Mariners Park is not native. As far as is known, the lupine native to Maine never grew much north of Portland. What we have all over the coast are lovely hybrids. To complicate matters even more, our hybrids have hybridized with those from British Columbia via the eager gardeners of England.

3:00 PM: and the afternoon breeze is now quite stiff. On warm summer afternoons sailors in Penobscot Bay can count on an onshore breeze. The air over the land heats and rises. Air over the water rushes in to fill the vacuum. Presto: onshore breeze. Sailors also keep track of the height of the thunder clouds that skim the head of the bay. If there is enough energy in those clouds to raise a tall anvil head, they had best prepare for the cold, sharp downdraft that precedes a squall. Lightning would be an even more unwelcome part of this scenario. Today we read only modest clouds scudding by, just enough to add lovely shades of lavender and interesting textures to the sky.

From a granite bench, iced tea thermos in hand, we ponder glacial geology. Mariners Memorial Park is a textbook example of glacial moraines, those gentle hills of debris left behind after the great ice sheets retreated. The steep banks overlooking the shore reveal layers of glacial till, the ground-up bits that erode out to form the gravel beach here. The University, by which locals always used to mean the University of Maine at Orono, has recently been providing the general public with excellent geological maps. This information gives great insight into where future housing development belongs. You wouldn't think it requires a map to realize that sprawling down narrow peninsulas with nearly one-way roads away from existing town centers might be a poor formula for growth. Maps showing soil types, however, can predict quite well where you can and cannot site septic fields.

It is amazing to contemplate how technology has changed what the average person can know these days. We have seen the results of World War II submarine explorations endowing us with enough data to demonstrate that the theory of plate tectonics is not far-fetched, but a sound description of what we cannot see. Modern biology labs have not only electron microscopes but lovely dissecting scopes that easily bring the macro world to students' delighted gaze. Ann's digital camera and home computer allow her to capture and manipulate this beauty.

Binoculars these days are better than ever, and much more affordable. We take for granted the many popular books on ornithology. These days we have plenty of bird song recordings available as well. Amateurs can and do take splendid telephotographs of birds of the sort that once cost Eliot Porter countless taxing hours in bird blinds. Amazing photographs of insects are now possible with the macrolenses of many digital cameras. Modern field guides have the potential to make us all accomplished naturalists. And that's all new in my lifetime. Yet we still do not know the host plant for a number of quite common butterfly species. I think about the myriad species of microlepidoptera out my back door yet to be described. We read in the newspapers quite frequently that amateurs are comet-spotters. Accumulating simple baseline data remains a challenge. Sadly, close encounters with the natural world give us the feel of a race against time. No wonder some people would rather not look too close.

I ought to go scout the edge of the woods for the tiny waxen parasols of Round-leaved pyrola, which have just opened. Someone phoned yesterday to ask about the mystery flower they had just found at Shore Acres—and it sounded like pyrola. The double tiny fairy lanterns of twinflower are also coming out now. That great Swedish naturalist Linnaeus gave us our form of binomial nomenclature, a genus and species name for everything. He so loved the twinflower that he named it *Linnaea*. I understand that he had his portrait painted with pink twinflower in his buttonhole. I like to think that Clark and Marjorie Hill would have enjoyed my thinking of their two daughters when the twinflowers bloom. I remember that I have in my pocket a copy of an e-mail from Judy Hill which she gave me to share.

I pass it to Ann.

<u>June 15, 2005:</u> Marnie Crowell stopped in yesterday to borrow an Eskimo basket for an exhibit…She asked what my thinking was in giving the land for the Shore Acres Preserve. I replied to the effect that, for me, it wasn't an idealistic process, but one more step - plunk, plunk, plunk - in what was happening in my life at various points in time.

In the 1960s our parents, Clark and Marjorie Hill, gave us some of their land (the woods on the north side of the farm to my sister, Lib, and the woods and shore on the south side to me.)

The only condition of the gift was that none of the land be developed in any way during their lifetimes, and that access to the land not be through their open fields. I had always wanted a camp out on the South Point, but making a road through the woods to get there was prohibitive - I was in grad school and had NO money. Grad-school friends, with whom I had sailed in this area for several years, offered to build the road in exchange for a spot where they could build a cabin, not too near mine. Dad liked these people, so I tested the "no development" idea on him, and he put his foot down, flat: "No, not in our lifetimes."

…I had no way to put my land to use. It just sat there, enjoyed only by a few hunters and me. I occasionally went over and puttered around, clearing out dead wood and stuff. But I have a fundamental philosophy that it's kinda immoral to just <u>own</u> something you're not using, when other people could be using and enjoying it.

When Dad died, in 1989, I was working in Bangor for the State of Maine, and a focus of my job was providing affordable housing for handicapped and low income people…. It became apparent to me that here I had 37 acres of undeveloped land, I had no great need for money, and I could turn it into a number of units of low income housing. I hired a soils-expert who found that the land could support only five residences, and told me that any attempt to develop it might well call in federal Wetlands people. A contractor pointed out to me that I might sell the land at low prices to low-income people, but that they, in turn, would probably turn around and sell it, at shoreland prices, to a couple of wealthy people or to a developer.

Marnie asked me why our parents put the "No Development" restriction on our lands, asking why they wanted that, and about their feelings about the land. I said something like, "Well it all goes back to the farm we had in Sudbury, about the same size as this, which the Army took, by eminent domain, at the start of World War II, to build an ammunition dump. We loved that farm …" It was on the shore of a large pond; it had acres and acres of forest, wide open hayfields, a peach orchard, an apple orchard, and a large barn, where Dad and his brother, Dick, raised Morgan horses, which they showed. They even had a night riding ring, until a band of gypsies went through one night and stole all the lights and wiring. (I'm not sure why, but there were quite a few gypsies around there in the thirties; I can remember seeing a brightly painted blue cart go through the road that divided our farm, loaded with kids and possessions, buckets hanging from the sides).

I gave her a brief reprise of what had happened to it. Ammunition silos and a railroad were constructed there before the Army found that the Port of Boston wasn't large enough, or deep enough, or something, to take the ships that were bringing in the ammo. It became part of Fort Devens, and was used for a variety of training purposes. I had never been back there until just before my Uncle Dick died, probably in 1998. I went to Sudbury to visit him (he was terminally ill at that time), and he had arranged a surprise for me - had permission to go see the property. We were both shocked beyond words (me to the point of tears)….

I think of tough little Judy again breaking into tears as she told me this. As I watch Ann scan the letter, I feel once again what an intimate revelation Judy has chosen to share. Dear private Judy in her own way has gone through life securely hiding much of her accomplishment as if behind a mask. Sadly, she has been physically not able to accompany us to the shore on our photographing jaunts, so we confined our recent

visits with her to the kitchen. On the wall in Judy's kitchen hang carved masks made by Indians and Western Eskimo. I recount now to Ann how I treasure the memory of Judy telling me with great indignation that she had been reproved by someone when she lent her masks to the prison that was being built. (In addition to working for the State Board of Alcoholism, Judy was also doing research at the new jail.)

"The masks were made by these peoples. Of course they could use these masks. They give a dignity, a sense of worth," Judy had said in her indignant and tolerantly amused and peppery way.

Judy did not tell me about the people there she tried to help. She never has told me about those here on the Island whom she has helped. But some of them have told me that she helped them in such simple and direct ways as seeing that they had access to medical things we often take for granted. I pick up here and there from various folks how Judy has over the years functioned as an informal source of support. No, we cannot guess who has been helped for hearing aids, braces for teeth, new eye glasses, an educational scholarship, or even animal welfare support. She has always just helped quietly where she could. To get any picture of the real, the whole Judy, one has to put together a mosaic from small snippets of information. Judy is not being deceitful or secretive about this; she simply represents an extreme of New England reticence, a sense of allowing people who need help to retain their pride. I have never heard anyone on the Island refer to her as Doctor Hill. I doubt many people know that she has that PhD from Boston University.

A gently smiling mask hanging in her kitchen is one she has retained from her Alaska years, the rest having been donated to the Hudson Museum at Judy's undergraduate alma mater, the University of

Maine. Its eyes are open but its lips are shut. How appropriate it is. It is one of my favorites.

However, since she wrote this letter both to me for telling her story and for her family, her heirs, I feel at liberty to share it. What a gift! Ann finds it as engaging as I had, for there is no way to take the letter from her, to draw some butterfly to her attention. Ann continues reading, obviously experiencing the authenticity, the immediacy, of the details of Judy's story.

… at what had become of our beautiful houses which, that day, were being used for urban-warfare training: two teams of heavily camouflaged young men were getting ready for a laser-beam battle, a team ranged on the porches of each of our former homes, which were barely recognizable. A couple of years ago, cousins visiting from Connecticut told me that Dad and Uncle Dick had never been paid for the farm, and how they knew that. Of course, the Army was just too busy fighting the war, and I'm sure there was no harm intended. Neither Dad nor Dick would have raised a fuss about it during wartime, and by the time the war was over, it was kind of a moot point. Dad had never mentioned it to us. Anyway, very recently I heard that the Army had returned land in Sudbury, Maynard and some other towns to the town governments. They've been combined into the Assasabett River Valley Nature Preserve - that would make both brothers and their wives very happy!

It all worked out for us, of course. We ended up in Deer Isle, and with a very different lifestyle - we had no electricity, no running water, one wood stove for heat; the house hadn't been lived in for 25 years, and it needed a LOT of work, which we all pitched in to do. Our affection for the land transferred fast to this beautiful farm and shoreline. But, no doubt about it, the experience of losing a wonderful place in the blink of an eye and with no say about it makes you look at things in a whole different way…

4:00 PM: the cat bird is singing in the alders. Ann has gone off by herself. I have just walked the Mariners' Mile in both directions. I find it such a temptation to record every species of bird, to census every species of bug or butterfly I encounter. This, however, is not a scientific disquisition. Ann and I have come to honor this place by recording its impressions on us. We would be delighted if we could influence some people to fall in love with nature wherever they are. Once in love, to learn, to chronicle, to protect, as we experience here. This is no wilderness. There are probably no endangered species here. However, this little pocket park, as you might call it, lies within a ten-minute's drive of everyone who lives on this island. It has the potential to make the healing gifts of the natural world available to anyone and everyone in the community. What a day this is.

5:00 PM: some butterflies still flit; some dragons fly. Their activity patterns often give away their specific identity. In the raking light the old farm apple tree trunks with green lichen seem especially poignant and lovely. I see Ann also documenting the tall trunks of poplars with their outrageously orange lichen spatters. I delight in pulling through my fingertips the silky needles of a larch. A sweet perfume drifts from the edge of the field. There is so much for the senses in this small park.

6:00 PM: we enjoy a picnic supper down by the shore. Once there were picnic grills here. Nowadays most people use gas grills on their own patios. Campers are often required to forgo fires and use any of the convenient new stoves. I am sorry my grandchildren will not have the same memories I do of campfire cooking and campfire singing and campfire dreaming.

    An SUV comes barreling down the lane, which is usually kept chained. Since the lobsterman who trailers his boat from here is still out, the chain is down. Two young men in baseball caps give us a jaunty wave. Somehow they appear to be on a mission, and obviously one they have done before. As we watch, they make a sharp right turn and drive up over the grassy hill to disappear behind a clump of trees. The car door opens and one of them gets out. We look questioningly at each other. In a few minutes he reappears making that tell-tale gesture of tugging at his pants. He hops back in the car which promptly roars another rut back down the hill and regains the lane. As they pass us in a cloud of dust, the young man who just took a leak leans out the window, gestures a "V" sign and says loudly, "Peace." A challenge? A mellow and perhaps drugged greeting? Who knows?

7:00 PM: hermit thrushes in the cool woods are tuning up, loveliest of sounds. A few gulls are straggling off to wherever it is they roost for the night.

8:-something: sunset. How you time it depends on which side of the hill you are. The golden glory spreads and changes for long moments. Fades. Colors further. Hush.

9:00 PM: I call this period of dusk the dusk impatience period. With luck we may spot a few bats, Little Browns, ready to take over the night shift from the swallows. It is too dark to still be called sunset, and other than one here and there, it is not dark enough for stars to be out. As we walk, we startle up several pure white moths the size and shape of a single bunchberry flower petal. Their wings have a sheen that reminds me of wet silk. These are white spring moths. What a prosaic name for the delicate little beauty, which is fairly common all summer long, and is one of those which often fly by day. Their caterpillars feed on apple and *Prunus* species. I think they are my favorites, at least for this season. The way an amateur identifies moths with a field guide is about like the way one begins to learn dragonflies. Look for a picture in the book that looks like what you saw. This is not a particularly efficient method, so when you finally make a perfect match, it feels like a significant triumph.

Various people have suggested that naming is a form of owning, a power play of sorts. I do not feel that. I feel I am paying homage to eons of evolution, recognizing the distinctness of a creature. I recognize that the small moths about me now share a likeness to priceless white jade with all the others of their kind I have ever seen. They partake in the emotional resonance of all the various lovely circumstances of our mutual past. This only enhances their value to me. That is quite enough to possess.

Tiny white stars shine from the sandy roadside grasses: three-toothed cinquefoil flowers in profusion. This sweet little plant is fairly uncommon in our state, but a hardy little herb of rocky soils. I have a special fondness for these, and other tough little natives, that "make do" with our mountain tops and sea shore habitats. Venus setting over the western horizon to my eye looks no less lovely than the glow at my feet.

10:00 PM: lightning bugs are rising steadily from the tall grasses. How I miss seeing them over on my spruce side of the Island. Fireflies were always part of my childhood. I still find bio-luminescence, light without heat, a miracle, whether I find it in the sea when I splash an oar on a night row or in these wavy lines ascending in a summer meadow's light show. The various species recognize each other by the number of seconds elapsed between flashes, 2, 3, or 5 seconds or whatever. These small black beetle-like bugs with their red-and-yellow collars are a slug parasite when they are larvae. Nature in balance; forget about control! They are the coolest.

11:00 PM: stars at last. The summer sky radiating down through clear heavens is surely one of the most glorious things the universe has to offer. Here we are far enough from light pollution to savor the full cascade of the Milky Way, a shimmering band across nearly the whole dome. There is *Corona Borealis*, the Northern Crown, a constellation so loved by me that I have taken it as a signature.

My day is complete.

July Second

Summer people arrive
like mosquito hordes

rocketing around the island
to get ready for the Fourth.

It seems to take some time
to wear off city soot

but that should most hug off
when we all meet
at the town parade.

Berry Picking

Press your fingers
down between the stems
and feel the heat
where small green factories
make sunlight into pie.

August — BEACHES — 6

August is prime beach month. Beaches here can be considered either pink ones or grey ones. Perhaps the best way to visit our pink beaches is to come by boat. That is because the very loveliest beaches may be those of the small islands south of Deer Isle, what might be called the Stonington Archipelago. Made of pink granite ground fine, they are bordered by dramatic granite edges as well.

A very satisfying number of the islands are now protected by conservation easement or are owned outright by conservation entities that allow public use. Maine Island Trail Association has been very successful in exploring how to open islands for the public to enjoy without seeing these treasures loved to death.

Many of the smaller islands are owned by the State of Maine. If they are used by nesting colonies of seabirds, they are closed to humans for at least the first half of the summer. Even the smallest rocky ledges may be similarly off limits to humans while seal pups are using them in early summer. Owners of islands are encouraged to develop similarly considerate policies for their private holdings.

But now, in August, we especially enjoy heading out to the islands to explore the richness of the season. Mackerel have been coming into the coves on the high tides, and the piers are a party with youngsters casting or hand lining for these lovely silvery-blue fish. It is quite exciting to watch when the silver surface of the cove starts to boil on a flat calm August-hot afternoon, some kind of small fish, herring perhaps, churning in a frenzy to keep ahead of the mackerel.

Just as ashore, islanders routinely wave to passing cars, lobster fishermen out on the water in these parts still return a friendly wave as we pass. Lobsters have about finished shedding this season. That means they are being caught with hard shells and fetch the highest prices.

An eagle comes flying over us, its white head gleaming in the sunshine. It is an adult, though many people would tell you that it's a male. The birds younger than four years are still mostly brown, not mostly female. We have seen eagles try unsuccessfully to rob ospreys of their prey. The young eaglet on Barred Island is about to fledge. It seems to spend part of every day now flapping its way from branch to branch on trees near the nest.

An osprey beats by, clearly intent on some mission. Ospreys have been making local news lately. Newspaper reporters and television camera crews were on the scene to record the power company's efforts to remove a pair of determined and troublesome ospreys from their nest site behind the school.

It seems that this pair lost its nest in the last storm in July. Nest, tree, and all blew down. Undeterred, the ospreys tried to rebuild atop a power pole nearby. This resulted in the ospreys shorting out the school's power system, with resulting damage to the school air conditioning system. The power company was called and came to remedy things. They brought small hard hats to a class of young children enrolled in a summer school program. The children were mustered out to watch as the crews fastened a round from a large wooden cable spool atop a utility pole. Sticks were laid on in what was believed to resemble a nest. What a great public relations opportunity. It even made the local TV news. We hear, however, that the osprey are being stubborn; they like the power pole better.

Porpoises bent on harvesting their own catch of the day come up for air. As much as we try to anticipate where they will next surface, we are never quite in time to snap the shutter. I hear their chuffing breathing sounds quite regularly these days. I fear that the dearth of herring is affecting their numbers as well as having a decimating effect on prey species throughout the food chain.

Sails dot the bay. I find their shapes, aerodynamic like that of airplanes, to be aesthetically thrilling. The scene is picture calendar perfect. August here can certainly look like what Maine fancies itself to be. A large sign at the border welcomes cars coming from the south with the message "Maine, the way life ought to be" and on a warm August day near the shore, anyone should be so lucky.

Cautiously threading our way in between submerged rocks guarding the little harbor, we ground out our hull upon the rough sand of our island destination. In short order we are trudging up the beach to put our gear well above the high tide mark indicated by the windrow of dried seaweed. I used to count this line of wrack as little more than a nuisance that smelled and sometimes seethed with the small crustaceans known as beach hoppers and the like. Current research, however, has found that the array of tiny arthropods which make their living in the shelter of rotting seaweed can spell the difference between life and death to migrating seabirds. Although it seems like high summer to me, most of the shore birds have already made their way down from the Arctic, heading south to their wintering grounds.

The island is a small replica of the mainland. That some species are missing out here makes the ecosystem a bit simpler and a bit more vulnerable than comparable mainland sites. Ken's research was on island populations, first of birds in the West Indies, and then on the mice on the various islands around us here.

At the back of the beach is a drift of rugosa roses and a line of yellow sow thistles and purple common thistles. Goldenrod and starry blue asters seem to clamor to have their picture taken. Songbirds are pretty silent these days but cicadas are singing, even out here. Their mysterious ratcheting sound winds up the warm air from somewhere off in the shadows of the trees. There is a thrill when the first sweet song of the crickets in the grass penetrates consciousness as a new sound. Grasshoppers clatter into us on every walk down a sunny path.

I associate black eyed Susans and goldenrods with the coming of autumn, but for a while yet am able to tell myself that they really signal high summer, nothing more. Lacey white flat-topped asters and a seaside goldenrod species have been found by butterflies even out here: white admirals, painted ladies, and a small species of fritillary. These meadow fritillaries are not as showy or as large as great spangled fritillaries but they make up for that with their numbers. They perch on the opening flowers, flapping their wings in delightfully slow motion as we walk by. We have seen very few monarchs so far this summer. Last time we noted a dearth of monarchs, it turned out that their populations had suffered a series of disasters over the winter. I tell myself it is early yet. This year and next could be quite different. That's what makes trying to study and predict populations so challenging.

In the tangle hang a few perfect raspberries. Only on the smaller islands offshore are there still any raspberries to be had. The ocean moderates temperatures so summer comes late out here. Blackberries are already beginning to ripen. Blueberries on the mainland are now nicely ripe. Ann reports that over "on the continent" by her the blackberries are nearly ripe and a mother bear and her two cubs have been seen harvesting. Ann has been bringing us ripe tomatoes from her garden. Perhaps we will be able to trade her some blackberries in a few weeks. It has been some years since a bear has been reported on Deer Isle. Like deer, bears are occasionally reported swimming from island to island.

A small, graceful young garter snake sunning itself on a rock startles me. I startle it, as well, so it quickly retreats into a crevice. Ken thinks probably great blue herons that used to nest out here before the eagles got too much for them were responsible for bringing out snakes as prey. Deer Isle does not have turtles, or bullfrogs. Most of the small islands have no snakes.

For many people a visit to the beach means hours of baking in the sun, with eyes closed. Not for the biologist. I was not born by the sea, so every moment I can snatch in this world between the tides seems especially precious to me. I am constantly searching, cataloging. That is not precisely the same as naming, but pretty nearly. I learned most of my botany in Virginia so I know very well to be grateful for Latin names. Common names vary with the geographical region. Up here the fishermen call sea birds coots and Lords n' Ladies, no matter what the ornithologists call scoters or long tails or harlequin ducks.

I have been teased about sounding forth on plants and animals at the slightest provocation. I suppose that is justified. I do. I find diversity thrilling. I particularly love the tall large-seeded grasses at the back of most beaches. Sea oats or seaside wild rye is what people call them, but that name strictly speaking belongs to more southern species. *Leymus mollis*, or sea lyme grass, is a more proper name. Sea lavender, which also is found where it only occasionally gets its feet wet, is also not a heather as the common name 'beach heather' would lead you to believe. It's not a lavender either, this *Limonium carolinianum* that we love here in Maine.

You find it in dried wreaths and soon it may be so over-harvested that you won't find it at all. Why is it that we have such trouble recognizing that the abundance of the sea has its limits?

Ann is happily photographing butterflies and then she quietly moves on down the shore to peer into tide pools. After looking closely at the patterns in the sand and nibbling on a few spinach-like orache leaves, I do what any self respecting beachcomber does. I stretch out on the warm sand, tip my hat down, and just listen to the wavelets pouring out on the sand. Before long, of course, I can't help thinking of the mechanical forces busily sorting out grains according to size and weight. Each beach is slightly different, not unlike a fingerprint. How much of it is made of barnacle bits? How much vegetable matter is there? Are there cobbles, round stones the size of golf balls or softballs?

On the horizon the blue silhouette of the Camden Hills offers a geology lesson. You can more or less read the track of the glacier some ten thousand years ago. The weight, sliding down from the north, carved a gradual slope. As the ice the mass pulled away to the south, it left behind a steeper face, with boulder bits plucked off and carried away. The islands out here on the bay often tell the same story in miniature.

The beach works its magic. Time seems to slow to a geologic pace.

* * *

Ann reports that this morning she found bear scat on the edge of her road. From the evidence it looked like the bear had been dining on blue bead lilies. The berries of that wildflower, properly known as *Clintonia*, are of a very special shade of blue, a color I know from nowhere else. I had been hoping Ann would get some photographs of the berries, pre-bear of course.

I had just been over to her place the previous day kayaking on the Bagaduce. We nearly never left the dock as I happened to take a close look at the growths on the timbers as we left. There, for the first time ever, I recognized sea squirts. As a former biology teacher and student, I was familiar with these ancestors of the whole vertebrate tribe, but I had never seen one. More accurately, sea squirts are known as protochordates, which means that as larvae they have a primitive notochord, the rod of cartilage, which is a first step on the way to what eventually develops in us as a backbone.

I had shared my wonder and enthusiasm with a friend who told me his houseguest, Dr. Page Valentine, was studying sea squirts. Wouldn't I like to meet this marine geologist from Woods Hole Oceanographic Institute for supper this evening? As I accepted, I observed that perhaps this man would enjoy tagging along with Ann and me as we took advantage of the afternoon low tide to go out with Dr. Robert Knowlton, a George Washington University professor from an old island family. Decapods, shrimp, lobsters, and crabs are his specialty, but he loves to poke around the beaches generally seeing what is there.

So today Ann and I have new partners for our beach expedition. We are to look at what I have called the grey beaches, two beaches of the north end of Deer Isle, the so-called Reach Beach at Gray's Cove, and the Causeway Beach between Deer Isle itself and Little Deer. Artist and basket maker Elizabeth Compton gave the beach to Island Heritage Trust, with an easement on the other side of the road to protect the marsh there. Mindful that there is so little public access on the Reach, Elizabeth likes to call this small beach Reach Beach at Gray's Cove. Looking in either direction—off across the Reach to distant Mount Desert, or south across the mouth of Fish Creek where it enters the Reach—you don't have to be an artist to appreciate the loveliness of Elizabeth's gift.

That vital processes go on around us unseen is nowhere more true than here at the beach. At first glance the beach itself is not very promising-looking, this gentle slope of steel-colored mud and blue-grey gravels and hardly anything a kid with a pail would call sand.

At low tide you can see elegant delta patterns threading between isolated rocks, which are colonized by barnacles. Large horse mussels and blue mussels, common, rough, and smooth periwinkles are all arranged in zones according to how many hours of drying air exposure they are equipped to tolerate.

The upper beach is more accurately described as small gravel. There is next that band I so admire of flats wet enough to sheen, dissected elegantly into dark lines of bifurcating deltas. I am reminded of the wide dark Olympic beaches of Washington state with their glorious array of deltas, images made moderately familiar in post cards and nature photographs.

    Bob demonstrates how he judges the character of beach by rubbing a bit between his fingers. Clay will sheen and stick to the valleys of your fingerprints. Silt to him is a size, less than 0.1 millimeter. Rub the beach bit between your teeth, and if it makes noise and you can feel the individual particles, it is silt, not clay. Clay is the finest grind of the feldspar in the granite we see so prevalently about the Island. The fine particles will sink where bays and coves and estuaries are calm.

    Out where the wave action is stronger, your bit of beach is likely to be really gritty. That is probably sand, what makes the pink beaches. Almost as pink as the beaches of Bermuda thanks to the pink in the Stonington granite from which they are ground, these beaches often have an interesting tweedy look thanks to bits of barnacle and other shells. As they settle out according to weight, they make lovely patterns of their own. Of course they have their own critters, but for sheer bioabundance, you can't beat this mud.

    Two ladies in lawn chairs they have set up by their car are eating sandwiches. I wonder what they thought of Bob's menu. They cheerily wave us off as we head down toward the water.

    Digging on the grey beach here is just like prospecting. Opening up the mud is like fossiling. Bob shows us how one can read coarse layers in the mud that tell of previous winter storms—and rising sea levels. The fecal pellets passed by the various worms that burrow in the mud are shaped differently according to who made them. In addition to the various holes on the surface, we find distinctive coils, rings, footballs, and lumps.

    Some worms live in tubes that point straight to the center of the earth, and others make slanted tubes. The tubes are their adaptation for getting oxygenated surface water down beneath the smothering layers of mud. Today their adaptation is to stay sensibly tucked in, deep in the shelter of the mud.

    I have brought an extra shovel. "Do you want your own shovel?" I ask the vacationing Page Valentine. He is delighted to accept. His wife Lanci is an artist who has come several times to Haystack. She is on the lookout for found objects to turn into art. As we slurp out across the flats, Ann suggests that I will have trouble accurately describing the sounds our boots make. Well, politely speaking, yes.

A variety of arthropods and clams and nemertine worms live here burrowed in the mud. Bob catches a glimpse of a retreating worm and pounces with his shovel. A bamboo worm, *Clymenella torquata*.

"Oh. I was expecting something like a night crawler!"

"But this is daylight."

"Look at the segments, just like a bamboo stem. We could paint that in the *sumi-e* technique, pressing the ink brush and lifting, pressing and lifting."

Bob explains that a bamboo worm can be up to some four inches long. It builds a sand grain tube in which it lives, head down. Periodically it extends its rear end out of the tube to defecate. However, a waiting fish may then grab a bite of the worm. As many as a fifth of the worms on the beach may show the insult-and-injury of this, regenerating the handsome crown-like frill at the bamboo worm's rear end.

"Here's a good one!" An unsegmented ribbon worm in its tube.

"Here's the head end," Bob explains, and the creature obligingly demonstrates, shooting out a red proboscis.

"Fantastic!"

Page is doing a good job with his shovel. He uncovers a surprise of golden worm called the shimmy worm, *Nephtys caeca*. It burrows into the mud head first, but when Page pulls it out, it goes like a desert sidewinder, even flicking out a snake-like pink proboscis. The shimmy worm has one high-energy undulating wiggle of a shimmy. It takes several worms, several tries, before Ann is in just the right position with her camera to catch the right instant. Tickle, dance! Shimmy and shimmer. Going, going, gone.

Preying on these burrowing tube worms are green crabs, *Carcinus maenas*. These invaders from Europe are themselves facing competition from *Hemigrapsus sanguineas*, the Asian shore crab, which apparently invaded from Japan. They first started turning up on the east coast of this country in the 1980's. Page says that so many species are from the East that they take field guides in Japanese with them on their research vessel. His work is mainly out on the Georges Bank, which was where he encountered an invasive colonial sea squirt species. Lanci tells me about a dish they encountered in Japan which involved a block of tofu into which live baby eels have burrowed.

Next we pull out of the grey mud a clam worm. These iridescent greenish polychaete worms of high school bio labs are much sought after by anglers for bait. Diggers here get $.25 apiece for them. Like some small dragon, these worms are covered with pairs of paddles. They capture their prey by flinging a long sticky proboscis out of their elaborate mouths. This is one gorgeous wiggle of a worm with a lovely name, *Nereis*.

"Its two chitinous pinchers might just startle you," Bob reassures us.

Next we find a bloodworm, another sought after bait worm here. We have a hard time making head or tail of it since it has no eyes. Bob demonstrates how a bloodworm attacks. He tickles it and it pushes the blood forward in its proboscis. A red zap—like a new year's noisemaker uncurling, only fast as a strobe!

"Good shot!' he exclaims in undisguised admiration. He cautions that bloodworms have four teeth with poison glands that can give you a zap much like a bee sting.

Clammers and wormers here each have their different favorite flats to work. In spring when the worms breed, the gulls know where they are and then we know. One night under an April new moon when the bay buoys report that water temperature has risen to the fifties, the worms swarm in the cove, males ejecting sperm and females literally exploding. Next morning the seagulls can be seen slurping up the worm bits. When the tide carries the worm fragments out to sea, the gulls float along, dipping their heads in a most desultory mode of eating that puts "peel me a grape" to shame.

Clammers who prefer to work with their hands like mud. Clammers who rake like sand. Wormers use a larger-tined rake than the clammers do because worms are apt to be found deeper. Such subtleties of this largely unfamiliar world.

To the east, this Reach beach looks across at Naskeag Point. The blue shape of Mount Desert defines the horizon. Laughing gulls fly over with a raspy cry. In the distance loons call softly.

At the next gently curving mound in the mud, one with a

somewhat bread dough look, we unearth a fringed spaghetti worm, a terebellid, *Amphitrite*. I consider this an inadequate name for what looks to my classics-trained eye more like it ought to be simply called Medusa. We are looking at a head full of ciliated tentacles, which it uses to transport food particles to its mouth. When it uncoils, Bob shows us its three pairs of red gills.

"Excuse me for a few minutes. I'm a shrimp person," Bob says, as he heads off slogging through the mud with a net. Before long he is back with a bucket from which he extracts a few delicate shrimp. Bob explains that these creatures, nearly transparent but with slight sandy markings, change coloration according to substrate. These are bay shrimp, *Crangon septemspinosum*, not *Pandalus borealis*, the Maine shrimp we enjoy in winter.

Next he brings out a creature that looks like a stretched-out seahorse. Peering closely we can see it is a pipefish. It is tiny but exquisite, delicately curved, with proportionately large eyes giving it a sweet almost Disney character look.

Bob makes the challenging trip back out to water's edge to return the creatures. Although they throw a good deal of Latin into their conversations, these scientists remind me of children in their enthusiasm. Their concern for the wellbeing of individual animals is touching. Their desire to understand the complexities of the natural systems is what keeps them returning to their work, tide after tide. Eventually we realize we have to tear ourselves away from this beach because we had agreed to sample the Causeway Beach on the same day.

A few miles drive takes us past blueberry fields where a family or two are

picking. The soaring arc of the bridge comes into view, and the sinuous curve of the causeway. Children are splashing in the waters their parents think are too cold. Other people are walking or simply sitting along the sandy strip.

Most of the animals at the causeway beach, as at Gray's Cove, may be too small to see or are hiding in the mud and gravel and under the cobbles, invisible but invaluable.

The causeway is what is called a tombolo, formed by currents from both sides, the bay and the reach. I explained to the Valentines that the islands just to the west have been recognized as nationally significant. Many of them are now protected.

Where we are standing is actually a mini-dune. The dry upper edge is porous, held together by the runners of the seaside grasses. A bit closer to the water is a zone that stays damp even after the tide leaves it uncovered, and beyond that is a resurgent zone, and then a low water zone, each with its own plants and animals. In the drifts of drying seaweed, we step over empty butterfly-like shells of blue mussels and the molted carapaces of crabs. We have both rock crabs, *Cancer irroratus,* and *Cancer borealis,* the Jonah crab. Locals distinguish between the sweet-fleshed ones they call sand crabs, and the rock crabs with their coarser flesh. Both are sold to the restaurant trade as "Peeky-toed" crabs. Less welcome but more common are the smaller green crabs, which Bob tells us consume soft-shell clams, periwinkles, dog whelks, and even mussels. The soft-shell steamer clams and razor clam shells are scattered here in abundance. The razor clams are well named if you know what an old fashioned straight razor looks like.

Common periwinkles, the two scientists say, are probably invaders from Europe. At least so far they do not seem to have made a nuisance of themselves. I enjoy eating them with garlic and butter. The small yellow or orange periwinkles known as smooth periwinkles live in the knotted wrack, grazing on micro-algae on the surface of the wrack. Occasionally we find broad pieces of kelp in the drying seaweed, tossed up from deeper waters. I am disappointed that none of the edible species commonly harvested in deeper waters a bit downeast of us are likely to wash up here.

This beach is a favorite place for Island gardeners to come get seaweed for mulch. The most common seaweed species, with a distinct midrib, is bladder wrack with its branching Y-shaped pattern and paired vesicles. Knotted wrack, or rockweed, is the darker, more stringy one. The air bladders, which can be read like tree growth rings, tell us that seaweeds can grow for ten or even twenty years.

A number of long razor clam shells direct our attention to an area that looks promising for a look at this species. We dig a few times but they are too fast for us. The incoming waters do not leave us much room to try. We feel quite expert now as we uncover a few worms which we recognize as the same species we saw on the Reach.

In answer to our questions, Bob says this is the general sort of beach where one finds sand dollars, *Echinarachnius parma,* but they are a species that collectors are prone to overharvest. They are so appealing for crafts. Back when we were more innocent about smoking, we all agreed we had possessed ashtrays that were once living surf clams, *Spisula solidissima*. Bob picks up a half shell and shows us the little lipped shelf that is diagnostic. I can certainly see it for a soap dish. I leave it to the waves. Logically I know that a discrete bit of harvesting here is not going to disrupt the ecological balance, but the whole idea of thinking of nature as objects, things, rather than as living organisms is something that really challenges me. Unlike the current rules at Acadia, our land trust is content, for the time being at least, to allow folks to fork their seaweed and to lug home beach treasures for art objects. That shows the difference a horde of visitors makes in what policies are necessary.

Bob has also found ribbon worms, *Cerebratulus* species, more than a foot long here. Ann and I exchange glances on that one.

He asks about the birds. Bob is looking forward to retiring in a couple of years so he can pursue his interests in natural history in a broad range. I tell him that as early as July some species of sandpiper and other shore birds finish breeding in the Arctic and come back through here on their way farther south for the winter, glad to pick over what they find here. A group of black ducks is commonly seen dabbling at the tide edge over by the Little Deer end of the causeway. Our common eiders are starting to raft up just off the islands here. Fall weather will bring us a host of black-and-white species: buffleheads, golden-eyes, mergansers, scoters as well.

We scan the trees of Carney Island but do not see either of the two chicks the bald eagles successfully reared here this summer. Often this summer you could see folks with spotting scopes set up to watch the eagles. Almost every day since the Causeway Beach was purchased and opened to the public you could see people enjoying the beach. It is late afternoon so there are only a few cars and one pickup truck here now.

The Causeway carries the only road onto and off the Island. It is both our front door, presenting our face to visitors, and the back door leading to the only beach of any size on the Island that is now accessible to everybody. A vehicle pulls off the highway and sidles up along side of us. The window rolls down and out pops a visored cap labeled Clam Warden. It's Dorothy.

"I just got a report that someone is out on the causeway flats trying to dig clams with shovel!' She laughs heartily. "I might of known it was you, Marnie."

I introduce her to the members of our party and Bob produces his clamming permit even though we are not really clamming. Traditionally this basin was one of the finest clam flats in the region. Dorothy tells us that the Deer Isle/Stonington Shellfish Commission's recent reseeding test plots here did wonderfully well. The Reach Beach at Grays Cove is next on their list. She wishes us well and then continues on her way.

Bob and Page decide to make a transect running straight out from the beach toward Carney Island. How scientific. Always on a busman's holiday I'd say.

Ann and I dally over the graceful patterns that the rapidly advancing waters make over the circles of eel grass. I cannot resist pawing over a few to look for the small green flowers which I have never seen, though I do know well that this *Zostera* is not a seaweed and not a grass. Bob and Page have both described watching patches of eel grass increase during the years they have been working as marine scientists. That may bode well for recovery of fish stocks. Bob says that he has found juvenile flounder on the Reach.

According to Ted Ames of Stonington Fisheries Alliance, this basin is used by a variety of fish when flooded by the tide. Below the intertidal zone, its greatest value probably is that of a nursery for the suite of fish and shellfish found in midcoast Maine, including cod, pollack, white hake, etc. Although most species abandon the area in winter, at various times throughout the year Atlantic herring, river herring or kyack utilize the basin. It took me quite a while to recognize what I was hearing when fishermen spoke of kyacks, meaning a kind of fish! Menhaden, mackerel, various minnows, juvenile winter flounder, horned sculpins are also found in the basin between the islands and the causeway. In the past, rainbow smelts and tomcod, also called frost fish, were also here. Minnows, flounder, horned sculpins, tomcod, and rainbow smelts are found below the intertidal zone all year.

While Bob washes out his nets after inspecting a few shrimp, Page gives us some insight into fisheries management. "Three years ago *Didemnum* showed up on Georges Bank. We put up a web site of marine nuisance species and heard back from Japan and New Zealand. We are now working on the DNA to see if they are all the same critter."

"How did they get here?"asks Ann.

"Perhaps when oysters were reintroduced to the Damariscotta River. *Didemnum* probably was on the whole oysters. Who knows? Remember, these things are very tiny. It's not until they form mats that we know they are there. The species you have on the Bagaduce, *Molgula*, is a solitary species, and it has been here a long time. You find it mostly on pilings and rocks, where the waters are pretty calm."

Page continues, "*Didemnum* is colonial. It grows on anything hard – wood, rock, plastic, stable sand patches. Mud would clog its siphon system. Out on Georges Bank it overgrows everything else. Nothing grows on top of it. It produces an acid surface and we find it produces some unusual chemicals that cancer researchers are looking into. Some scientists have tried grinding it into fish food pellets, but fish avoid them. This kind of sea squirt seems to have no natural predators."

"The tunicate terror," I offer.

"It would be for aquaculture," Page agrees. "If you are growing mussels on ropes you can haul up the ropes and dry the tunicates to death. Out at sea of course that is not possible. We could decide to turn the entire Georges Bank into a giant scallop farm. In 1994 fishing closures resulted in a huge scallop recovery. On the bank there are miles of shallow waters, just nine feet deep at the crest. The only way to harvest out there is by dragging. The scallop draggers tow through the gravel beds and that may mince up the *Didemnum* colonies and then every piece grows new ones."

"What a nightmare scenario."

"No wonder some people might not want to even hear about it on their watch."

"Fisheries management is really complicated, both scientifically and politically."

The only people left on the beach now are two who look like young parents and their two youngsters. In our group nobody needs to say out loud that it's their world we are concerned about. We are each in our own way dedicated to the joy of sharing life, with other humans and with other species.

Fronds of rockweed are now floating outstretched on the surface of the gently rippling incoming tide. I point to two tiny sea stars nestled on a branch which also hosts a colony of Bryozoa, tiny and ancient life forms. These are just the sort of creatures I love. These little "moss animals" are actually individuals interconnected with each other. The whole "lace" cooperates, waving its ciliated tentacles to feed at slightly different times, area by area. Although these creatures too are being examined for cancer-controlling chemicals, I do not demand of them that they be useful to humans.

"Sea lace!" exults Bob. "And it's another invasive." It's lovely so Ann bends down. She needs help as it sways. I squat along side of her and hold one end of the trailing weed.

As she clicks away, I hear a soft cursing from her. The next wave wets the seat of my pants, too, bringing me understanding. Cold! Damn wet! I laugh; I do laugh so hard I might wet my pants, but they're already wet.

As we make our way back to our cars, Page asks me to tell him about the beach. He has heard it's a good story. I can't help first pointing out the golden glow of the rose hips in such profusion by our cars. As we slip off our boots and pack up our gear, I launch into what has become a cherished story, a sustaining story in spite of the daunting challenges.

A few years ago when the Causeway Beach property came on

the market, town government officials opined that they did not need to purchase what had been traditionally used and was after all only a roadside strip. "Let the land trust do it."

Lawyers checked the deeds filed in the county house and advised us that the property was in fact vulnerable, no matter what we might wish. The local land trust could not simply buy it as the asking price was considerably higher than property's appraised value. In general, owners of shore property had their own and were perhaps slow to recognize that that was not sufficient for the Island as a whole. Islanders were already faced with pressing economic realities associated with the decline of fisheries, so they tended to accept the future closing of the beach as another of today's sad facts of life.

Bob agrees that rising taxes and escalating real estate values are forcing more and more Islanders into selling what shore access they have. Communities change into second home enclaves. Unwelcome and sadly plausible alternative scenarios for the beach were envisioned, ranging the gamut of keep out signs, attractive nuisances, and various exploitive economic enterprises. Individuals concerned that this was not how our future should look eventually managed to work out a possible alternative.

"Why don't we just buy the beach?" But who is "we" if the town won't and the land trust can't?

Our Island people are coming to understand the nature of land trusts, especially as there is obviously no justification for the old accusation of "just protecting the views from rich people's front porches." So a group of ordinary people banded together and bought the beach, which they then gave to IHT to steward forever. I enjoy telling the little group that is how I met Dorothy, what an indefatigable worker she was in the effort to buy the beach.

We later learned that our worst fears were well-founded. A developer—from New Jersey I think—had an eye on the beach to go with nearby properties, envisioning one appealing package, one more piece of the island scaled up and locked up. The beach purchase came just in time.

The beach is now watched over by the whole of the island. Look how little time it took for Dorothy to come check us out. Ordinary citizens are now beginning to notice when it looks as if commercial seaweed harvesters from over the bridge are ignoring protective regulations. Traditional harvesting high tide beach wrack to mulch one's garden is one thing; stripping the rocks bare would be quite another. The concept that groups need to partner because of their overlapping interests in our ecosystem is growing.

The concept of "cup and saucer" is a perfect metaphor for why this beach-and-basin conservation effort must be thought of as a whole—an aesthetic whole, an ecological whole, and a management necessity. Protection of the Causeway Beach will both guarantee public access to the beach and clam flats and preclude the adverse impact of any future development or inappropriate use. Now if only we can learn in time how to work with governments and with sea squirts…

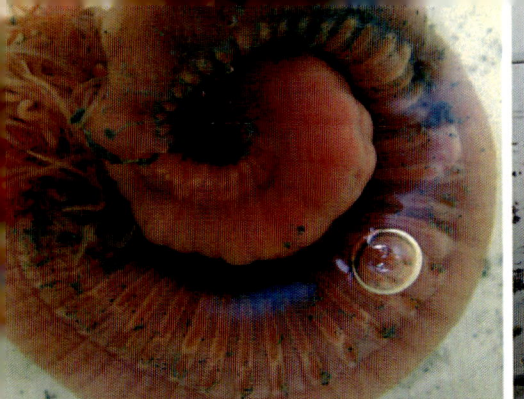 

Seaweed Sign

Here on the Island the harvest moon
Is a new moon, high wind up the bay
And a strong rinse of rain.

The road from the bar
Is windrowed with
Dark humps not roadkill

Lying there on the shoulder
Rockweed slithered off someone's truck
On the way to its next incarnation

Winter mulch
Slouching into summer
Lettuce and lilies.

Summer

The first round bales of hay
squat grinning in the meadow
while up the hill
the next field simmers
in a sun of black-eyed Susans
and on the porch an old man
observes that blueberries
are coming on good
this year and how sweet
the word for summer is.

September —— **PINE HILL** ———— 7

September has a special magic. For me September always has a new year feel, thanks to my own many years in school, then being married to an academic whose calendar was ruled by the university, and then sending two sons through various school systems. September has always meant organizing some array of new clothes, new pencils, new books.

Labor Day has always been the way we mark the commencement of this special era. When I was young, school did not start till several weeks after Labor Day so the day also meant a large gathering of my mother's family for a picnic. For Ann growing up in Aroostook County, school had already started earlier in August. Then school took a recess for most of September and some of October during the potato harvest because most of the potato pickers were community children. Some of the County schools still operate on that calendar although modern agricultural practices and machinery have changed the scene considerably.

At this time of year the squirrel instinct in me is very strong. I put away food. Having spent childhood years in southern New Jersey when it was truly the Garden State, I know what fresh from the fields bounty is. Living now on a granite ledge overlooking the ocean, with deer and hungry snowshoe hares eager to beat me to any meager harvest, I have had to content myself with farmers' market and a few wild gleanings. Wild cranberries of the upland type and chokecherries growing along old field edges for jam and syrup were among our favorites. I am feeling a loss as neither is available this year. It was too cold for the pollinators to fly back when the cranberries needed it, and the town road crew had cleared away the best stands of chokecherries. A bad year.

I identify with our Island fishermen as close counterparts to those who harvest from the land, who know both good years and bad.

Both farmers and fishers enjoy a measure of personal independence, take huge risks, face considerable danger, and are a culture unto themselves, a culture recognizably at risk these days due to ways we are managing our environment.

It's a clear bright blue day today, with a northwest wind. My spirits are high and the barometer registers high pressure indeed, just the sort of day that the hawks like to fly. Ann and I are meeting at the old quarry on Little Deer known as Pine Hill. It's also known as the serpentine quarry, if you live across the Causeway on Deer Isle; and if you are a geologist, it's the peridotite outcropping. Half of the hill has been cut away and was carted just down the road to build the Causeway between Little Deer and the main part of Deer Isle. Kurt and Pat Fairchild, current owners, have decided to make a gift of the promontory to Island Heritage Trust. With Ken and Dr. Nishanta Rajakaruna of College of the Atlantic over on Mount Desert, Ann and I are exploring the area.

It has been years since I have been here. As we walk up the narrow lane leading to the quarry I am once again awed at the tall cliffs sheer against the vibrant blue sky. It is only when we approach nearer and my eye travels the rock faces, that I see they have been defaced since last I visited. Urban style graffiti cover many of the surfaces. The quarry floor glitters with broken glass. Skulls, defiant but misspelled epithets, the letter A in a circle, the anarchy symbol, Black Sabbath and other rock band emblems of the subgenre favored by the Goth element of youth culture are spray painted everywhere. How utterly sad it is to ponder what this reflects.

How can I share with those angry young people another way of relating to the world? In my world, phenomenology, the study of the orderly progression through time of nature is remarkable and inexorable. It is September so plants will set seed, and birds will head south or stay, as is their nature. I find solace in knowing there are patterns greater than I.

In the sunshine we see tiny orange skippers now, flitting like campfire sparks. The striking black and alluringly velvety red admirals and white admirals wait till summer is ripe. It seems to take crickets most of the summer to really get going, and they are quite ready to take over when the cicada have retired. Shore birds are now mostly gone.

That plaintive cry is eagles or hawks—and they too come and go in their own progression.

Even our weather this month has its own bitter-sweet progression. It is always teasing, a warm-cold stirring not unlike the hurricanes, which we can expect to peak in intensity now. When the days are beautiful, the weather is matchless; when it's gloomy, the weather seems to press with the whole weight of winter, which we know is waiting for us.

Here comes Nishi. He is a native of Sri Lanka. His name is very musical—*Ni shan ta Ra ja ka run a*—but "Nishi" fits wonderfully. He is compact, very neat, and appealingly energetic. He's a natural teacher, explaining almost from the moment that we meet that scientists prefer to refer to the host of mineral here as peridotite parent rocks. That includes such slightly familiar words as olivine, serpentine, chrysotile, asbestos, nickel, and chromium. We have heard of soapstone, if not steatite, which is the same thing.

Nishi has studied the plant communities of serpentine rocks in California. In 1999 he also located a half dozen serpentine outcrops in Sri Lanka. When he was doing postdoctoral studies at Stanford, he worked on small islands where birds roosted and changed the chemistry with their guano. He mentions that plants restricted to isolated extreme habitats are often selfers, as one would expect.

"Selfer?" I can see Ann's quizzical expression.

"It doesn't need another plant to fertilize it," Nishi explains. He confesses that one of the reasons he took the job at CoA was that this Pine Hill quarry drew him like a magnet. Nishi is an evolutionary biologist, an ecologist of sorts, and is delighted to meet Ken who was the first graduate student of the distinguished ecologist, Robert MacArthur. Ken agrees to send Nishi copies of his papers on the mice of the islands. Robert introduced Ken and me at University of Pennsylvania back in the days when we were just figuring out how island biogeography operates.

"Now we think in terms of other kinds of islands as well, islands in time, islands along migration routes, islands in function." Nishi stops to point out a tiny strawberry plant nested among the shards of rock and broken glass on the quarry floor.

"These little strawberries here flowered within a month of snow melt. That's a common reaction to stress. That puts them well ahead of the other strawberry plants in the area. They will have only other strawberries of the peridotite population to pollinate with. You see what a powerful force that natural selection can be."

Ann is already down on the rocks with her camera.

"Serpentinite outcrops, mine tailings rich in heavy metals, and nitrogen-rich guano deposits all give rise to localized patterns of plant distribution. It's not that we have plants growing here that grow nowhere else: it's that these plants may look like the ones elsewhere, but their chemistry is different. They are morphologically identical but physiologically distinct. These plants, though small and stunted, have the trick of coping with heavy metals that most plants find toxic."

Ann is bent over a very small aster, focusing on its lovely lavender color.

"There is nothing here that is unusual for Maine," Nishi says, "but everything here looks stunted, physically stressed, sad, if you will. This substrate effect is not as spectacular as it is in California. The rocks here have been exposed only some thirteen or fourteen thousand years—since the islands emerged from the sea, maybe less if you're counting from the glacier's most recent retreat—so we probably do not have full-fledged species differentiated here yet. Genetic accommodation to extreme edaphic—soil—conditions can take place quite rapidly, even within a few generations. These conditions are potent agents of natural selection."

"Only thirteen or fourteen thousand years!" I think to myself. I have read that the rocks in serpentine formations are from the mantle of the earth, thrust up from deeper, older regions. This has happened in a few places along the Appalachian Mountain chain, near Washington, DC, near my old stomping grounds by Philadelphia, in Vermont, and in Greenland and Scotland, to name places in this hemisphere. The idea that I have seen special windows into the mantle of the planet pleases me. The idea that conditions here at this small serpentine quarry can teach us about evolution occurring in my life span awes me.

Nishi guides us over to the vertical rock face. He hands Ann a lovely stone flake, shining a waxy green in the sunlight. "This is what people call serpentine. And look at this Resurrection plant," he says with undisguised enthusiasm. "*Selaginaella rupestris.*"

I usually think of selaginella as a trailing moss-like plant in greenhouses. This small silvery plant looks more like tall haircap moss stems, and Nishi assure us it is now very green after our recent rains.

"We hope to do a complete, all-season vascular plant survey. If we get a grant from NASA we can have these plants chemically analyzed."

"Why would NASA be interested?"

"Well, peridotite makes up the mantle of Mars."

"Why would a plant find it an advantage to take up heavy metals?"

"Perhaps as a defense against pathogens or herbivores. Heavy metals are very toxic to insects."

I'm impressed. Nishi points out a charming wood fern, *Woodsia ilvensis*, clinging to the rock face. "Here is a particularly interesting possibility." Ann thinks so too as her photo frames not only the diminutive plant but the wild colors of the graffiti painting.

"Nishi, what would you do about the graffiti? Leave them or try to clean them off?"

"I would hope people would value this site and not make any more, but I definitely would not apply any chemicals to try to clean them. You might also think about encouraging people to walk on a designated path for the view. Soil compaction can be something of a problem where a site gets loved to death."

We have scrambled up to the top of the quarry. The sun is warm on our backs. An eagle soars by, looking for all the world like a diving board just half way to the moon. We perch on the bare ridge top. Even the grasshoppers also taking in the sunshine look like rocks. An occasional buffy dragonfly clatters helicoptering by.

We look directly into the tree tops, an unusual perch for bird watching. The tree canopies filled with flocks of twittering small birds seethe like kettles of bubbling jam. This batch sounds like it must be young goldfinches. Plain and tiny, most of these are what ornithologists call "confusing fall warblers." In the autumn, warblers have a drab plumage that makes most of them very difficult to identify. Without such field marks as "bright yellow breast" or "conspicuous rust streaks under the wings," you have to look sharp for the remaining wing bars or eye rings which make one species recognizable from another.

Ken says that the birds with dark olive backs are probably blackburnians. In spring a blackburnian warbler has a bright neon orange throat patch, but for now we will have to take Ken's word for it. The distinctive silhouette, spectacle-like rings around the eyes, and its silvery call makes us fairly sure we are watching a solitary vireo as well. I can't really care just which ones we are watching because it is such a treat to be up high, tree-house style, watching the birds.

The sky is a gorgeous blue. To my eye it looks like a good day for hawk watching, but so far, we see none. The wind is almost out of the northwest, so it ought to be a good flight day. We had heard of the hawk watching programs at Acadia National Park. Maybe we should be at Acadia.

This year we went to the official park hawk watch for the first time. From the Hawk Migration Association of North America web page, Ken found just about anything we might want to know. Weather forecasters think we may see something of Hurricane Ophelia by the end of the week so we decided to head on down, as they say around here when one heads down east with the predominant wind direction.

Deer Isle folk are slightly smug about being different from Mount Desert Island. We take a special pleasure in Ellsworth saying we are from The Island. They of course assume we mean MDI—and we do not. We are very glad that we are off the beaten path. We have our PFA's, persons from away, here on Deer Isle, but not many JPT's, just-passing-throughs. We could be talking about tourists or migrating birds it turns out. To our dismay there were still crowds of humans aplenty, the air uncomfortably warm and distressingly smoggy. From the top of Cadillac Mountain we could barely see Deer Isle as ought to be possible on a truly clear day.

The beaten path was certainly well-beaten. We were impressed with the very nicely worded signs about not trampling fragile and special vegetation. Visitors are urged not to pile rocks on top one another to form cairns. That is the equivalent of posting false road signs as cairns placed by the park service are meant to be read for guidance in the fog. We ask our stewards here on the Island to dismantle any free-lance rock piles when they find them along the trails. Here we are not so much worried about misdirecting hikers lost on mountain tops in the fog as trying to encourage folks to be considerate and not spoil the scene for others with signs of man-made intrusion.

According to the online report yesterday was a record day at Acadia, with 88 sharp-shinned hawks and an amazing 483 broad-winged hawks tallied. Comparing notes with area birders we think it is possible that the broadwings tend to follow the Reach or cross Sedgwick farther inland with the lift they get from Cadillac Mountain. We see relatively few broadwings here on Deer Isle. On days when we have checked nearly simultaneously at our own Hawk Hill, at Settlement Quarry, and at Pine Hill by posting friends at the various sites and doing some fancy commuting ourselves, we have found pleasantly satisfying numbers of hawks in the air, but not hundreds.

As we pick our way up the shred of trail that skirts the cliff face, rock by rock, Nishi and Ken keep up a conversation about Ken's work in the Antilles. At the top they continue while Ann photographs near and far. I enjoy the sun and the eavesdropping. "We have been worrying about islands in the neotropics and islands of habitat," Nishi is saying. "Perhaps we also should start worrying about loss of diversity due to our having created islands in structure."

"The lollipop mentality," I curse to myself. I hate it when I see landscapers chainsaw off all the branches they can reach on trees, leaving nary a bush for a bird to nest in, to rest in, thanks to some misplaced human enthusiasm for neatness or the manicured look. Migrating birds rely on that ordinary diversity of structure for shelter. They have no reservation system allowing them to choose where they will spend the night on their long trips. Nishi says he is trying to interest his students in the possibilities of backyard sanctuaries with less-manicured habitats, simple ideas that enrich ecological diversity.

How encouraging it is to meet a young scientist like Nishi. As we start back down the trail, I hear Ken and Nishi discussing the high number of endemic plant species in Cuba. Endemics are plants that have evolved *in situ*, and soil indicators are plants found in fairly restricted area, wherever serpentinite soil is found, for example. Nishi says 99 per cent of the plants here are what are called *boden vag*, or soil wanderers, from the Scandinavian words for wandering home.

I pause to write that unfamiliar term in my notes on my clipboard.

I am part way down a slide on my rear from one boulder to another. I hear Ann behind me laughing as I hang up.

"Hold up! Marnie's always on duty."

My notes are heavily laced with technical terms. Edaphic races, phylogenetic taxa, serpentinite endemics, hybrid inviability, ecotypes, etc. and that is not even counting the Latin names. And I am aware that as biologists, we are slightly guilty of glossing over how exciting this area is geologically. It is all too easy to glaze over when geologists enthusiastically name and describe the collisions, pressings, squeezings and volcanic squirtings that they easily envision over millions of years. They are comfortable with the changing names for the comings and goings of the oceans and continental plates resulting from all this bashing.

Precambrian sounds incredibly ancient, basically before evidence of living organisms. When those oldest rocks have eroded into sand and pressed into sediments and cooked, we have what geologists call Ellsworth schist. The grey-green crumbly rocks of the north and east of Deer Isle are Ellsworth schist.

Little Deer's rocks are the result of somewhat later Cambrian volcanic explosions and take their name from what the scientists call Castine volcanics. The mixture rocks that look to be made of many sorts of pudding stuffs may date to this period.

By the time we get to the Silurian Era, granites have boiled up to form Cadillac Mountain and the greyish granite rocks in Sedgwick and South Penobscot. In the Devonian Era, Deer Isle Granites, the "newer" granites of Stonington, distinctively pale pinkish, and Oak Point granites, more salmon-reddish, are intruding. This is the era that could be called the Great Age of Sharks.

Then comes Jurassic Era, which everyone thinks they can visualize thanks to the popular movie, *Jurassic Park*, in spite of the fact that dinosaurs came later. This may be the time that gave us the dark green serpentine-like peridotite, the lovely green flakes which litter the trail.

Whether this is a slice of ancient ocean floor or the core of an ancient volcano, as the locals say, this distinctive silhouette, like a camel's hump, brings joy to vacationers and residents alike when first spotted on the horizon above the sparkling bay. What makes the camel's hump, this earth sculpture, is the fact that half of the hill has been carted away. It was not mined for any of the interesting minerals, but for rocks to build the causeway between Little Deer and the main island of Deer Isle.

On the highway we see distant yellow school buses, while through the trees we glimpse sails of yachts making their way under the lofty bridge. Today there is just a hint of autumn glory in the colors of the deciduous trees that stand out from the deep black-green of the spruces around us and on the rolling mainland hills. We have had many warm winds up from the south, but no really cold nights to bring out the colors. Gasoline prices have been high and suffering in our own Gulf states has been enormous, thanks to hurricanes Katrina and Rita. How will the shoulder season be this year? Will those folks known as leaf peepers come? Lobstering was only fair. This could be a cold winter.

Nishi heads back to his own Island, Mount Desert, and we return to my Sunset home to grab some lunch and spend some time on our own hawk hill, adjacent to and functionally part of Barred Island Preserve.

When we arrive home, the crows are hollering "Hawk! Hawk! Hawk!" The woods lane dead-ends at our house so the driveway turn-around creates an opening in the spruces. The hawks work these edges to flush small birds. The crows so firmly claim the fringe of spruces and the small point of land between us and the nearest neighbors that we have labeled it Cape Crow.

Like so many fighter planes, sharpies, and the crows swoop out into the bright blue sky to challenge each other, dog fighting just above our heads.

Why on earth don't the hawks on their long distance journey save their energy? They do not avoid a fight. They veer out of their way to challenge other hawks or the crows or even the occasional raven which lends its big baritone fighting yell to the fracas.

"Hawk! HAWK! KRAWNK!"

Sharp-shinned hawks, why are you here and not at Pine Hill? I think serpentinite plants are not the only mysteries yet to be unraveled. Our world is very subtle.

Only reluctantly can I tear myself away from the birds above the driveway to thread through the birches up a hundred and some feet above the sparkling sea level to a more inclusive vantage point. It's really hard to count the hawks on Hawk Hill. Even from the knoll at Barred Island Preserve where you can see in 360°, the hawks don't really cooperate. In the first place, by far the most numerous species are kestrels and sharpies, the small ones. They move along the ridge in spirals, dipping down into the trees to snatch their prey, the small birds who were also about to head out over the bay. So, is that the same bird circling back again?

As we sit quietly under a tree, I turn my head to peer in the direction of a small keening cry. A small swift hawk hurls itself over my shoulder and disappears among the trees in front of us. Ann cannot possibly lead fast enough to capture the image. She mutters under her breath. I pick a bird and follow its spirals around and around the hillside, waiting to watch it finally head out over the water. But then the bird slips around in back of me so I might count it once again.

I am glad for the sake of science that they are getting fairly reliable numbers up at Acadia. For me it is sufficient to know that this small area of cut-over spruces and birch is of importance to a good number of hawks. That is reason enough to rejoice in the knowledge that conservation easements should keep it available to the hawks and warblers for years to come.

The experience of hawk watching here is quite different from the Acadia hawk count. Instead of the thrilling parade of hawks soaring up the mountainside to pass overhead in an awesome stream, here the watcher is almost a participant in the drama. The experience feels quite intimate. Like everything else about comparing Mount Desert Island and Deer Isle, theirs is definitely on a larger scale. The pink cliffs are bigger, the beaches are bigger, the "cottages" are bigger, and even the crowds are bigger.

As if to heighten the jewel-like effect of the September afternoon, a few sails still grace the bay here too. For many sailors, this is their favorite time of year. I watch a large and lovely white lobster boat send up paired rooster-tail wakes as it circles to pick up traps. There is wind enough, cool and crisp, to stir up the bay sufficient to make it fairly rough work hauling traps. But in the light of this autumn beauty, I know the lobsterman would shrug and his eyes just perceptibly twinkle if I were to praise him to his face.

Our own chores of the workaday world finally exert their call, so we head back down through the woods. On the silver spear of an overturned spruce root, a black plastic pail is impaled. The sheriff has left his calling card, a warning to whomever it was that was growing marijuana out here. A few weeks ago, the hill echoed to thumping growl of a helicopter ranging slowly back and forth, back and forth. The next issue of the local paper reported a sizeable pot bust. The overflight was apparently timed for when the plants would be large, but not yet ready to harvest since we have not yet had a frost. Well, the sheriff and his machete have taken care of that.

Ken, as steward of the Barred Island Preserve, followed his nose yesterday to find evidence that this year's deer poaching has begun. As in past years, a black plastic bag was dumped just off the road, inside the concealing fringe of bushes. In the bag were the guts and boney parts of a deer, shot, hastily butchered, and telltale remains quickly disposed of. I am distressed. Legal hunting seasons will begin soon, but for some that is not soon enough.

We here lead parallel lives. Like the hawks flying over us or the shorebirds who travel in the night, our destinies are linked.

A Camden architect friend of ours bemoans the loss of community there, where wealthy Shoreland Ordinance-breakers just pay the fine when they choose to chop out a grand view from their grand house, their trophy. Recent studies have found that the disparity between the top income bracket and the poorest is at its worst here on Deer Isle. I have noticed that the general appearance of what was once known as Tarpaper Alley has been much improved in appearance in recent years. Cosmetic appearances aside, however, anyone who comes here to work, young Islanders who wish to remain here, young families—they all will find acquiring affordable real estate on Deer Isle a real challenge.

On a recent walk here we encountered an Island family walking the land by a favorite spot once used by all. Their cousins who own the land have moved away but now are selling out at a price that only the wealthy from away can afford. The Island is changing too fast for local comprehension. We can't stop the changes. We can only hope to steer the changes to minimize the painful consequences to our community and maximize the good things that can come.

* * *

Another sweet fall day lures us to Little Deer. We decide to go see Pat and Kurt Fairchild, the Little Deer folks who are donating Pine Hill Quarry to Island Heritage Trust. They have a lovely home overlooking the Reach. The sign in front of the house on the hill still displays Pat's parents' names, "Emily and Monroe Wiegand." Pat stills refers to this as "Mother's house." Sparky, their Petite Bassett Griffon Vandene, a French hunting hound, greets us. In the kitchen Pat gives a pot of chowder another stir before we settle in to visit. She is making it to take over to one of her neighbors, an elderly woman of about hundred. They have just sold this house and are in the midst of packing their belongings to return to their winter home in Arizona. Boxes line the hallway, but Pat is obviously not worried about chowder-making taking time from their packing, and she is equally unperturbed by the prospect of a visit interrupting.

Kurt comes in from his shop. His full beard is longer than it was last time we saw him. "Now that we are getting things here properly wound up, I can get my beard trimmed," he laughs, settling into a chair. Out the window we see bright fall foliage and impressive air traffic of small birds at the feeder on their deck. Both Pat and Kurt keep track of what birds are there as we talk.

We discuss the fact that my brother has been looking in on his friend, Arthur Haskell, a.k.a. Dud. A master mariner and yacht captain, Dud is now retired from the Merchant Marines. He lives in Deer Isle village across from the Shakespeare School. The school house was named in honor of the crew of the schooner *Shakespeare*, lost at sea in 1818. Saving and restoring this one-room school house, which operated from 1858 to 1921, is a project dear to Dud's heart. Pat's father, Monroe, was a generous contributor to this work. As with so many other people that Monroe came in contact with here on the Island, they became good friends.

I observe that the metaphor of beads and string has occurred to me to describe the interconnections, which are so enriching. Dud met Monroe when he was hired to bring Monroe's yacht up to the bay one summer. The two subsequently enjoyed each other's company, partnering insights and resources to make local enterprises of good will effective, and dining out together quite regularly.

Monroe Weigand was a vice president of the Avon Company. "Don't you know his arrival on the Island put a stir in the local Avon lady?" Dud liked to say.

The Wiegand family loved the people here for what they are. They had no desire to change them, to make them more like the folks of Suffern, New Jersey where Pat grew up, or Greenwich, Connecticut to which her father was eventually transferred by Avon. The list of caretakers, neighbors, town officials, etc. whom Monroe befriended is long.

I say to Kurt that an impressively long list of folks have told me about something Kurt fixed for them. Family tradition.

Modestly he deflects my praise saying, "The Lord blessed me with an ability to figure out problems and fix things."

Pat laughs, adding that "He is the one who knows where the valve is, who it is that has the keys, where the corner markers are, even where the septic tank is buried."

"I understand you are very generous with your help, and your gift of Pine Hill is very generous," I say.

"I made a good living at being a site manager for Honeywell Corporation in the Phoenix area. At one time I oversaw maintenance and construction in six factories there, twelve shops, as a journeyman electrician, tending plumbing and heating. I figure it is time for me to give back. Besides, it's Pat who is generous. It's her family land."

Pat sews enthusiastically for the craft sales for the church on Little Deer. Kurt is volunteer sexton at Hardy Hill cemetery, mowing, trimming, setting markers. She explains that her father had Dick Buxton survey out some land to give to the Hardy Hill cemetery association land to expand. I wonder if Dick and Monroe talked about Dick's project, a preserve at Holt Mill Pond. I wonder if they compared notes about loving this community and the need to think about the future. I ask about other plots of land I've heard Monroe was involved with, and Pat and Kurt explain.

"Monroe fell in love with it here in 1966 and decided to retire here and built this house in 1987. Over the years he acquired a number of properties and sold and gave parcels as well. Someone needed to relocate a road, needed a place to live, you know, things like that. He was genuinely interested in the community."

"Pine Hill was used by the whole area. People liked to climb up for the view down the Reach, even before there was a quarry, before there were trees grown up."

"It always belonged to the community. It was never really just ours," Pat says.

Kurt says he too has heard that the stones for the Causeway came from the quarry, and perhaps for the bridge abutments as well.

Pat adds, "We hope now Pine Hill will always be a place for the community to enjoy, where they can come to take pictures and leave nothing but footprints." As a teacher of third, fourth, and fifth grades, Pat has always had an interest in the natural sciences. She and Kurt are very aware of the botanical and geological value of the quarry. I'm sure they will follow Nishi's researches with great interest.

I ask how their children feel about the gift. Between them and the children's children, there are nine: Kurt's two sons and two daughters, and Pat's children.

"Well, when the property was inherited, the bank trustees urged us to sell to developers," Kurt begins to explain.

"Over our dead bodies!" Pat declares.

"We knew the same pressures to sell would eventually be on the next generations."

"What the kids said they would miss most was that we were selling the shore. How will we see the water? Climb Pine Hill. The Trust will see that you can always do that. That works, they said."

I note that we are all looking out over the blue expanse of the Reach. Kurt says softly that they are going to follow with interest the results of the beach by the bridge being sold to developers. "Where locals always went to enjoy the beach and launch their boats, where I read in an old 1894 book at the church that folks used to use the piers and slips for coming to church."

"I would be lost now if you put me back where I grew up, "says Pat. Being originally from New Jersey as well, I know what she means. "When we drive back and forth to Arizona it just breaks our heart to see the farmland plowed down for development."

"You try to come up with some sort of protection for the land, but it all comes down to what some sharp attorney can turn around."

Silently I think about the struggles over the years that made the land trusts of the nation band together in a national association and retain the finest legal minds possible to deal with precisely this phenomenon.

Kurt breaks the silence saying "The city of Phoenix has been chasing us for the past 40 years. Farther and farther out. We once lived 18 miles out past the city line. We moved further out when the city swallowed us. Now they are developing the Sonoran desert as well. We've seen six thousand acres of wonderful desert plowed and paved. It's the fastest growing city in the nation I think."

"They say we need the tax base," Pat says scornfully. "You could see it, if it wasn't that there are empty houses and empty office buildings remaining empty there," she says. "It's all just a question of profits, lining the city's coffers, not what is good for the people who actually live in the city. Development *costs* the towns. This world is beautiful. We don't like what people have done to it."

A new wave of goldfinches twitters up to the feeder on the deck. A purple finch hangs onto the thistle bag. As the last of the afternoon light gradually shifts to that particular fall gold, which is like no other season's light, the air temperature takes on a special crispness. No wonder they call those who winter in warmer climates "snowbirds." We and the tiny birds can feel it coming.

Kurt and Pat express their sorrow at leaving soon. They plan to keep ownership of enough land for an RV pad. Parked outside even now is the vehicle in which they plan to spend future summers here. How well I remember the days in our own life when we had a foot in two boats, Deer Isle and Canton, New York. Though I loved my life in both places, I always found the transition most uncomfortable.

Kurt is looking forward to elk hunting with his sons in December. Ever since his own boyhood in Michigan he has been an avid hunter. He is proud of the fact that he and Pat raised their own chickens and beef and live off wild game. "I never hunt for horns. If we don't eat it, I don't shoot it. Pat hunts only with the camera, and we travel with field guides in the van. We love animals."

Tree shadows lengthen as we make our way home. Both golden leaves and green grasses are backlit in a charmingly theatrical way. I know from experience that hawks have found roosting places in our hillside birches for the night. Deer have stepped out of those same shadows to nibble the summer grasses in the clearings.

The scene, with or without human observers, is quite like a Garden of Eden. The fall from grace will happen soon enough. Hunting season, tomorrow's challenges of migration. But tonight is golden. I am glad to be where I am.

Lee

In the island lee
a hundred white-winged scoters
just-arrived,
strange as Taoist scholar's rocks
in the sheen of bright September noon.

On the lee slope, goldenrod
igniting orange flares of Monarchs
by the dozens gathering,
not needing to be noticed
before they cross the bay.

October — **HOLT MILL POND** — 8

October 1, and still no frost. Mushrooms, which seem to me a late summer occasion, are still sprouting up. Why do I think of late summer, when I know very well that it is always just this time of year that "Halloween" fungus appears? By that I mean witches butter, a bright orange jelly fungus on stumps and cut ends of logs. No doubt that's why the merchants too have begun putting out Halloween decorations. Some years about now we have had a crop of boletes as well. The Italians call them *porcini*, or ceps, the King of them all. So far, however, I have not spotted a one. I know they are under there, deep in the ground, minding their own calendar. Maybe next year.

By the sounds of it, the crows have begun "densing up." We have not seen the last hawks yet, nor the last pale lavender asters. Dragonflies still buzz and clatter in the afternoon sun. Chickadee and nuthatch families are loud in shriveled birch leaves. They are gleaning feasts of leafminers and other insects, which have been quietly burrowing in the leaves all summer.

Ann has long ago finished putting up the last beans from her garden, and she has been busying herself with other less rewarding tasks. She has been plowing through the piles of paperwork associated with her clinical psychology practice. We need to take Ann for some managed care, a restorative paddle! I call Nat Barrows, owner of the island's only newspaper, *The Island Ad-Vantages*, and confirm our date. Yes, he can take us out on Holt Mill Pond in his canoe.

We arrive to find that Nat has just finished splitting his wood. The splitter stands amid a small pile of neatly split lengths of wood. Nat, with his wife Ann and daughter Hanna, has succeeded in getting most of the wood moved into the woodshed. He is ready for a break and greets us with a great grin, wearing a warm sweatshirt atop his bathing suit.

The tide is right for a canoe ride up into the marsh. Sea duck hunting season started yesterday: inland starts tomorrow. Deer season has not begun unless you are using a bow, which not many hunters around here do.

From Nat's place we can look south to see the bridge where the highway passes over the mill run. Bright buoys mark the latest experiment in aquaculture. Bits of eel grass float by us on the water, their green calligraphy hinting at promise of fish stock recovery. Ecologists in the past half century have come to belated recognition of the crucial importance of estuaries as nurseries for many of the creatures of the sea. Perhaps this small salt marsh does not strictly qualify as an estuary, but it's all we have here. We must not underestimate it.

Looking up to the left, more or less northwest, we see the cove ringed with salt marsh. This is the only stand of salt hay of any size on the Island. To an early settler with a cow to feed that must have looked like gold. No trees to cut and burn and clear and plant before a pasture grew. Maybe not quite a land of manna and honey, perhaps, but close enough, a definite advantage over everybody else trying to scratch out a foothold on this coast. (And the native peoples who already lived here might ask, in what sense a promised land?)

Henry Holt was born in 1644 in Andover, Massachusetts, according to the Deer Isle-Stonington Historical Society records. He came here and built a mill somewhere near where the present road crosses the mouth of the cove that bears his name. We can be sure the significance of the island's only salt marsh of any size did not escape him. He would have known the value of salt hay.

The air is so clear and calm that we can see the sailing spider webs as these aerialists float ballooning across the water. Nat points out where the winter's ice has worn an overhanging spruce to bone white. In winter he has seen otter slides along here.

Ann points her paddle at a large rock. Nat says, "We call that the Ice Palace Rock. In winter the ice piles up around that rock in sheets like four walls. When it rains over the ice and then freezes, we have come out and skated across here."

We pull over to the shore so Nat can point out the eroding bank. "See those white shell layers? That's an Indian midden. I like to come here and sit and think about those who lived here before," he says quietly. "Somebody has been digging here lately, so I'd better get around to dropping another tree or two as protection on it."

We hover over the gravel at the mouth of Indian Brook, one of the four streams that feed into Holt Mill Pond. It is the precise and fluctuating blend of salt and fresh water, both its chemical and physical properties, that determines the fate of the organisms adapting to this fragile environment that in turn feeds the sea.

There is a shimmer of light waving on the trunks of the trees here, reflections from the sun on the ripples.

"Doesn't it look like a spirit glow?" says Ann.

"It's almost like an aurora," I add after we have sat and gazed a while. The clatter of a kingfisher calls us back from our silences.

The water music, currents sliding under the canoe bow as we head up into the marsh, works its magic. A ripple of tiny fish splashes sparkling in the grasses in front of us. The sigh of the hull on the grasses, the wind in the trees—it's a sweet sound.

The channel is a mere thread here, maybe two or three feet deep at most. Somehow I had expected to look up at deep clay banks. Of course when the water level is high enough to float our canoe, it is high enough to cover the banks. We have prowled the marsh with Professor Knowlton, the invertebrate specialist, i.e. our friend Bob the mud man, and I must admit that in some ways the view of the marsh is more dramatic from land, from the preserve nature trail, at a low tide.

"At a moon tide or a storm, the water might be twelve to fourteen feet deep here," Nat explains.

Nat has spotted a group of four ducks landing beside us on the next turn of the channel. He signals to Ann to ready herself and camera for our approach. With the breeze behind us, we drift silently toward the four plain, dark ducks now floating serenely on the glassy surface. Delicate and graceful, I think they are black ducks rather than mallards. Technically the field mark that allows you to determine which species you are looking at is the color of the speculum—that color patch on the wings. However, in practice, one comes to recognize the "look," whether it is ducks, your child, or an old acquaintance in a crowd.

The ducks cock their heads, come to a halt, and then take off in shower of sparkling drops. They circle around us, then pass overhead, the pale pearl grey of their under wing feathers lovely as moonlight. Four satellite moons orbiting the marsh.

I remember once going duck hunting with a friend in Montana. As now, we rounded a bend in our canoe and flushed a small group of ducks. I recall watching the graceful arc of flight change in a wing beat to the straight line drop of a stone. "Drop like a stone" is so descriptive that it's no wonder the phrase has become a cliché. The words so accurately describe the instant when living muscle and nerve and blood give up the magic that is life. We ate that duck well-prepared and with appropriately feast-like ceremony. There was a real sense of partaking in sacred ritual, the taking into one's own body that which had so recently been another life.

I understand. But nevertheless I am pleased to watch the iridescent blue wing patches of these four black ducks winging safely away through the bright sky. A number of duck species enjoy dining on the tiny poppy-seed-like bounty of widgeon grass which grows in pools at the head of the marsh.

They seemed quite tame, almost curious about us, until we floated too close for their comfort. It is as if they are totally innocent of the fact that hunting season for them begins tomorrow. Of course they are innocent; they are ducks. How then to explain the skittishness of the sea ducks just now? Their open hunting season began yesterday. For over a week the large flocks gathered on the bay had become noticeably skittish. Whenever our boat approached, even distantly, the entire gathering departed in a flurry of foam and flapping.

Walter said he too had noticed that the large flocks of eiders and scoters had seemed to be disseminating into smaller groups. "It's as if they are getting ready for hunting season, making themselves harder targets."

How could this be? Might the groups have some sort of aggregate memory? In a large flock, more individuals are likely to have lived through other hunting seasons. To them this particular length of day, cast of light, may signal something threatening. The innocent young of the year may pick up on that.

The sea duck flocks are particularly attractive just now, the scoters with their chic black plumage set off by white patches and bright red-and-yellow bill patterns. Immature male eiders too sport a particularly dapper half black-half-white new plumage these days. I regret that for the next four months I will have to give way to the hunters who flock to the bay for guided slaughtering sessions. Not surprisingly considering their diet, these birds are reputed to taste fishy. Not infrequently their carcasses end up tossed on the town dump. That may even be legal, and it would not be legal for me to go out just before dawn and spook all the ducks away from the hunters. Go figure. Four months of what seems like World War II Normandy Beach reenactment seems awfully long by the end of January.

The grassy swales are pressed in wondrous patterns. Bands of color and texture paint the scene as if with very painterly brush strokes. Even from here we can see that vegetation has sorted itself out according to how the various plants deal with salinity. We recognize the russet glow of ripe seed heads of the *Spartina* grasses. Salt-water cord grass, *S. alterniflora*, tall and stiff, grows along the banks. Marsh-hay cord grass, *S. patens*, short and fine and matted, grows on the flats. The swales look like big green cowlicks. Farther back, at the very edge of the marsh by the tree shadows, is a dark band of black grass, *Juncus Gerardi*, actually a rush.

We are enchanted by the lavender mist of beach heather, *Limonium*, attractive in a ghostly way. From this vantage many of the plants look coated with gray silt and clay from the muds. Where tall grasses overhang the bank I urge Ann to reach out and pluck one. "Feel the rough saw-toothed edges. That's how you tell *Spartina alterniflora*."

"It's rough," Ann agrees. As she inspects it, I urge her to lick it. "Those grey splotches are the salt that the plant excretes. Taste it; it's like a pretzel." Ann is dubious, but game.

As we bask in the full heat of the sun and admire the artistry of the back-lighting, we are buzzed by red dragonflies and serenaded by crickets hidden off in the green billows. Green grasshoppers crawl and skitter through the grasses. The marsh is an amazingly rich detritus-based food web, a peat formed by plant matter ranging from purple sulphur bacteria,which are responsible for the characteristic rotten-egg smell, and filamentous green algae and cyanobacteria to the array of grasses and herbs growing, decaying, and being recycled. Large brown dragons dart by, and the bright males with distinctive white wing blotches earning them the name ten spots. Here and there what look like lightning bugs fly up. They are actually ctenucha moths, creatures with fancy feathery antenna and bright yellow-orange thorax. They look to me like Zen priests in their dark robes.

That summer is gone seems hardly believable, but the chittering of chickadees flying back and forth over the channel say it is so. The touch of red in the swamp maples confirms the arrival of autumn. Spruce shadows seem particularly dark, a heavy blackness slightly foreboding. Winter.

"I find it interesting each spring to see how ice has changed the marsh. We get quite drastic changes when ice moves quite sizeable chunks of vegetation around and drops them when the ice goes out." Nat says how he is fascinated by having become more aware of the diversity of ecological niches of the marsh over the years he has lived here. He came to the Island in 1968 to take ownership of the paper. In 1970 he bought his property along Holt Mill Pond. Over the years from 1983 to 1987, he and his wife Ann built the house.

I find it interesting and not a little amusing to think that young people of today might assume that Ken and I, our late friend Dick Buxton, and Nat might all be representative of the wave of hippies that came here in the seventies. Free spirits, yes. Countercultural? Somewhat. Psychedelic? Hippies? No. Gives me a point from which to think about Henry Holt and the other early settlers here.

"Never in 35 years have I seen anything like the way the deer now eat our gardens," says Nat as we inspect what are clearly deer grazing meadows. Salt marshes are said to produce more biomass per acre than an acre of wheat field—some ten tons per acre compared with a measly one and an half tons of organic matter produced by the wheat field in a year—but I do not think I will offer that as consolation to Nat.

Over the tops of the trees we can just make out the graceful white arms of a small windmill. Nat explains. "That is Dennis Saindon's windmill. He's the high school shop teacher, you know." No sooner have we said his name than the man himself appears.

"Isn't this a top of the pyramid day!"

"Not even any bugs."

"Sometimes here at the head of the cove, the mosquitoes can be so thick they'll pick you right out of your canoe."

"Well, I made a special arrangement with the swallows and flycatchers that run the concession at the bridge."

Dennis tells us how pleased he is with his windmill, only having to turn on the diesel occasionally to charge the battery. He's glad to hear of our project, visiting the island's natural areas, celebrating them. "Keep at it, Marnie. We've lost so much of the environmental sensibility we had back in the seventies," he laments. "You heard about Ted getting that MacArthur award. I hear others talk about how that will help the country take us seriously. It is my hope that may help us here to take ourselves seriously as well."

Ted Ames is our mutual friend, a lobsterman who hailed originally from Vinalhaven, next island over. A gentle man, an educated fisherman, Ted is the ideal recipient of a prize, an honor, and a financial reward, which he will have no trouble putting to good use.

As we talk, the tide has turned. The change is barely perceptible, but now the waters gently move us away, back to the sea.

"That daylight, the clear space just behind the trees, that's Georges Pond," Nat explains to Ann. "Dennis, are the beaver still at work back there?"

"Yes, and the ATVs as well," he answers ruefully. "Trouble is, when anyone breaks a path, it's an open invitation to others. These guys just don't have a clue that what they think is harmless fun is actually connected to their fathers, their brothers, out breaking their backs on the water trying to wrestle a living from fishing.

"There's some hope for getting an ATV club started at school this year. That ought to help. The Stonington Conservation Commission, which advises the selectmen on environmental issues, arranged two assemblies at the elementary school. ATV owners are being encouraged to start a local ATV club. The state warden service, which has jurisdiction over ATVs, came to the school and tried to get kids to understand what is actually at stake when a few bad eggs spoil a sport for others."

The presence of Dennis on the marsh has been invaluable. Dennis doesn't add and I don't say what we both know: some of those riding the

ATVs are no longer kids in school. They are old enough to know better. The wheel ruts destroy the vegetation. The erosion and runoff degrades the nursery for several species of fish. We literally lose the grass roots of our marine resource base.

We notice that tacked up on the side of a tree overlooking the marsh is a lawn chair. "Yup. The guy even has a cup holder fastened there," laughs Nat. It is someone's hunting seat. "Dennis, can you see if there's still enough water for us to turn around at the hairpin?"

Dennis stands, unfolding his lanky frame, shielding his eyes against the sun, and pronounces it worth a try. At the worst, we'll just get hung up and have to get out and wade and carry the canoe through the mud.

"Go for it!"

Nat has been most courteous, even courtly, on this journey, paddling stern so Ann can have the bow. She wants none of us in the way when she points the camera at the next great shot. That relegates me to the center, where seated on the canoe floor amid the thwarts I feel like some Egyptian queen, ruling with a clipboard of course.

We manage to turn without having to ignominiously back out to preserve our assigned ranks. Once assured we are not stuck, we float briefly to peer over the grasses at a pair of shallow pools, one with a whitish surface layer—bacteria—and one without water. Bob Knowlton and the marsh scientists would call them a classic panne and ruppia pool. *Ruppia* is the scientific name for widgeon grass. Just as the bulrushes of the salt marsh are sedges, not rushes, and black grass is rush, not a grass, so too the widgeon is not a grass. A panne is a pan-like shallow depression which has evaporated, a plant and animal community with

its own set of adaptations for dealing with the tidal fluctuations here of wet and dry, salinity, and interspecies competition.

We consider clambering out of the canoe to take a closer look. Nat, probably concerned about the logarithmically falling tide, suggests it might be more prudent not to.

Conversation turns to honey pots, those mysterious sink holes the clammers told us about. This salt marsh has its ways of exacting revenge on those who would trample its integrity. First there are the usual hordes of bloodthirsty mosquitoes, but no less menacing are the treacherous ditches and holes lying in wait invisible under the grass thatch or under a mud surface of deceptive depth.

I recall watching Bob Knowlton plunge the handle of his dip net into several feet of one of these elephant trap ruppia pools. We kidded him for announcing, "That mud's a solid three feet deep at least." Decidedly NOT solid.

He retaliated by pointing out a tasty wild salad green, orache. He pronounced it by clearing his throat. "Orrr," and imitating a convincing vomit. "Rrrrach!" Clammers have no corner on honey pot humor, the sulphurous wit associated with this salty region.

As our canoe glides past a channel winding off through the marsh, Nat points out that the town line runs right along here. The shore on the north side is the Town of Deer Isle; on the south side, it is Stonington.

"Nat, speaking of lines, do you think being a surveyor had something to do with why Dick Buxton got the Holt Mill Pond project started?'

"I can't say for sure, but he certainly knew the land better than anyone else on the Island at that time. If anyone could see changing land ownership patterns, it would have been him."

We startle a wraith-like school of what are probably tiny killifish. I would love to have Ann see some of the tiny eels I know are down there as well. At this stage of their life, they are each about the size and shape of a nut pick. But so lithe and quick! Their dark eyes and narrow heads are reminiscent of salamanders. Same innocent grins too. When these young eels were just coming in from the ocean, they looked more like transparent willow leaves, so-called glass eels.

We duck into a cove and Nat whispers that there is a doe standing at the shore. Sure enough. We drift in silence. We watch her lift her head. Her ears begin to twitch. She flicks them twice. She bounds away with a great white swish of tail and long leap of elegant legs.

Ann laughs in that triumphant throaty call of which I have become very fond, "Got it!"

A lone eagle soars over.

"We've seen as many as five eagles here at one time," Nat says. "Let's go over and have a look at that gauzy spruce, okay? Wouldn't that be a good shot, Ann?"

She nods in approval and picks up her paddle.

"My mother was an artist and a gardener. She collected and nurtured many plant species." Nat paddles softly for a while, then adds, "I find a spiritual value in looking at the natural world, just being in it."

At the water line a row of reddish-tinged plants catches Ann's eye. "Marnie, what is that?"

Everything looks slightly different from this perspective. I have to study the stout stalks protruding out of the water for a moment. Then it comes to me. "Oh, fall color comes to the marsh too. I think those are marsh samphire, pickle plant. You can eat them. They are surely adapted to having their feet wet. Some people call them chicken toes, or saltwort." Ann leans out to pluck a taste. We hug the shore looking for organisms. We paddle and float, peering down through the shallows. Periwinkles are slowly wending their way.

"Look closely and you can see that some are not just snails; they have been taken on by hermit crabs. They sort of scuttle along," Nat points out. "I don't think we can get you pictures of the eel grass, Ann. The water's still too deep."

We had earlier expressed interest in the fact that Nat had seen very healthy looking patches of eel grass growing out near the mouth of the cove. The eel grass, with the salt hay, is the emblem of the importance of this salt marsh complex. Neither may look like much to the uninitiated, but both are significant beyond measure to our marine resource base.

"We will have to make do with these sea snakes, then." Long fronds of the green weed float round us now in serpentine rows. These too are eelgrass, fronds that have been broken off. The plant looks as if it ought to be a seaweed, but it is a flowering plant. No, Nat has not seen just what the flower looks like, nor does he think there is still any of the old fencing left that once separated two pastures here. When we first came to Holt Mill Pond all those years ago, a line of fencing stretched from land to a blind end at water's edge. What looked to my eye open, to any grazing cattle looked a barrier indeed.

Ahead of us a catspaw, the wind, sends ripples across the water. It looks like alligator skin. A raucous grunt "Grrronk!" and another. Then a great blue heron comes over the trees from somewhere just out of our sight. We are properly awed by its size and strangeness. I try to see if it has a white fringe of long feathers on its breast and a white crest on its head. "The immatures don't have the fancy white trim," I explain. "I am always amazed at this time of the year to think that the young of the year have probably already headed south, making the journey they have never made before."

"Are the herons still nesting out on Scraggy?" asks Nat.

"No. Apparently they moved the whole colony elsewhere after the eagles took over the area. I am always delighted to see any heron now," I reply.

Ann asks about my book, *Great Blue, Odyssey of a Heron*. "Is Scraggy the island you wrote about?"

"Yes. It was just this time of year, just that sort of noise, which decided me to write that book, even though I did not realize it for some months later. Ken had a sabbatical and we were going to head off to the West Indies and Bermuda to revisit some of his research sites. He had worked with flycatchers of the genus *Eleania*, on St. Lucia, St. Vincent, and Grenada. I was sitting out in our yard, here on the Island, packing and feeling slightly apprehensive about taking our two small boys on such a long trip, when three herons flew over and made that great qwonking sound. I remember watching them go over and thinking, 'You are making the same trip I am headed toward—and you don't have maps, no one to tell you where to stay. You have to do it all yourself; you don't even have an airplane.'"

It is all so clear to me now as I recount the tale to Nat and Ann. "From that moment on, the story just seemed to write itself. The first leg was flying out of Boston to Bermuda. A commercial pilot had the seat next me. He leaned over, pointed out the window and said to me, 'See those shadows on the clouds down there? Those are migrating birds, herons probably.' Then when we arrived in Bermuda our friend, David Wingate, who was going to meet us, was late. 'I'm sorry I'm late,' he said. 'I've been up in the radar dome helping NASA. They have stationed US Navy ships from here to South America and they are tracking some herons that flew over Cape Cod. These half dozen or so passed right over Bermuda. They never even landed. There are ships anchored off the Antilles. We'll see what the birds do next.'

"We expressed surprise that the navy was suddenly turning into bird watchers. 'Oh,' Wingate explained, 'They had me up in the dome using high-powered binoculars to identify the birds. Then they correlated that with what they were seeing on the radar screens. It was so they could learn to distinguish between migratory birds and enemy airplanes.'

"We know so much more now about what birds do in their travels. We *Norte Americanos* are coming to realize that our birds are perhaps even more theirs. Birds may be more accurately thought of as visiting up north to lay eggs, rear young, and hurry back home. At that time, however, there were many gaps in the story. In my own edition, so to speak, we encountered a man in Trinidad who made his living guiding birdwatchers into Caroni Swamp to see the scarlet ibis, which roosted there in spectacular numbers. He told us about the tame great blue heron he had for a number of years. He had rescued it and nursed it back to survival but not to full recovery. He had the bird for a number of years. About then I realized the story was, as they say, almost literally writing me."

We are all quiet for a time, as each of us had experienced something of that same instruction by what men like to call the muses. Ann must be thinking about our current Beads and String adventures. Talk about a work writing itself, this time with photographs no less.

"The irony of it all was that a well-known ornithological reviewer wrote of my book that the writing was nice enough, but it was a shame I did not know that herons did not actually fly the route I had described. I have always wondered what he thought when subsequently the scientific papers describing the migration research came out."

Along the ridge of a spit of land grow seaside goldenrod, salt-marsh aster, and a handsome bayberry bush or two. I comment on the fact that there is a snail with lungs that goes up and down the salt grass stems, grazing, as the tides rise and fall. As we paddle along and look up at the vegetation I recount Bob Knowlton's remarks that a salt marsh grows vertically on its own peat, and, so far, faster than the sea level has been rising. Scientists at the University of Maine have found, however, that the Greenland glacier is melting much faster than we thought, which means that in our lifetime we may see Gulf of Maine sea levels rising much more significantly than we thought. Ann and Nat paddle along silently, none of us caring to discuss the big global warming question.

An osprey and then another flies over. "Several osprey hang out down at the bridge. I think they know that lots of fish funnel through there on the current." Nat says next how pleased he is that the Island temporarily has a stop light. I am thinking that the next nearest one is forty-five minutes away in Ellsworth, and thank you very much, let's keep it that way.

Nat continues, "Often I am driving home and the light turns red and forces me to stop. Just stop. And I turn my head and look up Holt Mill Pond and I remember to take time for a good look."

We nod, knowing just how special such a moment is.

Nat continues, "There's all sorts of neat stuff under the bridge. For my kids it was a sort of rite of passage to jump off the bridge. I keep thinking I will put on sneakers and wade under the bridge. Well, now we all wear Tevas, but I should have done that this summer. When the tide is low, you can see another world there. Sponges, sea anemones, green crabs."

Ann and I do not say how we hope he will not find a certain new invasive sea squirt species matting out everything down there. Bob Knowlton did report the more benign kind just there by the bridge.

We can feel the air cooling as the afternoon sun slants, the sweet cool draft rolling down the shaded bank. Tonight will be clear and our precious heat will radiate away.

"When our son Ben was about twelve," Nat says, voicing thoughts of the coming cold, "he and I went out one winter-spring evening just at ice out. That can be pretty spectacular here. We cut some spruce poles and rode the ice cakes out with the tide. Then we walked home."

We, too, have returned from our marsh journey. As we disembark and pull the canoe up on shore, a tiny red berry catches Ann's attention. It is a single berry of *Mianthemum*, the wild lily of the valley. The fading sun rays endow it with a clear red gleam. Ann pastes herself along the ground to meet it eye to eye. She has a marvelous knack for capturing the beauty of the humble. One more shot. The last bloom of summer, a lone ruby on a stalk.

On my way home I ponder all the people with commitment to this community where they have put down roots as strong and humble as the salt hay that holds the marsh together. Perhaps being from away they have perspective to see what is special, what is not the normal elsewhere. Handsome, personable, and dedicated to the Island environment, Dick Buxton, for example, was well thought of here. Originally from New Jersey, Dick graduated from the high school in Bucksport where his father owned the newspapers, and his brother still presides.

Dick died young, aged fifty, of prostate cancer, but not before he had seen Holt Mill Pond safely transferred to the care of others enough like him in their dedication to this Island. His children live here now. Son Peter is a boatbuilder, and Richard, mentored by the Island artists, now works as a jewelry maker among his other trades. Their sister, Sandy, has generously shared her vivaciousness and talents teaching Islanders to value physical fitness.

Nat Barrows grew up in Connecticut, but his family has its roots in southern Maine. His father before him was a newspaperman, one who gave his life in the line of duty as a matter of fact, working for the *Chicago Sun Times*. Nat has used his paper to speak forcefully for keeping the Island as a healthy year-round community rather than degenerating into seasonal playground for the wealthy.

Ken Crowell came to the Island from New Jersey via Cape Cod on his father's side and Bath and Surry, Maine, on his mother's side of the family tree. Retirement is not a very accurate word to describe what Ken does here now that he is no longer teaching.

Clayton Gross was another of that early bunch who joined together gathering private contributions, writing grant requests, and convincing the town to put up some money for preserving the salt marsh. Clayton was born and raised here, but he finished his education away. I jokingly say even a long weekend away in Massachusetts will do that to you, make you a person from away. Emily Muir, from outside New York, who summered here with her parents and then moved here when she married an artist, was another of what I call the Stonington Force.

For some years this Holt Mill Pond Preserve, the town's property, was not big in the selectmen's minds. To this day, many in town do not understand the ecological significance of the Island's only salt marsh. With no more cows, we do not see the need of salt hay. No one has put out nets for elvers for the past several years there. With no one smelting, and not even an ocean view, Holt Mill Pond Preserve may seem just an out of the way place for riding ATV's. There is really no public place for launching canoes and kayaks on this salt pond. The fragile marsh is best served by the nature trail, the lightest touch of recreation. The classic salt marsh view down the cove from the highway bridge where Holt's mill once stood is in itself worth all the trouble.

Understanding and cooperation are coming. We are learning that everything in our ecosystem is connected to everything else. This is a state-wide pattern, a nation-wide pattern. We continue to hope. My generation thinks education will make us all good enough citizens. Others have joined Nat in his passion for keeping the island a wholesome, stable, year round community. We are coming to understand and accept one another. We are coming to recognize who our allies are. Our little twelve by twelve mile island has two town governments, two landfills, two phone exchanges, but we are making progress: we have one high school basketball team these days. Hereabouts, that is really something to cheer about.

The sunset sky to the west over the dark silhouette of the spruces is a delicate glow. I have recently learned that there is out there, invisible to me, an especially strong band of polarized light near the horizon at dawn and dusk. It stretches across the globe from north to south, and apparently the migrating birds will be using it to calibrate their internal compasses. That is a comfort to me although we humans cannot see that light. I ask what should we be using by which to calibrate our inner compass to guide our way? We have GPS, infrared sensors, ultrasound imaging—oh, yes, we are living in an age of marvelous new technology, but our ways of treating one another and the living world around us have not evolved with the same lightning speed.

Sometimes it's hard to look at the golden glow of sunset and feel that it symbolizes a rosy future for us all. Autumn afternoons leave us particularly vulnerable to melancholy. After the setting of the sun come small keen knife cuts of cold, and then the dark. I will have to hold on to the notion of noticing the healing effect an outdoor outing has on my mind and body. I will hold in my heart the marvel of the self-correcting systems in the salt marsh. I have the humility to accept that humans make short-sighted choices. I have the will to try to influence the direction of our future choices. It seems that given who I am, I may have no more choice about whether or not I try than the elvers have about making their invisible way through the salt marsh, up the fresh water stream, and into the secret places at the heart of the Island.

Fall Weave

The gallant
little spindle
of a bird, brown creeper
fluttering down with the
rain-driven leaves

begins again
its persistent ascent
on threadbare birch
weaving life, the only
anti-entropic force
in the wintry universe.

November — SCOTT'S LANDING — 9

I am alone. I have come here to Scott's Landing several times with Ann, and with others who share this story with me, but I feel the need to come alone today, shortly before Thanksgiving. Hunting season is in full swing, so the fact that this is not woods is in my favor. I do wear a rusty orange jacket, but largely because that is the color it came in. At this time of year, some folks get quite "fetishist" about their day-glow costume, reluctant to appear behind the wheel of their pickup or at the post office in anything less than International Orange.

I suppose the story is apocryphal, but at Barred Island Preserve one hunter a few years ago supposedly reported that he had a huge furry animal in his sights, but fortunately lowered his gun when he realized it was just a city slicker in a fur coat. I can understand why the out-of-town visitor feels safe on a preserve, but that would be an error—most preserves do not have a no-hunting policy. Hunters, however, understand the significance of the bear story whether it is literally true or not. They are all too well aware that there is now precious little left of what they regarded as their traditional hunting spots. New houses are hiding in the woods now.

All this month the woods have been twittering softly with the calls of mixed flocks of tiny birds keeping in touch with one another as they move through our area. I do not know what they find to eat now. We have had several killing frosts. The large flocks of robins that came through recently feasted on the bright red berries of winterberry, our native holly, which lines the roadsides. I have several times encountered metropolitan types, recently moved here folks who were enthusiastically picking bouquets of the berries. One woman asked me anxiously if I thought the berries were poison. In all honesty I had to reassure her that they were not. I did tell her gently that the robins would be along any day now to feast on the berries as they moved south.

I could not bring myself to point out that where she was standing was actually someone's yard. The owner, the resident, may indeed have been planning to pick a few of the pretty branches for their Christmas decorating. Well, perhaps not. The owners had probably by now become quite used to the passersby who also pick all the fat roadside pussy willows for their Easter decorating come spring. To some eyes, if it is untrimmed, it looks unclaimed.

Recent storms have stripped the trees of their fall color. Waist-high billows of alizarin crimson are the sole exception; huckleberries, last to turn color, seem to be last to lose their leaves. Against the stormy skies they make a fine show.   Flocks of chickadees, juncos, a last yellow-rumped warbler, and a golden-crowned kinglet are chirping to one another and buzzing about, hiding or finding food. Off in the distance I hear a flock of geese. A great blue heron is silently fishing in the nearby cove. I am sitting on a ridge of land that affords me a view to the west of the bay, Causeway Beach and the basin and causeway itself. Due north lies Little Deer, and to the east I look across the Reach to the mainland. Just a short distance away, the waters of the Reach pour out in gentle, quick succession. Only a few tattered brown leaves cling to the oaks and a red leaf or two mark the sumac stems and blueberry bushes. Since I am dressed warmly, I feel the air as a crisp sweetness on my face. Ann says she loves this time of year because you can see so much farther now that all those green leaves are no longer in the way.

Mushrooms are pretty well gone by now. There is the occasional ink stain where certain species once were, and what look like stubbed cigars mark where another type persisted. For me, this is the season for lichens. The storms have brought whole limbs crashing down. Roads and paths are strewn with lichen specimens I usually cannot see. I always think of rain forests with their secret trove of epiphytes aloft. I have read that a single tree of ours can have more than thirty different species of lichens; no match perhaps for rainforest diversity, but more than enough for me.

Lichen identification is particularly frustrating. They mostly look more or less alike—a grey-green which at least distinguishes them from those other lowly overlooked darlings, the mosses and liverworts.

The names of many have all been changed so any book I had decades ago is now no help. I do not have a compound microscope or chemistry set so I could not make an accurate species determination for most of them even if I cared.

Of course, I cannot bear to leave it quite at that. I have worked out for myself what I call The Pasta System of lichen ID. Back when I was in high school we were taught that lichens are a symbiotic association of an alga and a fungus. Nowadays biologists are more precise and prefer to designate the association as being between a fungus and a photobiont. That is, the partner may be a cyoanobacteria, what we used to call a blue-green alga. We were taught that lichens came in crustose, fruticose, or foliose forms, as if that meant something from a classification standpoint.

With much more chemistry done and much closer looks, we now know that those forms are merely descriptors. Hence I feel perfectly justified in classifying the lichens I see as lasagne noodles, fettucine, linguine, or if they are round, spaghetti or capellini— all based on how wide they seem to me. Crustose lichens, of course are sauce, and perhaps the squamulose lichens ones are "with cheese." I am quite willing to turn up the noodles to see if they are black or pale underneath, and I delight in making up impressionistic names for the obviously different lichens I see. After all, if scientists when pressed for common names call various members of the genus *Cladonia* by such names as British soldiers, I am comfortable attaching my own for them, at least until I get home and can look in a book or on a web page for matching pictures.

Today I am applying my own system to the lichens of Scott's Landing. The open meadow sweeping down to the Reach is quite different from the spruce forest where I live. Because this was not too long ago a farm, the apple trees are still here. There is a lovely horse chestnut or two, some oaks, and a grove of poplars. There are lichen-coated remnants of stone walls, and here and there a glacial erratic boulder that was too large for farmers to move. All have lovely lichen coatings.

The trees quickly impress me with how like an island each one is. Each species of tree has some lichens growing on the bark and limbs which look somewhat different from the kinds I usually find growing in the spruce forests. Many, however, look familiar. There is the dotted fettucine one with the black underside, called hammered shield lichen. You can indeed see what look like hammer marks on metal. There are the starbursts of linguine, black underneath, with narrow fingers stretching out as if by a rolling pin. These I lump as "starbursts."

The poplar trunks all have round grey paint-like stains that on closer inspection appear to be dotted with tiny black structures. The maples and apples have several well-lobed and luxuriant kinds with light undersides. On the maples some are so deeply lobed they are called "lung lichens." The lone spruce in the middle of the pasture sprouts starbursts and dark-rimmed rolled out narrow straps with dark brown cups of fruiting bodies. Could they really all be the same species? If not, how in the world would you ever tell them apart? Of course, the answer is with chemical tests and a microscope. The biochemistry of lichens is very interesting and one thinks naturally of future medical uses. That lichens are extremely susceptible to air pollution should give us pause.

The tufts the spruce tree wears of old man's beard lichen are mistakeable. I never can resist tweaking the hairy growths. I am only trying to see if I have made the correct identification. *Usnea* species have a solid and elastic core. They stretch like rubber bands. Other similar species do not. It is such fun to tweak those beards.

I go to walk the shore. Here I keep my eye out for arrowheads or pottery bits that might have washed up. There are rocks that are quite obviously granite, but different from the Deer Isle granites—no pink. The geology map labels the bedrock across the Reach as Sedgwick Granite, and it is quite likely these grey granites have made the trip across to the island in the days before the bridge. I will have to tell Ann. She will come. This is a fine place from which to photograph the elegant arch of the bridge.

The largest rocks at the back of the shore have lichens on them. Bright gold ones encrust the rocks and even a wooden post still standing from the old ferry landing days here. One grey granite boulder is sprinkled with a crustose lichen poetically called Fire Dots. Like garnets, like drops of burgundy wine, these lichens.

Today might be dismissed as cold and grey and lonely, but a closer look reveals a day that is a treat, something I am glad not have missed. I give thanks. Ordinarily giving thanks is not hard for me to do. That Abraham Lincoln was the one who officially proclaimed a national day of thanks giving seems very fitting to me. That our traditions now involve both the Native Americans and all of us who came later also seems appropriate. That we fantasize about a First Thanksgiving with Pilgrims and Indians while another part of us knows full well they did not live happily ever after also fits my picture today.

The sky is heading toward overcast, as it so often is this month. The pewter skies of November offer a special beauty. The nearly-celadon green of the lichens is a perfect hue of choice to feature this month. Wind and waves often combine to give us a picture of the steely blue-green Atlantic, which several painters have found irresistible. Whenever I watch fishing boats out there breasting the cold grey waves, I think of the ingredients of heroism.

This "place of the fish weir," where the tide waters flow over the bar between Little Deer Island and the bigger island of Deer Isle, must have been a convenient and promising place for the first peoples here. There they could embed a line of brush in the shallow waters that would act as a weir, a funnel. Ground fish swimming here would be channeled into an area where they could be speared or otherwise caught.

The map of today's Maine tells an interesting story about Maine's past. You can fold that map along a line where the cities line up, Portland, Auburn-Lewiston, Augusta, and Bangor on the crease. To the east lies the coastal fringe of lands, below the falls, the tourist destinations, a calendar-pretty maritime Maine. Wherever there were falls, the early colonists saw the potential for setting up mills, grist mills and saw mills. There too the native peoples had known they could go to capture sea-run fish that made their way through channels to upstream spawning grounds. Treaties trying to restrict the native people to areas where they would not be in troublesome competition with the powerful newcomers drew this same line on the map: Native peoples should stay up beyond where the tide reaches.

Geologists and biologists draw a similar crescent along our coast, according to their own interests and knowledge. Today the newspapers often refer to "two Maines"—not The County and Downstate as Ann knew it growing up, but two distinct states of mind, of economy, and also of biological, geological and historical reality. The physical reality of a place always bats last.

When we boated around the islands a few months back with my brother, I remember our amusing impromptu three stooge routine when I called this spot to Ann's attention.

"There is Eggemoggin, the place of the fish weir," I'd said.

"Ware," my brother corrected, using the local pronunciation.

"There," I said, with a gesture.

"Where?" Ann quipped, joining our act.

Today, as I sit and gaze across the causeway I think about Bob McCloskey and his daughters who so generously gave The Nature Conservancy an easement for protection to their beloved Outer Scott Island where sea birds nest. The sign says the pull off is called the Bowcat— a reference to a ship of that name which went aground here— but as I observed when we sailed by in June, the point of land at the Little Deer end of the causeway also stands as sort of a memorial to McCloskey's love of this island panorama.

Next in my view comes Causeway Beach, the tiny strip of sand that a group of interested folks bought recently and gave to Island Heritage Trust. That is the island's largest and certainly most visited beach. In every season, in all kinds of weather, you are almost sure to see a car or pickup truck parked there while the occupants take a stroll, walk the dog, shovel up some seaweed for garden mulch, or simply drink a cup of coffee.

There has been almost no vandalism in what is clearly a popular spot. Recently someone has taken their truck and driven quite deliberately in crazy circles over the fragile sand dune-like sea grasses. If that keeps up, the entire strip of land may well vanish, wash away into the sea. I can picture all too well that the climate now may be changing rapidly and I may live to see rising sea levels. I cannot picture why the individual persists in ruining the beach for others, any more than I can picture why my nation is so reluctant to consider what part we may have in accelerating climate change.

I drag my thoughts back to the ridge where I sit, back to the time when the Indians lived here. Which Indians? Those most ancient of peoples of the tundra who followed the melting of the glacier? Their large fluted spear points and the bones of the mammoths they killed are not found here. Their lives are too hard for me to imagine. Fast forward to Algonquian-speaking Etchemins, arrowhead makers and hunters of game in the mixed hardwood forest of their day. They are not those earlier, more primitive peoples, but also probably not exactly the same as the Penobscots and Passamaquoddy peoples who were here just before Samuel de Champlain in 1604 and when Captain John Smith in 1614 sailed by here. Nor do I picture the exact same people as the Penobscots who came here in the 1890's to sell baskets to the Victorian ladies of the cottages. And I am not exactly daughter of the Scots who later moved in and helped make modern Maine, but we are all beads on those strings.

Archeologist Steve Cox tells me that I cannot project my mental time machine for Deer Isle's clamshell middens too far back. In the time of what are called the Paleo-Indians, those who first came to the lands after the glaciers retreated, perhaps ten or eleven thousand years ago, this spot was undoubtedly not water, not even clam flats. Then came the sea creeping in, and the period in Maine from 10,000 to 3,000 B.P.—before the present—we call Archaic. The period from then until contact with Europeans in the 16th or early 17th century we call the Ceramic Period. As I sit, I am aware that the sea is even now washing away the land. Those ancient Indian camps are gone, washed into the sea, but their stone artifacts are often found on the beach here.

I choose to imagine being here with those who made pots of clay. The prints of their fingers are still in the pottery fragments that no doubt lie buried under layers of shells beneath me now, their bits washing out on the beach after winter storms. Together we will pat and smooth the clay, mark it with a stick, a wooden notched comb, a twined cord. Together we will scrape deer hides and moose hides with our flakes of stone. Together we will fringe and color and decorate our garments with porcupine quills, bright dyes and pigments.

We will sing and laugh. We will make wigwams of poles lined with deep beds of fir boughs on which to lie in our bear skin robes. We will sew birch sheets to shingle our wigwams and we will stitch birch containers for cooking and birch canoes for our trips up and down the great river and even out to sea. We will tend our fish traps and make sets of bone points for spearing flounder. We will lace snowshoes. We will play games, sliding snowsnake sticks in grooves in the frozen snow, tossing bone bits like dice in gambling games. Some Novembers will find us fat, and some winters we will starve. And when the white men come, we will lose the toss and sicken and die. All life is a gamble, and it still is.

Whoever it was, they lived here long enough to accumulate layers and layers of clam shell garbage. A number of folks are most eager to find out just what messages have been left for us, what relics have washed out of the bank of shells here. The owners who are selling this property to the trust, Nathan Pitts and his wife Ellen, have offered to share their artifact collection with us for identification. Ellen mailed me some photos of the collection. The neat rows of artifacts, both points and pottery, indicate middle and late Ceramic components, ca. 2000 —500 years ago. In general stemmed points indicate middle Ceramic period, and side-notched ones come from the late Ceramic period. The collection included one large pecked and ground stone tool that was likely Archaic or what is called Moorehead phase, ca. 4,000 BP, but one can't tell for sure from the photo. Meanwhile, all too clearly, looters have been at their destructive work here in the midden in spite of the sign stating that digging is not permitted.

We met Ellen when she was a young girl, moved here from Brooklyn, New York, when her mother, Anna Osterby, decided to bring her children and return to the Island. Not only were they our neighbors, but Ellen's brother, Karl, worked for Ken on his mouse population research for a number of years. Across the causeway at Harbor Farm another of Ken's former research assistants is probably at this very moment sitting at his desk. Spud, a.k.a. Dick, McWilliams is another of the boys and girls of the island who worked for us over the years in the mouse research project. There's Milton who worked at the Post Office, Leslie who was killed in Vietnam, Dick who now lives just down the road from us, David who went lobstering and now does landscaping, and Jane who now lives in Belfast. Most people these days would never guess what they all have in common with each other.

Ellen and Nathan have worked with Island Heritage Trust in a most generous and patient way in the past year in what is probably the last big conservation project on the island. Maine Coast Heritage Trust had identified as a priority preserving something along the Reach. When you sail the Reach you notice not only the increase in homes along the Reach, but the fact that so many of the homes are very large ones. There is no longer any large, undeveloped stretch along the waterway, very little hope for any sort of access for the public.

Nathan is a descendent of the Scott family who were among the first settlers here, the region between Deer Isle and Little Deer. They held from the king a grant to the exclusive right to run the ferry here. Scott descendents ran the ferry that carried people from here to the mainland until the bridge was completed in 1939. From their property you get a splendid view of the bridge and the boats sailing down the Reach. What a spot this would be for the older retired seamen to come and look out at their beloved boat traffic. The land is gentle. The very young and the very old alike could handle a trail here.

In July the fields here glow blue with blueberries and flame with a very special plant, the wood lily, which looks like a freckled red sister of the tiger lily, only one that looks up, one that is native. As commercial

blueberry barrens get aggressively managed with herbicides, I fear for the continued existence of this lovely bloom that I have never seen growing anywhere except beside a boulder left by the glacier, surrounded by blueberries. These days, even the boulders are at risk, as they are being sold off to landscapers and fields are cleared for mechanical harvesters. It does not seem to occur to anyone that there are unique microhabitats being lost. Since we know that there are species of microlepidoptera, very tiny moths, associated only with blueberries, I would guess that there are yet undiscovered species awaiting us at our very doorstep.

At first called the Gateway Project because the collective area around the basin here at the causeway was so designated by the Transportation Department, this preserve has been a very tough sell in the community. Very misleading information circulating as local gossip and even incomplete articles in the local press have had an unfortunate effect. At the very time that the Pitts family were being besieged with developers flying up in their helicopters to pressure them, others were working just as diligently with a generous—and anonymous—conservation buyer to secure the property.

If all goes as hoped and all the Scott's Landing property is secured, I have no doubt that the public, the Islanders in particular, will eventually be most grateful. The Pitts family now lives in Cherryfield. Their two boys would be unlikely to be able to afford that property in the future, but as Trust land they will have access to it. We hear that story over and over. Their own descendents were in the mind of Dr. Tennis and the Fairchilds. The children of their friends and neighbors were in their minds as well. Judy Hill and Carolyn Olmsted and Emily Muir were each quite outspoken and specific about generations to come as well.

Why is it that some folks have such a hard time understanding genuine philanthropy? They grouse about what conserving two or three percent of our land does to our tax base. Don't they recognize what is their golden egg? Why does someone destroy the beach? Why does someone steal from the middens? Why take what is not rightfully theirs, especially when it comes to pitting short term profit for a few against long term benefits for many? So I am saddened at the same time as I have come to give thanks.

I walk down to the little beach curving at the base of the shell midden. White bits of clam shells spill out over the grey gravels. I look, but I do not see a bit of bone harpoon or a shard of brown pottery or the glint of a flaked arrow point. Steve Cox pointed out that this could be an exceptionally good site as perhaps not much has eroded into the sea already. Although the site is near the shore, the sea here has not much fetch; it is only a short distance across the Reach so strong waves do not pound in from that direction.

After he comes with a team and does some tests to see how extensive the midden is and how extensive the pot hunters' damage is, Steve will consider offering a summer field school here. Offering would-be archeologists and enthusiasts a week-long training in return for a fee which helps support the research is a pattern he has used most successfully, both over at the Tennis Preserve for the Asbornsens and across the Reach at Flye Point. What archeologists have learned here, on the archipelago of islands off Stonington, and over on North Haven, is that this area was once extremely important in the culture of the northeast coast of this country.

Cox and other scientists at the University of Maine where they are studying the geology and glaciers of Maine's past are very concerned about the rate of rising sea. They estimate that in only fifty more years virtually all of the island coastal archeological sites will have vanished, taking with them valuable ecological information. Can we learn anything about why the great auks vanished? These were large cousins of our puffins. How about the sea mink? Or huge swordfish that were once so plentiful here in shore that people could go out in their canoes and spear what they needed?

Looking at the remains of animals is called faunal analysis. In recent years scientists have learned to tell much from analyzing the teeth of animals found in the middens. Not only do they tell us what animal species were there, we learn about tools the people were using. Beaver teeth were often used as wood-working tools by the Ceramic Period people. Surely they are the prototypes for the historic "crooked knives" used by Indians and sailors, and still used for woodworking today. The shells of clams that piled up in such astonishing numbers in these middens can be thin sectioned to read the growth rings for seasonality just like tree rings. From this information we learn not only which seasons the people were living at the site, but the age demography of their catch.

For the price of one luxury car a year Maine's scientists could be supported in their ecological archeology researches before the window of opportunity closes.

I want to get Ted Ames together with Steve Cox. Ted did such remarkably useful work interviewing the older fishermen about past fishing patterns that he and Steve would no doubt have a most useful interchange. When it was announced that Ted had won the MacArthur "genius grant," our local television station realized that they had some wonderful video footage of Ted. He and I were standing on the wintry beach at the causeway. In his lovely gentle way and musical accent, Ted explained to the camera how significant the interface between land and sea is. He explained that it was a group of interested citizens from all walks of life who were joining together to buy the beach that could then be turned over to the land trust. The few small grants there were came thanks to the Stonington Fishermen's Alliance and the Island Fishermen's Wives being willing to stand as fiscal sponsors.

The causeway basin here was once one of the Island's most productive clam flats. Could it become so again? Since the Clam Committee, our impressive marine shellfish committee of the two towns, found that their reseeding efforts here are phenomenal, they might be on the right track. Toxic runoff from ill-considered projects on the land might, however, halt any recovery efforts for our marine resources. We do know that everything is connected to everything else, but we seem slow in figuring out what to do with this knowledge as a society.

My spirits lift as I study the sea edge. There under the roses lies a scattering of bright red rose hips among the stark white of clam shells of some thousands of years ago. The blue of this summer's mussel shells and the grey of the water-rounded rocks make a lovely tweed pattern. Being outside, with no particular agenda, is a very healing experience. That should be available to all of us, no matter what real estate we can or cannot afford to own.

That healing landscape belongs near us. It is one thing to plan and pack and save for a once a year vacation to a national park, but it is quite another thing to be able to walk out your back door to healing or take a short walk to healing, or to take a short trip to the solace of open spaces where one feels welcome.

Frederick Law Olmsted and his Deer Isle friends were most conscious of sharing the benefits of open space with everyone. The nearer one was to the full dawn of the Industrial Revolution in England, the more clearly some saw what a two-edged gift industrialization was. My favorite Olmsted quote comes from the *Maine Olmsted Alliance for Parks and Landscapes Journal*. Olmsted is saying about public parks, "There is probably no custom, which so manifestly displays the advantages of a Christian, civilized and democratic community in contradistinction from an aggregation of families, clans, sects or castes. There is none more favorable to a healthy civic pride, civic virtue and civic prosperity." The language is not exactly mine—though I admit I can read it better than I can read any Wabanaki tongue—but the sentiment about open space shared is ours.

We picture Indians as inhabitants of some sort of pre-industrial Garden of Eden. November is called "the moon when the ice begins to freeze at water's edge" by the Passamaquoddy. That is at once a poetic observation and a shiveringly ominous warning. This month might even have been a particularly tough time for the Indians, not as challenging as February and April perhaps, but it comes after the runs of fish, long after the nuts and berries, well before the winter hunting benefits of frozen, snowy ground.

Steve agrees with me that one of the things about Native Americans that appeals to many people is not the sorry story of how Europeans supplanted them on this continent, but our somewhat romantic notions of the way those first peoples connected, first with their environment, and secondly with each other. Their relationship with the environment differed from ours in the fact that there were nothing like the population densities we see around the finite globe today. They had to be quite closely connected with their surroundings because their food and clothing source was never a grocery store or a clothing store. The nearest they came to such exchange centers was possibly trading at the grand gatherings for which Steve unearthed evidence over on Naskeag Point. Or sadly, the white man's trading posts in the recent days of the Indian past, and we are all quite familiar with the pitfalls of that arrangement.

That Indians really did have ideas that differed from Europeans' ideas of ownership seems quite apparent from the misunderstandings that came right from the beginnings of contact. Any sort of Thanksgiving reenactment poses some questions we would rather not look at too closely. Whose land? Whose caches of stored food? What items were offered in trade? And, if we let you live among us, what will that mean? (Whose diseases?)

I realize with some unease that I am no longer able to feed us on the fruits of our own labor. When we lived on a farm, I put up most of our food. The Asbornsens were quite proud of the fact that even though Matt was a practicing physician, he ran a capable tractor. They produced most of what they ate. The Fairchilds, too, expressed satisfaction in their food source. Pat gardened and Kurt hunted. I suspect that a thread common to those who have been able to share their land is that they all had an intimate connection with it.

I find quite interesting the customs of our European ancestors in caring for the children or the widows or elderly relatives of one's relatives. That the Patten brothers of Bath, who were Ken's forbearers, routinely invested in one another's ships, captained those vessels, and sent sons abroad as cabin boys on those ships, sharing both the risks and the profits, shows an interesting closeness we do not see much today. Of course we admire and long for imagined benefits of a more closely knit society than ours.

It is not just a network of relatives which binds us. We have another network, often one of choice, our friends and neighbors. Islanders like to say "We take care of our own." By that they mean anyone who lives here. Some quite unlikely alliances are formed in the face of adversity. Any fisherman will tell you that any man on the water is his friend, even if it's someone he really dislikes.

When Ken and I arrived in Maine we were amazed and delighted to find that there were still Indian basket makers here. We were appalled to discover that these baskets were considered humble items fit only for carrying out the trash, saving bits of string, or holding cufflinks on the dresser. Baskets were left to deteriorate outdoors. We found baskets spray painted gold for flower arranging. The indignities led us to undertake a most quixotic rescue mission on a faculty salary.

We had a wonderful time going to yard sales, junk shops, and even the occasional antique shop. The proprietor of the Island's only antique shop became interested in our quest and began to help, educating us, alerting us, and sequestering for us good pickings. Before we knew it we had hundreds and hundreds of baskets. A collection. Now what were we going to do with a collection?

At an auction where Ken had gone to check out the baskets, he noticed one particular fellow bidding against him for all the good baskets. In conversation Ken learned that it was Bruce Bourque, state archeologist who had been assigned to get some baskets for a Maine State Museum collection.

"Well, don't bid against me," laughed Ken. "We are going to give you our baskets." And we did. When Bruce came to the Island to look at the basket collection, he brought with him Steve Cox. When Steve Cox came to the Island to go diving on island sites, Marshall Rice agreed to take him out in his lobster boat. We were invited to come along and watch as Steve suited up, donned his scuba gear and jumped over. I must say it was a procedure not entirely unlike dropping a freshly baited lobster trap overboard. What wondrous items might come up from the sea! Scallop draggers were always coming up with fascinating finds from what we regard as our own version of Atlantis disappeared beneath the sea.

In the seventies, archeologists in general mounted a fierce campaign against shell midden disturbance. They were almost too successful. Nowadays few will admit to having an artifact collection. At least one of the major collections has been sold off the island. Somehow I resent having to go to Washington DC or New York or even to Mount Desert to see what I regard as "our" artifacts.

Sadly, our baskets did go off the Island. At the time we offered them to the local historical society, but the tiny old Sellers farmhouse had no room for them. Robert Abbé had made a collection up at Mount Desert, but the building housing that collection also was tiny. The state museum at Augusta seemed the next best thing.

Subsequently the Abbé Museum has relocated from Acadia into the center of Bar Harbor in a very glamorous and spacious building. Recently they were given a huge collection of baskets collected a bit further down east. When we went to look, it was a very emotional experience for me. Some of the baskets were identical with ours. Clearly they had been made by the same hands, on the same molds. It was like meeting a lost cousin or sibling you did not even know existed. To me the real value of there being two collections is much more than twofold. To see a basket twice means that it was not a one-off, an exception. It was the way that basket was done.

Basket makers today now sign their baskets and command good prices for their craft. A young couple on a faculty salary these days would not even contemplate making a collection like ours. The traditional basket makers now find sons and daughters more interested in keeping the traditions alive. Artist basket makers like Elizabeth Compton who gave the Reach Beach at Grays Cove collect and venerate the traditional Indian forms of baskets but do not imitate them. The young Indian basket makers are managing to work out new touches of their own without losing what made the baskets a distinct form of their own heritage.

Island youth today face that challenge as well. How do you equip yourself with self confidence and skills for today's world? The life path today may take you to the far corners of the globe. How do you learn to value what we have here so it will stand you in good stead no matter what comes your way?

I hear the "out oodle ooo" call of long-tail ducks in the cove. The winter ducks have been appearing here all month. The first winter we spent here, I was most surprised at all the lovely and confusing species of black-and-white ducks that winter here, come down from the Arctic. I set to sorting them out, in part so we could reinstitute the National Audubon Christmas Bird count here. Ken and I devised a small book that we called a *Quick Key*. I had a pretty good idea which bird features Ken was sure to ask about when someone called excitedly describing a bird sighting. Those were the field marks and the behavior observations that I pointed out. We were able to use data from Acadia National Park to eliminate about half the species usually listed in bird guides for east of the Mississippi. Quite a few people new to birding have plucked up their nerve and joined in the Christmas counts here.

The great blue heron, which has been working its way slowly

around the cove, now soars overhead in a nearly soundless rush of its enormous wings. I could not see if it had the distinctive long white plumes on its breast that would mark it as an adult bird. One or two adult herons hang around most years well into the winter but by now the young of the year have left, making their first trip, leaving before the adults did, going where they had never been before. Amazing.

Since *Winged Migration* proved such a hit in theaters, the public has a better understanding of the annual migration of what we used to think of as "our" birds as they make their way back and forth from the neotropics. Without attention to both ends of the string, the bead necklace is broken, the world impoverished. Ann and I try not to be discouraged at the evidence of ecological impoverishment we document.

Perched on a shell midden made by people some millennia ago, it feels logical to take the long view. It seems logical to accept change as inevitable. At the same time, we feel it is important to document the good things in our world today so that as a society we can take stock. What do we value? What is important enough to treat well? For these gifts we express thanks.

* * *

Often when we cook something that one would not make for a single person, we take dishes out to share with Judy Hill. Judy has never precisely divulged the nature of her breathing problems. She now wears a nasal cannula and accompanies herself everywhere with a cartridge of oxygen carried in a satchel as if it were a fashion accessory. Being both private and proud, she would hate to be in the position of asking for our help, but she is always unreserved about thanking us warmly when we appear at her door.

The light is on at her porch. Judy's car is parked in the drive. But no one answers the door. We can see through the glass of the kitchen door that the cardboard carton of our most recent culinary offering is still sitting on the table. No one answers the door when we knock.

We determine that she seems likely not at home, but we are very uneasy about what to do next. We cannot call the ambulance squad for further information. They are by law required to observe strict patient confidentiality. We do not want to call Judy's sister in New Hampshire and alarm her if it is unnecessary. Should we break in and search for her? We satisfy ourselves that Judy is not there needing a rescue. We go home.

Eventually our phone rings. "Judy asked me to phone you and tell you she has called the ambulance and has been taken to the hospital. Don't bring her any more food just now."

We learned that in fact she was fighting for her life. The Blue Hill Hospital emergency room has one of the best reputations in the nation. They managed to put Judy as right as possible in as short a time as possible. Indomitable Judy headed off for Thanksgiving Day with her sister in New Hampshire as soon as she was released from the hospital.

To our dismay, however, the day after Thanksgiving, before Judy's return, we spotted a for sale sign on the lawn of the handsome house next door to the Salome Sellers house, the Deer Isle-Stonington Historical Society. Buying this house to keep the Sellers farm property intact had been Judy's dream. What was going on? A few more phone calls.

Judy had been overwhelmed. She called Carol Bridges and had her put the house on the market. Ken and I took a deep breath. The handsome Greek Revival house must not be sold out of all possibility for a proper civic destiny. Of course it was too much just now for the current dedicated-but-small crew managing so heroically to run the historical society. But in the future, some arrangement might be made for the lawn, the parking, the space for outdoor events in summer, for large meetings, for off-season storage, for a place to put all the treasures that are currently residing in Judy's barn. Clearly all these dedicated volunteers of the society have no intention whatever of dying. But what happens when tomorrow catches up with them as it inevitably will?

We discuss the matter with Carol. After a quick tour of the house, she explains to us that she already has several appointments to show the house as soon as the Thanksgiving holiday week has passed. Judy has just returned home. A short discussion confirms that she has only reluctantly given up her dream, overwhelmed by her drastic descent onto hospital care. In short order we arrange for Carol to meet us out at Judy's kitchen with a sheaf of papers so we can make an official offer. If

Judy accepts it, there will be a binding agreement and Carol can tell the other prospective clients that the house is now under contract.

I can see that our cardboard food box on the kitchen table is safely empty. Judy looks perhaps a bit peaked, but not much the worse for wear. She is so delighted that we will take on the house we can scarcely keep her from accepting our offer on the spot. Tough, reserved, private Judy alternates between grinning and wiping tears. Carol shoos us out so she and Judy can conclude the transaction of offer and acceptance in honorable seclusion.

Oh, what have we done? Just when we were hoping to simplify our lives, with the Scott's Landing project heading toward to a satisfactory conclusion? A house? Of course. A campus actually. Details to be arranged later.

Sky Poet

Too human to hear words,
I glimpse pulsing thoughts
as the sky poet works,
bold line of dipper-handle stars
asserting meter, faint
on the wild cadence
of aurora shimmer.
Just before dawn
the saucer of old moon
balances aloft a stack of
planets,
Venus and Jupiter
echoing that linear meter
of night's earlier stanza
before sun reasserts
the radiance
of its own intention.

Thanksgiving, Deer Isle

I
It was easy to give thanks
when the monarchs winged
steadily over the sparkling bay,
when rosy apples bent their branch,
fat deer, ripe berries beckoned in the sun.
How rich we felt when mushrooms
like gold coins gleamed among the fallen leaves,
ruby, mahogany, ebony wealth,
great underground galaxies, comets
from an unseen realm we do not see beneath the roots.
We thought each being individual,
but they knew
we are all
one.

II
Now that nor'easters have felled our trees,
lichen-laden boughs dropped like
rainforest canopy across the roads
while we huddled powerless indoors, facing winter, world up-ended,
it's harder to give thanks.
Fisherman tossed on the steel-grey bay
calculates anew the high cost of being his own boss
though he can't help but smile at the lords 'n ladies, the coots,
all those black-and-white ducks from the arctic down for the winter
bobbing nonchalant on the heaving seas.

At lowest tides the kelps wave their dead man's fingers,
rockweeds curl around the silent ledges…
He hears the waves sigh,
Give,
and the shore answers,
Thanks,
Give thanks
Give thanks,
with each breath of being.

III
And sometimes at a windless dawn or quiet dusk
comes a slack tide moment
when all the bay, Island, world, holds its breath,
when roily seas stop their warring struggles.
The water clears like glass
and you see clear in,
to the deep of things
to that holy center,
beyond where there are names for things
 —my god or yours—
where we hear without words,
Give thanks
Give thanks
Give thanks,
with every living breath.

December — HERITAGE, MAN-MADE —10

Since it will not be clear for some time just what will be the best use for the modest but handsome old house at 420 Sunset Road, Ken and I have taken to calling it Heritage House. On this island you cannot simply tell people what they ought to want, what they ought to do; thank you, no thank you. We will have to buy that house and patiently, slowly, proceed to explore how it might best be used. We have tentatively shared the idea with the historical society board, the land trust board, and a few friends who have spent all their lives here on the island. They have all been most encouraging, sure that somehow the house is part of our heritage and should be shared in some civic purpose.

Ted Ames and Robin Alden have already expressed interest in having some exhibit space there to introduce the public to their Penobscot East Resource Center. They are working on what they call a community lobster hatchery and renovating a building for it on the Stonington waterfront, next to the lobster co-op. Our lobstermen wish to try to supply baby lobsters for seeding areas in Zone C, from Matinicus to Blue Hill. Successful local zone management of our lobster resource makes a persuasive case for extending local management to our other fisheries. Any partnering with the fishing community, the arts community, the land trust and the historical society would be worth all the trouble.

Our sons, too, tell us they think this crazy idea of their parents is one worth doing. Funny how kids always think they are the ones focused on getting approval from their parents. The boys have no idea what hoops we jump through whenever they are about to visit us. Both boys are ready with ideas of how the house could help IHT serve young families better.

On the opposite side of the coin, the Scott's Landing Project seems clearly off track. Sufficient moneys for the December closing are not in hand. What a shame if this piece, the most family-friendly piece of property on the Island, is lost to the developers so eagerly flying up and pressuring Nathan and Ellen.

Maine Coast Heritage Trust has gone into high gear. Our trust members meet and phone and e-mail almost constantly. Nathan and Ellen have agreed to postpone the closing till January. The anonymous conservation buyer has agreed to hold the property only temporarily. We can identify with that as we hope not to own the dear old house we are purchasing any longer than necessary. In the Scott's Landing case, however, the stakes are much higher: a million dollar matter, not thousands.

All property on the Island has now reached what to us seem practically stratospheric price levels. In the eyes of the world "out there" however, this is one of the last great undervalued places. Developers realize they can still turn a profit here. Some have even begun flipping properties, which could have been considered by our young islander work force. We are pathetically unprotected by our local lack of zoning and planning. Nathan and Ellen are being not only patient but generous to accept the land trust offer, which is less than they can get from the most greedy but ruthless developers. Instead they want to do right by the Island where they grew up and where their own sons and their children may one day wish to return as visitors.

When Nathan and Ellen married, they moved up to the north end of Deer Isle, to the family's Scott's Landing property. They had come to trust their neighbor, Jean Wheeler, who runs the Inn at Ferry Landing, a bed and breakfast which had once been the Scott family home. When Nathan put the property on the market and Maine Coast Heritage Trust came a-calling, Nathan was favorably disposed to learn about options that would benefit both his immediate family and the generations of the future.

It has, however, proved a huge task to approach a project of this size. Unfortunately for all philanthropic enterprises just now, the giving public is feeling insecure in the wake of 9/11 and the Iraq war, causing us to revise our hopes for the future. Generosity itself is not well-understood in a land of frugal Yankees, generations struggling to make ends meet. Still far too few folk understand the nature of land trusts, so the Island Heritage Trust has proved vulnerable. It's amazing how challenging it is to do good, even with the best intentions. However, it is too soon to be really discouraged.

I know I can count on the great outdoors to sustain me through these small periods of turbulence. Today is no exception, the Island dusted with its first snow, holiday decorations blooming. I am always amazed by the look of the first significant snow flurry of winter. First snow also signals the end of lobster fishing near shore. Becoming aware of the seasons of the sea has been one of the lovely, unexpected, bonuses of living here on the Island.

Today Ann and I are making the rounds of some of my favorite old buildings here on the Island. I can't say that my interest in these structures suddenly arises because we are now owners of one such small gem. It's more that we've recently watched some of the best of them be torn down or built-over to such an extent that they have vanished. Documenting and appreciating what we have feels like a good idea.

After years of renting office space in various places that became temporarily available, the Blue Hill Heritage Land Trust has recently purchased an old house on the edge of town. Jim Dow, Executive Director, says that since they are in the business of owning and caring for lands in perpetuity, they felt they needed a permanent headquarters that expressed that. The house they have acquired is a sweet old cape of a restrained, modest style revered in the past and largely overlooked these days. Our local land trust has taken three equally important words as its name: Island, Heritage, and Trust. What we hold in trust for future generations is not just land, but our finest old buildings, and even, I would say, the knowledge and skills that are part of the cultural heritage we have been blessed with here.

Our first "favorite old building" is at Burnt Cove. Ann and I meet Bob Williams as he is hanging wreaths on the Burnt Cove Church. We find him aloft, with his wife Diane holding the ladder. It's a lovely crisp sunny afternoon and both are in a chatty mood. Since Ann is a new acquaintance, they happily fill her in on all the stories they think I already know. I would say that Bob has taken his boat out of the water for the winter, and Diane has not yet gotten caught up in the swirl of visiting far-flung family at Christmas.

For almost a month now folks have been going out into the woods and cutting the tips off fir balsam branches. These are wired onto a metal wreath frame in layers, either "single-face" or "double-face," depending on whether the wreath is full on both sides, front and back. Of course it is more economical to do only the side which shows, but not surprisingly, such corner-cutting is scorned here on the Island. You can imagine what Islanders have to say about single-sided wreaths that come from Canada, cheaply made with staples! Sadly, I have not seen anyone lately making the garlands of fir tippings fastened around ropes. These were heavy and quite magnificent decorations popular for "greening" the church balconies at Advent.

Burnt Cove Church is a small church building of classically perfect proportions, unsullied by later improvements and additions. Inside, acoustics are wonderful, and the pressed tin décor is authentically delightful. In the sense that chamber music is different from but not in the least inferior to a symphony orchestra, this is a wonderful space for a small gathering. The church steeple guides mariners home from sea, not to mention pilots landing at the tiny airstrip. It had not been a functioning church for years when the Baptists gave it up and passed the deed on to Bob's mother, May.

Diane seconds my observation that May was certainly an Island dynamo. She would never take no for an answer. When the school said they could no longer afford to pay her a salary for teaching music, she did it anyway. She scheduled her classes before the school began, and then went around herself to collect the children. Having lost an uncle at sea, May was determined that all the children of the Island should learn to swim. She convinced the Muirs to allow swim classes at the saltwater pool they had created on their shore.

May no doubt came by her enterprising determination naturally. Bob tells us that the story goes that her mother, Edith, had heard about the handsome young minister at the Congregational church. Edith hired a horse and buggy and drove herself up there to church. The dashing young minister with the handsome black mustachios proposed before long. They married and eventually raised seven children. May's father had his own interesting story: an Armenian, he'd been raised in an orphanage in Turkey—until he ran away. He caught the eye of some

Congregational missionaries who offered to sponsor him if he became a minister. The young man agreed, came to America, studied at Andover Newton Theological School, and then decided he would prefer Bangor Theological Seminary. Hence, Maine.

On her mother's side, May's family were Fifields, one of the original families awarded a Kings Grant of 100 acres on Deer Isle. The Fifields were among those who founded the society to build Burnt Cove Church in 1867. The ladies of the church aid handed out eggs to be hatched and yarn to be knitted into mittens. The 'increase' was then sold at considerable profit, sufficient to begin the church building in 1870.

Though no longer at Burnt Cove, there are still Baptists on the Island, but they struggle to keep the doors of the Oceanville Baptist Church open. About this time of year, some time in Advent, the Baptists hold their "Ship of Zion" service in Oceanville. I love to see the ship model in the sanctuary, lights twinkling in its rigging. These days the pastor comes down from Bangor or Brewer to minister to his flock, most of whom are quite elderly. Still they manage to put on a good feed at their church suppers for the benefit of some Island family in need. My grandchildren love the blueberry jello I learned at one of these suppers: the contents of a can of blueberries mixed with dissolved, heated gelatin. That's the recipe.

I consider food a part of our spiritual and cultural sustenance. Old recipes give us a window into the past, our heritage, by way of the craft of cooking. Perhaps my interest stems from the fact that I learned to cook here.

At Nat Barrows's annual Christmas party last week I fell into conversation with Linda Shepherd about Island recipes. Over the years she has spent her summers on Devil Island as cook for the group who summer there. She prides herself on producing good cooking from local ingredients. The Slow Foods movement would love her. She is a true artisan in her approach to cooking. She confirmed my impression that here one would expect biscuits rather than any chowder crackers, oyster crackers or pilot biscuits with chowder. She agreed that the local secret to a velvety mouth feel in chowder is evaporated milk, as I had been told by Carol Small who used to be one of the cooks at the school.

The first year after Ken and I were married, we rented a tiny cabin overlooking Crockett Cove from Martha and Lewis Small for the summer. Lew's son, Jimmy, lived next door with his wife, Carol. Carol took pity on new bride-me, giving me both her 'receipts," her domestic know-how, and her cheery company. Since their son, Milton, worked for Ken on the island mouse trapping project, Ken always got a good look at whatever Milton brought for "dinner." Milton called it dinner and would have it eaten well before eleven AM. "Blueberry muffings" were perhaps the gem of Carol's repertoire.

Over the years, Ken kept his boats moored at Burnt Cove. He became friends with Allen Fifield whose nephew Willie Fifield ran the business at the end of the wharf, buying from the fishermen, selling them bait and boat gas. Allen's wife Dora picked crabs and made wonderful braided rugs, which we still cherish. When she died, Allen at seventy, maybe eighty-something, single-handedly built himself a small house perched on a rock overlooking the shore. There he could look out his picture window at the cove, knit bait bags, and tell me stories while I waited for Ken to come in from the sea. Allen used to go lobstering under sail, in a small locally-built sloop. He would visit the lighthouse keeper out on Saddleback Island, a rocky nubbin you can just see from here on clear day. He described a bosun's chair out there, rigged on a mast and spar to haul goods and the occasional visitor ashore.

Every spring the light keeper hauled out tubs of "loom" to replace the scant supply of garden loam washed away by the winter storms. This was just enough so they could plant a fresh garden for the most indispensable green stuffs. Nevertheless, any guest arriving with goodies from land was most welcome.

Allen had a wooden orange crate rigged up with his equipment for making bait bags. He had what he called a mash board to serve as gauge for the mesh. He had a shuttle that acted as a needle. The finished products hung festooned on nails. His gnarled hands were fascinating to watch as they flew about their work. His accent was so thick it always took me some weeks to relearn it anew each summer. Bait bags—or pockets—are now made by machine from bright synthetic cord, and, with herring scarce, any bait is now hard to come by.

I wish I had asked Allen more about salting and smoking and

drying fish. Back then it was quite common to see racks called fish flakes drying in the sun. Cod were even pinned up on clotheslines to dry for making strip fish. You could pull off a strip of just what you needed. Did the practice of smoking fish have anything to do with trying to dry something in our foggy weather? People assure me that they ate cod and haddock, dried and smoked. A Sunday meal with baked potato, onion, and squash, and fish with a dash of vinegar, oh bliss. Although I never heard anyone use the phrase "finnan haddie" in the days before artisan food became popular, surely the Scots stonecutters come here to work the granite did. I'm told that is what the dish was always called here. It is a term I have heard in Scotland for smoked, salted haddock, as they do it in Findon on the Scottish coast, served on boiled potatoes, with a cream sauce. Fin and haddock? Finny haddy? It was amusing to read the different versions of signs advertising the smoked fish for sale here over the years. It is also most interesting to make inquiries now. "Oh, my husband's family ate salt fish; my family never did." Make of that what you will.

Cod was the fish of choice for chowder and for hanging up to dry for strip fish. People then spoke often of fish hash, which meant bits of a white-fleshed fish, diced onions gently caramelized in an iron skillet, with a "junk" of salt pork cut into tiny bits and "tried out." The whole might be doused with "white sauce," a.k.a. "cream sauce," or if you put hard-boiled egg in it, "egg sauce." Imagine my surprise to read in Abigail Adams's letters a mention from her friend George Washington describing his favorite dish of fish and egg sauce.

Add enough milk or cream and you get chowder as they do it here. (Plus of course, that secret ingredient, evaporated milk for the distinctively silky texture.) I didn't know to put scallops or shrimp in seafood chowder until we were living here in the winter. Nowadays I cannot even find cod cheeks in the store, let alone cod racks, the vertebrae, which when boiled give a distinctive viscosity to fish stock, but I still use salt pork, not bacon. I dice onion fine and fry it after the salt pork has browned, and I certainly put in no untraditional spices. There weren't any spices here but salt, pepper, and cinnamon in the three grocery stores! No fancy spice racks.

Not everybody on the Island a century ago had their own cow, but cream was readily available to put on breakfast oatmeal or to whip for topping that treat they served on the Boston boat—gingerbread. Gingerbread was served with a cornstarch-thickened lemon sauce or with blueberries or whipped cream or even cranberries. A Scandinavian friend puts cranberries, fresh or dried, into her gingerbread for a delicious cherry-like version. I think lingonberries may be the same genus, perhaps even species, as our Island's small upland cranberries, so gingerbread with berries is like periwinkle snails and other so-called circumpolar species: the same on both sides of the Atlantic Ocean.

Sand Beach Farm, just along the shore from Burnt Cove, took in summer boarders (Ken's mother for one, and it was Nat Barrow's first home here on the Island). Norma McGuffie gave me her recipe for her sister-in-law Vangie's biscuits famously served there. Quick and easy, made from the winter's barrel of flour, biscuits could be fed to a large family, even providing food for the dogs. Lucky dogs! Biscuits here were usually made with baking powder but some folks used Bakewell Cream. Baking powders often were a family secret, the formula handed down from one generation to another. The various baking powders —the tartrate ones, the calcium phosphate powders, and combination or double acting baking powder which contains baking soda—are all interesting chemistry, but that is sufficient to say. Ask people here what they remember most fondly in the way of island food, and they are most likely to list chowder, biscuits, and gingerbread or molasses cookies.

Vegetables were, are, a challenge. I would not have thought of sending Ken to the store with a list in the first decades we spent here. You had to go see what there was and then make decisions. When she was expecting company, our neighbor at Felsted, Phyllis Pashley would plan to take all morning making the round of all three small stores. Most summer ladies had a well-stocked pantry of favorite canned goods as well, but for fresh veggies they were stuck with late-blooming kitchen gardens or in their mother's day, the slimy greens in the spinach barrel.

In later years I would make blueberry muffins and share some of the batch with Phyllis. We put them in a cardboard box panniers we had rigged onto an old wide-tired Schwinn bike to ride the dirt road between our houses in what Phyllis called "pedal post." Her son David worked for Ken as a boy. Then came years when David was off at school, off at jobs, and Phyllis held the fort at Felsted alone, with only us down the lane for company.

Felsted is certainly one of the Island's outstanding examples of architectural heritage. Designed by William Emerson and completed in 1896 for the Olmsted family, it was converted by S. B. Knowlton into a hotel in 1926. Knowlton also owned The Firs, another summer resort hotel in Sunset. Emily Muir and her parents were guests at the Firs. Small world, this island.

Bob Knowlton, the marine biologist who still summers on a remnant of the Firs property, points out the irony of people decrying preservation as cutting into the tax base. He should know how important it is to look at what may be unintended consequences. The Knowlton family was forced to tear down the Firs because they could not afford the taxes. They had asked the selectmen for a stay of taxes during the war years and post-war gas rationing, and been refused. Actually, I'm told, they simply removed the Firs roof as the result, that being sufficient to remove it from the town tax base. Doug Knowlton sold the Felsted Hotel in 1941 to the man who had been best man at his wedding, Bill Pashley, who was able to have the hotel addition removed and return Felsted to its original grace. Ever frugal, these Yankees, the Islanders moved the lumber from the addition up the road and used it to side a barn at the Sellers farm, the barn which is attached to what we now call Heritage House.

Bill's widow, Phyllis, was a gracious hostess, a Wellesley graduate from New York. Phyllis was a tiny woman with carefully styled hair, gold bracelets, crisp white peter pan-collared blouses, and almost inevitably, navy blue slacks. Her father was a buyer of rare woods from around the world. Phyllis could point out with both knowledge and pride the original greenheart paneling in Felsted. The Pashleys have been good stewards of this home, winterizing it with discretion, but after this year they will put Felsted on the market and hope to build a state of the art energy-efficient house next door.

Felsted, like the Bar Harbor cottages, was designed in what is now called Shingle Style, rather fanciful geometry, sheathed in natural grey shingles, contoured to fit the land. The handsome home has starred in two movies, one, *Man Without a Face*, produced by Mel Gibson, and the other more recent, *Finding Home*, by an independent producer couple. The rent from the movie companies helped pay for Felsted taxes and repairs, but Georgia still winces recalling the long, long days of fall and winter that they spent in a camping trailer, awaiting completion of the filming. And yet, she says they'll go through such an adventure again in order to "go green."

    Georgia Pashley invites me to stop in for a cup of tea while Ann photographs the house from the beach with snow on it. Long active in Eastern Star, a veteran of elementary education, and now a grandmother, Georgia retains her love of childlike enchantment. She has unpacked some of her extensive collection of miniatures for the tiny Christmas Village, a miniature world recreated in Felsted's paneled dining room, handsome with its arched fireplace and views across the bay. Georgia also still puts out her mother-in-law's sand trays—table centerpieces created with shells, driftwood wharfs, sea glass, and miniature lobster traps and boats.

    Georgia's mother-in-law, Phyllis, epitomized an era, a style of doing things, now largely vanished here. Phyllis entertained often for lunch and sometimes for cocktails. I keep her recipes in part because they meant so much to her. For me they recall an era. Summer People food, not madeleines, but Proust would have understood. Every summer Phyllis would announce with great glee her stock of new recipes gleaned from the women's magazines. One such recipe still shows up here at potluck dinners, crab pie. One might think it a local creation, but my friend Anne Cushman still has her mother's magazine clipping for the recipe.

    It feels a bit odd to chronicle the "orthodox" versions of recipes now, because tastes have so changed. All manner of "fusion" recipes are now touted as regional. Brooke Dojney, who lives just across the Reach, wrote a cookbook entitled *Dishing Up Maine*, which is a delightful exception to the plethora of cookbooks that do not make a distinction between local and traditional. She labels the old way clearly as such, and goes on to share each best new thing.

    Food fashions come and go, originating perhaps from an intelligent designer, but most certainly evolving according to natural selection. This year it is goat cheese, made at Yellow Birch Farm, served with Nervous Nellie's fabulous chutneys and spreads—cranberry, rhubarb, blueberry, etc. Variations of sushi are gaining favor thanks in part to the award-winning smoked salmon of Stonington Sea Products.

When Wilda Eaton is not busy being chief of the Memorial Ambulance Corps, she runs a small business called Isle Cater. For years the tiny rolls for her signature crab finger sandwiches were supplied by an off-Island bakery. Since the bakery has gone out of business, Wilda now makes a dainty white sandwich bread version. Crab sandwiches are part of wedding receptions, showers, or funeral receptions here. You know then that this occasion is considered really special, honoring someone especially loved and significant.

Crab is traditionally mixed with mayonnaise here. For its Fourth of July sale the Congregational Church ladies don't bother grilling the buns with a little butter, as they probably would do if they were making them at home, and they do some years add a tiny bit of finely diced celery—no onions as some people do—and they definitely serve the mixture on the kind of top-loaded hot dog rolls popular throughout New England, the lengthwise, rectangular kind, split vertically. Some people serve crab on hot dog rolls of the oval kind, split horizontally, and some even go for the round hamburger roll. And of course some do any of the above variations, only with pure chunks of lobster meat. Finest kind, as fishermen here really do say.

Forty years ago, you would likely have had to order the crab well ahead. The woman who so skillfully picked out the meat, saving the intact ovals from the claws to decorate the top would have to ask her lobster-fishing husband to bring crabs home rather than tossing them overboard as so much nuisance. She would boil up the crabs in her own kitchen in those days before current inspection regulations. Tapping with a small wood or metal mallet on the crabs on a scrap of polished granite from the quarry, she could produce a superb product which the summer people were quick to appreciate.

Pickytoed crab, or peekey-toed crab, is now a fairly common marketing term based on locals' description of the "peak-ed" ones, pointed walking legs of the crab, the picket ones, not the legs with the pinching claws. You will also encounter opinions about the deep water reddish Jonah or rock crabs with rough hairy claws and coarse flesh, versus the smaller sand crabs, the ones on sandy bottom. There is definite thought locally that the cold water and hard bottom here in Penobscot Bay produce scallops and crabs of higher quality than elsewhere. All we really agree on is that none of our species is the same as the blue crab of the Chesapeake. Now too, we have two species invading our bay, the small green crab which has been here for some years, and a newer one from Asia. Neither of them offers much culinary promise, and both have the potential to be quite devastating to our ecosystem. What a complicated web we find when we cast our nets in the sea.

I have long favored what is known as Ed Muskie's recipe for crab cakes. I have no idea whether this illustrious Maine senator ever had anything to do with the recipe, but I suspect it at least reflects tastes in Maine. The secret ingredients are cracker crumbs with a tablespoon of mayonnaise and one small egg as a binder and not a great deal else camouflaging the sweet taste of a half pound of Maine crabmeat.

When I go down to the Felsted beach to join Ann who is still busy photographing, I tell her of my reaction to the Mel Gibson movie, *Man Without A Face*, filmed here: "Who is that strange guy up there on Phyllis's porch? What's he doing there? Relax, Marnie. It's a movie."

Mel and his movie crew—and their eighteen-wheeler on this narrow wooded lane—made quite an impression around here. I described my meeting with Mel Gibson on the road to our son Tom. "Gibson was smaller than I had pictured, and there was something about his accent, sort of like the telephone company or weather forecast machine-made neutral. And his clothes, a new Yankees baseball cap, a new tee shirt, new jeans, new sneakers…."

Tom interrupted, laughing. "Mom, you have never ever seen anyone wearing all those particular items of clothing brand new, not even Japanese tourists. I bet he was wearing what his Hollywood staff had cooked up for him. That was in his Maine native costume, but of course it should have been a Red Sox cap!"

Ann and I can hear the sound of the horn on Mark Island from the Felsted beach. I love it that people all over the Island mark the weather by the sound of the foghorn. We are not unlike Italian hill towns in their affection for their church bells. There is not much out there on Mark Island in the way of historic building now, although the square stone tower built in 1858 still stands, The lightkeeper's house is gone, however, burned to the ground in a 1958 mishap.

Mark Island Light was the epicenter of Ken's mouse population research so when it came time for someone to write the application for the light, we were drafted. The only other people to venture onto the island were US Coast Guardsmen. Landing on the island is very difficult. The lighthouse keeper had rails stretching from the boathouse to the tide line on which his boat could be slid. The crews in the days after that just came close and jumped when they came to do routine maintenance on the automated light equipment—and harvest a little rhubarb while they were at it.

Benjamin Franklin introduced rhubarb to this country in 1777. A century after that, the keeper of the new light apparently had rhubarb growing in the garden on Mark, and a hundred years later Ken was competing for the rhubarb harvest with the Coast Guard crews. Given that rhubarb is propagated vegetatively and once begun, a patch is very long-lived, we could say the Mark Island rhubarb is a very old plant, with greater longevity than Franklin, the US Coast Guard, and the Crowells combined.

We can document at least the outline of this story, as Melissa Colby Holden is said to have burned a rhubarb pie left in the oven when her elder children helped her deliver her son Amasa out there in the light house. A 1933 newspaper clipping shows lightkeeper Capt. Elmer E. Conary and his family on the veranda. Daughter Alice tells in the accompanying article of making rhubarb and wild strawberry jam out there on the island. The wild strawberries out there always seemed to me especially sweet, amid the rugosa roses and salt spray.

My recipe for Rhubarb Cream Pie comes, however, from Dorothy Carman. I always think of this dignified former Latin teacher as Aunt Dot, although I certainly never called her that. She grew spectacular flowers by her small house on Pressey Cove. Her rhubarb grew exuberantly, keeping her in good supply for what many Islanders called simply "garden sass."

Dorothy's sisters, Neva Beck and Arlene Kydd were the Sylvester Girls, whom I knew. One, Norma, married and moved away—to Sunshine on the eastern side of Deer Isle. On what would have been

Dorothy's birthday last month, the surviving sisters and their daughters gathered for a tea party and they served molasses cookies. Some brought the kind called molasses crinkles; some brought the crispy ones. Small ones we call spice drops or ginger cookies. Large ones we call molasses cookies or lumberjacks or even nicknames with rude reference to cow pastures. Isle Au Haut-style ones may have ginger bits in them. The Sylvester grandmother, I know, made them thick, which is the way I do. I'm not much interested in funerals, but the tea party commemorative celebration is a sweet practice I can appreciate.

Dorothy then, and Neva now, and her daughter Linda, all were driving forces first in buying and then in conserving the Salome Seller's house, starting back in 1960 when this classic Cape Cod-style farmhouse became the Deer Isle-Stonington Historical Society. How interesting that Sylvester descendent Carol Kydd Bridges is now the agent involved in selling to her ever-so-distant cousin Ken Crowell the part of the Sellers farm on which Salome's son Norman built his lovely Greek Revival home.

Aunt Salome lived to be over a hundred. She had a brother named Crowell Sylvester, a fact which we found intriguing as Ken's family had a Sylvester Crowell, not the two most common first names in the world, even in those days. Eventually we learned that the Sylvesters and Crowells shared a common Cape Cod Crowell grandmother. The volunteers at the Stonington-Deer Isle Historical Society and their archives can help tease out who is who on family trees as well as who had shares in what ship for the past centuries.

I make molasses cookies for the Crowell grandchildren from the same recipe as generations of Sylvesters used and still do. The recipe may not be in the archives, but just ask; they can get it for you. Of course, you have to realize when you use this grandmother's recipe that you do or do not put in eggs, or use cloves, or allspice, or black pepper, or candied ginger bits, and you may use just light or dark molasses or part brown sugar and part molasses—or nowadays, part Sucralose—and you will use butter or lard or Crisco or even oil or applesauce—depending on what is in your cupboard or in fashion at the time. And then there is that question of patting or rolling or scooping, to roll in sugar coating or not, to aim at thick or thin, crinkly or.... I also still have my grandfather's pocket watch. He got it from his father who carried it for years. In all that time it only needed a new case a couple of times, and new workings once or twice.

When Ann and I showed up to take photographs at the Sellers House, some of the volunteers were busy in the archives. Neva was there, along with Tinker Crouch, the energetic and delightfully-dedicated descendent of a lighthouse family. We talked about island favorite recipes and they told me that I should not forget Grape Nuts pudding. Ah, yes. Ken has the Grape Nuts pudding recipe that he was given by Dick Bridges. Dick is a most successful Island fisherman. Lately he has achieved some fame or notoriety because a New York Times food writer did a splendid piece on him and his delicious chowder. His mother, Connie, ran one of the favorite places for fishermen ashore to congregate. Her Grape Nuts pudding is famous: Mix together 1 cup sugar, 1 cup Grape Nuts, 1 quart scalded milk, and cool. Add 2 beaten eggs, a dash of salt, and a teaspoon of vanilla. Bake at 350° for an hour in a baking dish set in a pan of hot water.

On the lawn of Salome Sellers's house, now the historical society, is a large brass bell. It is the lighthouse bell which Bob William's dad, Francis, helped Dr. Waldron of Goose Cove bring from Curtis Island. For years the bell called guests of Goose Cove Lodge to meals. The recipe I have for Goose Cove Lodge chocolate bread pudding reveals the long-established practice of the lodge of using local food products, and local cooks, to produce fare fancier than usual for the guests. Pudding has long been locally made but often with biscuits, not bread, and usually it is not made with chocolate, so this recipe is considered really decadent. That it is delicious with whipped cream is, of course, very island-appropriate.

A week ago Ann and I made our way up the Penobscot River to Orono, for the annual Indian Basket December sale and show, sponsored by the Hudson Museum. Micmacs, Maliseets, Passamaquoddy and Penobscot basket makers gather to sell their crafts. One of the things I particularly enjoy about the event is the opportunity to have moose meat loaf, hull corn soup, fried flat breads, and blueberry or molasses cake-like deserts, sold for the benefit of the Penobscot Nation's Boys and Girls Club. This meal is not exactly a delicacy; it is a window of insight into a way of life, a place at the table of history.

In upstate New York, we often had the opportunity to sample *onensto*, a similar hominy stew. When we first came to Maine and met old basket makers from Indian Island on the Penobscot, they were still fairly conscious of the Mohawks as their Iroquoian enemies. The Mohawks revere the trio of Corn and Bean and Squash, and it shows in *onensto*, with its rich mix of hominy, red beans, broth, winter squash and root vegetables such as carrots and turnips. Perhaps more significantly, the New York version had meat. There was always pork and venison, and probably hamburger beef in their hominy soup. Penobscot hull corn soup is by comparison, plain, sometimes just pale beans, salt pork, broth and hominy.

Here on the Island, folks tell of their own favorite version of baked beans. They recall not the salt pork which commonly enriches the mixture of molasses and small white Northern beans, but it's the venison that makes their version perfect. The deer meat is mixed with the beans, cooked low and slow, set out on the back porch for the rest of the week, and then and only then was it considered ready to be reheated for the table. How direct the lineage seems to me from the First Peoples and their clay pots to the New Englanders and their bean pots.

The first summers we were here, there were no prime cuts of steak, and no yogurts to be had in the markets until after the Fourth of July, when the summer people were here. After Labor Day, the yogurts and steaks disappeared as well. When we first moved here year round, I went to the Hancock County extension office in search of the Maine equivalent of Cornell University Extension bulletins. The clerk huffed somewhat primly, "We don't have bulletins like that to give out. New York is rich. Maine is a poor state." Yes, our recipes do reflect our circumstances. And money matters, and what we do with money matters.

We remodel our recipes and we remodel our houses. There are few old Capes left unremodeled on the Island, few old churches unmodified, but Ann and I are headed to photograph an essentially unmodified classic, the Opera House. Like the Squire Ignatius Haskell House, now the Pilgrim's Inn, the Opera House is named on the Federal Register of Historic Places. The slight renovations here include plumbing and insulation and heating upgrades, all welcome consequences of modernization.

This is our last stop of the day, timed for the golden winter light of late afternoon. From the water this building appears to rise like toy blocks above the other buildings, a sort of billboard, announcing OPERA HOUSE in huge letters, complete with a period at the end. What a classic and unique touch—quintessentially us!

The Opera House Arts organization, a 501c3 community nonprofit, was founded in 1999 to restore the historic building to its original purpose at the heart of the community. OHA offers residents a chance to work alongside professional actors, dancers, and musicians in dance productions, readers' theater and other live productions. Their Imagination Project trains young people and community members in audio and video production techniques. Active in the community planning processes, Opera House Arts is the creative economy at its best. And now we don't have to go all the way to Ellsworth to see year-round, first-run movies!

Originally built to entertain the thriving granite-quarrying community, this is now a decidedly funky beacon. The current Opera House gang coalesced around a group of four women—Linda Nelson, Carol Estey, Judith Jerome, and Linda Pattie—with New York City connections, who rescued the building, which had fallen into disuse and disrepair.

In its prime the Opera House was a center of community activities. The rows of seats could even be pushed out of the way for dances. That is not to say that there were not kitchen dances as well; there were—the Island version of a Scottish *ceilidh*, with fiddle playing, shared cooked dishes, and homespun fun. Before the days of the automobile, winter shut people in if there was not enough snow for sleighs.

Almost certainly someone would have brought gingerbread. Gingerbread was traditional in this seafaring community. Even as recently as the days of the steam boat from Boston to Bangor, 1942, gingerbread was featured with pride. Many is the summer person who, like the young Emily Muir, looked forward to gingerbread on the Rockland boat as the definitive signal that summer was about to begin.

About the same time that the Opera House came into being, Captain Al Shepard built his trim mansard-roofed house overlooking the harbor on the Indian Point road. His ships—several bay coasters—carried cobblestones from the quarries to Boston; fish, coal, and pulp to the mills in Brewer and Bucksport.

Ann and I trespass, one wintry afternoon, walking up the bouldery hill behind the house to see if we can get a good shot of the yellow house, the attached ell and barn, and the view of scattered islands, just like one of Stephen Pace's paintings. A storm door now closes the front door; the Paces are gone.

"In 1972 when Stephen Pace and his wife Pam bought the Shepard house as their summer residence, there was still a photograph of one of his vessels in the parlor," I tell Ann. "The Paces gave it to the Shepard family, in a gesture of generosity that was totally characteristic of them. They have given the house, now listed in the National Historic Register, to the Maine College of Art in Portland who plan to use it for a study center for young painters."

For years both Paces were readily recognizable figures in our landscape. They get their signature dress from L. L. Bean, beginning back in the days when the only outlet was the Freeport store: Pam has three red felt crush hats, various cloaks and oversize sweaters. Stephen has three jean jackets, some lined, some not, so he is set for any weather. He too wears a characteristic small hat, a canvas pork pie from Bean's. One might easily overlook this unassuming man, but his paintings hang in the premier museums of the country: the Metropolitan Museum of Art, the Whitney, the Corcoran Gallery, the Hirshhorn Museum of the Smithsonian, the Museum of Fine Arts, Boston— to name just some of them.

Stephen was drafted in WWII, and spent time in Paris where he even managed to find time for some painting. It was at his easel that Gertrude Stein spotted him and took him in tow, inviting him home to lunch to meet Pablo Picasso. She asked Picasso to give the young artist a free critique, which he helpfully did. After the war Stephen returned to spend more time in Paris with his new wife Palmina Natalini, Pam, from Springfield, Massachusetts."

One afternoon last summer Stephen invited Ken and me over to his studio in the barn. This airy space on the upper floor of the barn is wonderfully full and at the same time well organized, one section for oils, one for watercolors, containers of paints orderly, with impressive rows of brushes. He had put out three chairs facing a huge easel, illuminated by a spot light, behind which were stacked a number of watercolors, full sheets.

He had in mind a private showing, because he had selected several dozen of his paintings he thought we might like to choose from. We realized he was sharing his life's work, spanning his entire career, from early expressionist painting to recent ones. As Stephen pulled out the first several paintings, we were afraid to comment, afraid to stop the succession of wonderful images, afraid to break the spell.

When Stephen asked if there was an image we felt drawn to or some we were not interested in, I finally confessed that I could not live with the painting of the horses; it made me feel too anxious, Stephen nodded. I would never play poker with him because he can keep such a straight face, but I sensed my reaction was just what he had hoped for. He explained these black and white horses, identical in all save color, represent his commitment to our nation's confronting the uncomfortable issues of racial discrimination. I said I was sure I would always go see it at any museum, every time I came to visit, but I could not live with it.

I could also see that the nudes made Ken squirm. They were so bright and clear and sunny, exhibiting such enthusiasm for the female form that I was quite comfortable with them, even as Pam cataloged who modeled for each one. Ken was, however, much drawn to the early strong, intensely-colored abstracts. By the mid sixties Stephen had moved his painting style on from that of the other American early Abstract Expressionists. He told us of the days when New York's artists met routinely in Washington Square. There he met John Marin, whom Stephen describes as pleasant and quiet. That from a laconic man himself!

Stephen recalls watching Marin painting on the porch of the Sand Beach Farm boarding house. The islands in the view—Second, Andrew, Mark—show up in several of his paintings. I told Stephen that we always call the overlook just a bit further down the road the Marin View. Since he could not purchase the house he had rented here, Marin had left Stonington after painting around town for several summers. Marin went further down east to Addison, which Pam declared had not nearly as nice a view as Stonington.

The Paces were good friends of Milton Avery, friends with Jackson Pollack and the deKoonings. They knew Mark Rothko and a host of other names we don't recognize, members of what came to be known as the New York School artists. The New York artists' scene at Washington Square eventually disbanded due to the emerging drug scene making the area unsafe, according to Pace.

As Stephen pulled out sheet after sheet of watercolors, Pam commented; Stephen smiled. I was much captivated by the simple geometry of a truck and highway and black rectangle of burned blueberry barren, as well as one of a mysterious black storm cloud hovering over the delicate shape of our bridge with boats safely huddled in the harbor, but still somewhat ominous. Which to choose?

While we pondered I asked, "How did you discover Deer Isle?"

Stephen described how he and two artist friends were painting on Monhegan in 1953 and on a whim, drove on here to the Island. Stephen fell in love with the place at once. It took some years before circumstances conspired to bring him back and allow him to acquire the yellow house of his dreams—and of his paintings.

Stephen's abstracts have mellowed over the years to lyrical, Zen-like brush strokes which lovingly depict friends and neighbors, and beautiful ladies, like Pam with the kohl-rimmed eyes, Pam in her red hat gardening, their pet dog, their Burnt Cove neighbors, and then after 1973, their own yellow house. Stephen painted self portraits, himself picking blueberries, studies of clammers, of fishermen, and their boats, images very much woven into the fabric of this place.

Perhaps modeling herself after her good friend Sally Avery, wife of Milton Avery, Pam has spent a major part of her energies creating what she calls "an artistic bubble" of freedom in which Stephen's main concern is to paint. She is a big fan of Stephen's painting. In her mind she maintains what seems like a complete visual catalog. As we went together to Kneisel Hall Chamber Music Festival Concerts in Blue Hill, Pam labeled each vista with the title of one of Stephen's paintings, and she probably commented on who has it now. It was fun to be with her as she rounded each corner and remarked, "How lucky we are." As we passed one scene after another she said, 'I love this house, this field, this tree...' and Stephen nodded in agreement."

As she finishes photographing their house, Ann asks me, "So do you have a Pace recipe too? It seems every place we go is associated in your mind with a recipe."

"Oh yes, mushrooms. That's how I first met Pam. She is very knowledgeable about mushrooms. She had invited me to their kitchen to look over a table spread full of various boletes, some edible, some not."

"Ah, I should have known."

Like many Italians, she is knowledgeable about many more species than *cêpes, Boleteus edulis*. Stephen has painted her with the bright orange chanterelles she also loves. Pam likes to sautée her mushrooms lightly till just tinged with golden brown. If she feels like it, she may add a dollop of cream or white wine, and serve the mushrooms with a mild vegetable dish such as new potatoes. Like any serious mushroom gatherer, she has her own secret places for finding them. (It is nearly impossible to get people to understand that our preserves—all but the town and state-owned one—are not publicly owned in any sense. Wouldn't eating a stolen mushroom threaten your conscience with poisoning, or at least indigestion?) I've never asked Pam to divulge where she found her mushrooms. Mushroom gatherers are no less territorial than fishermen!

When Pam realized that her memory was slipping, she vowed not to collect any more of the subtle boletes, but to stick to the almost unmistakable chanterelles. I admire her for that. So many people completely deny it when they start to have problems that may come along with aging. Even more, perhaps, I admire Stephen's quiet acceptance of the situation. When Pam would chide him over some detail, saying 'How could you have forgotten that, Stephen?" he would just shrug and gently say "I guess it's just me, Pam, the way I am."

Pam used to have a wonderful garden and she was a superb cook. They were delighted when Causeway Beach was acquired and given to the trust because they used to go there to collect seaweed for mulch for the garden. Stephen has lots of paintings with veggies and lilies and their high bush blueberries, with Pam and even himself doing the picking. They used to walk every day to the pink lily pond, Ames Pond. Stephen has lots of lily pond paintings.

The Paces always had a good eye for what is special about this island, what needs protecting. Pam has been a valuable IHT volunteer, especially good at soliciting funds. Who could resist her charming request for support? She was also keen to support Habitat for Humanity's local projects as well.

Pam herself, one of five, was raised in modest circumstances, but she is someone who was recognized for her sophistication. With delight she told me of meeting someone in Italy who corrected a friend on introducing Pam, *No questa non e' una donna; lei e' signora*, No, this is not a *donna*; she is *signora*. Lady Pam, a founder of the Deer Isle Artists Association, would be sure she and Stephen went to all the DIAA shows on Sunday afternoons before the Kneisel Hall concerts. She and Stephen were always most supportive of artists, even the most innocent of neophytes.

"Ken and I finally settled on the painting that Stephen titled *Fisherman Inspecting His Boat*. Pam approved of our choice. A very lyrical one, she said. Afterward, I sent the Paces a copy of a poem in which I had written about precisely the same gesture, a fisherman patting the hull of his boat in early spring."

"Spring fever," Ann laughs.

"Spring feels far away just now."

The Paces were fêted all summer when it was learned that this was to be their last one in Maine. Characteristically, Pam observed that it was wonderful to feel so surrounded with love.

Shortly before their move, on a gorgeous sparkling September day when Ken had just come by with a box of freshly-picked blackberries for them, Stephen took down from the wall a lovely oil painting entitled "Spring Shower." A nude stands with her back to us, her skin echoing a blossoming fruit tree and the hint of a rainbow.

The painting was to be a contribution to Island Heritage Trust. The Paces expect that the painting will be sold for the benefit of the land trust. Some lucky owner will have a reminder of Stephen's philosophy: We humans too are a part of nature and we honor this special place by taking care of it, surrounding it with love, as Pam would say.

Ken is busy with arrangements for the Audubon Christmas Bird Count, which usually happens in the week after Christmas and before New Year's. Everyone is a bit distracted by the combination of all our daily business, the holiday preparations, and celebrations. Everyone I know feels they have just too much to do and wonders how we got into it all.

Ann and I have been working at the Opera House recording studio to produce a show for a February Opera House Valentine Coffee House. For May we are also planning a web launch party in the two front parlors of Pilgrim's Inn for www.threehalfpress.com. Built in 1750, the imposing block of a building was known for a time as the Ark, before George and Elli Pavloff bought it and set up shop as Pilgrim's Inn. Elli figured any traveler was a pilgrim, hence the name which has nothing else to do with Deer Isle. May seems comfortably far away, so we think we will have our poems and photographs ready.

The idea for the web launch with three community sponsors came into being during a conversation with the previous owner of the Inn. He came to the Island from Sanibel Island in Florida. He had been very active there with the Chamber of Commerce, the artists' community, and the local equivalent of land trusts. He declared that here on Deer Isle these three factions of the community were not in sufficient partnership with one another and would come to rue that. A party with no further agenda than getting together in celebration would be a step in the right direction, and he volunteered to host it.

Not long after, the Inn was sold. Ann and I wondered how the new owners would feel when they discovered that they had bought a lovely old property, probably a not-lovely septic system, and—least of their worries—a promise to give some strangers a party. Would they want to do that? The new owners, Tony Lawless and Tina Oddleifson, were pleased to continue the idea. Tina had worked for The Nature Conservancy so she knew very well that such cooperation was important for keeping citizens committed to maintaining the natural integrity of our natural resource base.

Island Heritage Trust, Haystack Mountain School of Crafts, and Penobscot East Resource Center have all agreed to act as sponsors for the occasion. Stu Kestenbaum, director at Haystack, is not only a fine poet, he himself is no mean ecologist, self taught as he may be in that area. Stu understood at once that the idea was to highlight Island artists speaking for our natural environment, and that Ann and I are using Threehalf Press as the guinea pig for this effort. After opening the show at the Inn, we will then take it down and move the effort to Heritage House where it will be on exhibit for the summer.

IHT has been much too busy with the Scott's Landing project to consider the outreach possibilities yet, but everyone agrees that the artists of this community are already acting as ambassadors for the beauty and welfare of the Island. That's what brought them here to settle. That is what they want to see preserved.

Amid all the bustle, some of us know that it's already time to get ready to gear up for the winter production called Cabin Fever. This annual effort brings out singers and actors and all the back-stage folks to put on a musical which packs the house at the Reach auditorium. When folks on the continent inquire doubtingly, "What do you do on that Island all winter?" I always want to answer, "Oh, we sit around and tell summer people jokes." Only we don't; we don't sit around. December days signal winter, and the dark days are just too short!

The influx of artists and craftsmen has changed the community. The summer community, once principally Bostonians, has now become more cosmopolitan, and not limited to summer. In Scotland they would be called "incomers," largely wealthy Londoners buying up the lovely landscape. In Montana they came from California, and here on the Island they came from Manhattan and Massachusetts, and now the world. These newcomers change our taste in foods, our taste in architecture, and in all the arts.

The only thing that does not change is that all of us—those born here and those who come later—recognize on some deep level that this is a special place. Conserving our heritage, both that which we create and that which nature creates, is something in which all of us can participate.

Crab Pie

Mix 8 oz cream cheese, 1 tablespoon of grated onion, 1 tablespoon of Worcestershire sauce and 1 tablespoon of mayonnaise. Line a 9" pie plate with the mixture and pour on a catsup-horseradish cocktail sauce. Sprinkle on ½ pound of crab meat and chill overnight. Garnish with parsley and serve with crackers.

Blueberry Muffins

Melt and cool ¼ cup of Crisco or butter (or these days you might substitute 3 tablespoons of oil) Mix 1 ½ cup flour,½ cup sugar, ½ teaspoon salt, 1 tablespoon of baking powder. Mix 1 egg with ½ cup milk and quickly stir in the cooled shortening or oil. Add a generous cup of blueberries. (If you use thawed frozen berries, drain them first or you will have funny-colored muffins! Even still frozen, they tend to color the batter slightly. But who cares?) Stir just until mixed. Bake at 375° for 12-15 minutes. This makes about ten in the old-fashioned-sized muffin tins. That was before supersizing!

Aunt Dot's Rhubarb Cream Pie

Fill a cooked plain or graham cracker pie shell with 3 cups of sliced raw rhubarb. Mix together 1 cup of white sugar, ¼ cup flour, ½ teaspoon nutmeg, 1 tablespoon of melted butter and 3 large eggs. Pour this mixture on top of the cut up rhubarb. Bake at 450°for 10 minutes, and then at 350°for 30 minutes, or until custard is set and slightly browned.

Sand Beach Farm Biscuits

Mix 2 cups flour with ½ teaspoon salt, 4 teaspoons baking powder, ½ teaspoon cream of tartar, 2 teaspoons sugar. Cut in ½ cup Crisco or butter for shortening, and stir in ¾ cup milk all at once. Pat out rounds ½" thick, and bake at 450°for 10 or 12 minutes.

Mushrooms á la Pace

Brush the mushrooms clean of the bits of moss and soil. Sautée lightly till just tinged with golden brown. Add a dollop of cream or white wine if desired. Serve with a mild vegetable dish such as new potatoes.

Gunga's Gingerbread

2 cups flour, sifted, 1 teaspoon ginger, ½ teaspoon salt, 1 scant teaspoon soda, dissolved in ½ cup hot water, 1 tablespoon melted lard (or butter) ½ cup molasses and ½ cup sugar (or 1 cup molasses) Bake in a greased 8"x8" pan, at 325° for 35 minutes. Serve plain, or with whipped cream or lemon sauce. (Lemon Sauce: Stir together ½ cup sugar with 1 t cornstarch. Add 1 cup water, and cook till thick and clear. Stir in lemon juice to taste. A dash of salt and butter and lemon rind may be added.)

Molasses Cookies

Mix 3 cups all-purpose flour with 1 1/2 teaspoon baking soda, 1 teaspoon salt, 1 teaspoon ginger, 2 teaspoons cinnamon. Mix 1 cup of molasses with 1 cup of butter, Crisco, lard, or ¾ cup of your choice of healthy oil, and 2 eggs or the equivalent egg substitute and stir into the dry ingredients.

Form teaspoon-sized balls and bake for 12-15 minutes at 350°, or until the tops just crack. Roll warm cookies in granulated sugar. You get wonderful ginger stars for Christmas cookies if you use butter and add an extra cup of flour with some ginger, allspice, and cinnamon, and roll the dough very thin.

Goose Cove Bread Pudding

Soak 2-3 cups of crumbs (6-8 slices of bread) in 2 cups of milk for 30 minutes. Mix ½ cup unsweetened cocoa, ¼ teaspoon salt, ¾ cup sugar, 2 tablespoons butter. Add 2 eggs beaten with 1 teaspoon of vanilla. Pour into a well-greased dish and set in a pan water enough to come up a half an inch. Bake at 350°for 1 hour. Serve with whipped cream.

January — Crockett Cove Woods — 11

My New Year's resolution: I will go to the historical society and see what I can find out about Captain Al Shepard, who owned the Pace's house. In the winter the society Archives are open on Mondays. Among a certain set, the work of cataloging and filing the society's impressive collection of genealogical material, old photographs, and memorabilia is an irresistible magnet. A good time is had by all.

I meet the usual group of volunteers quite willing to talk, including Paul Stubing, Alan Gott who grew up in Stonington, and Stan Hardy from Little Deer who had known Captain Al and had worked on his last vessel, the *Endeavor*. Shepard had owned the granite carrier, *Annie & Reuben*, and the *Enterprise* as well. She'd had her two masts moved aft to make more deck room. The men look up the dates the various vessels were built; they speak of the date of launch, rhyming it with tree branch.

These men are local authorities beyond doubt, telling me how they remembered seeing the harbor full of masts—the 4-master *Nancy Hanks*, which worked at the Settlement quarry loading cut stone for building, and the 3-master *Fiheman*, built at Bath for Goss, which carried granite for years. Until they take me next door so I can read the label on the model of it, I think they were saying "fireman." The air of the Marine Room put to bed for the winter steams with our breath.

Bay coasters, the men tell me, liked to stay in the bay carrying their loads of coal, fish, pulp, stove wood, driftwood for the Rockland kilns, whatever would bring in some money. They explain to me that driftwood with its impregnated salt burned hotter than other wood, so it was much esteemed at the lime-burning brick kilns across the bay.

Stan Hardy says that the *Enterprise* masts ended up on Al's new boat, the *Endeavor*. When I ask about this recycling, Hardy says his uncle had then bought the *Enterprise* from Shepard after Shepard had sold the hull minus the masts, all a question of timing and cash flow. The uncle then cut new spars on Pickering Island. He rhymes 'spar' with 'ah.'

Then we look at the handsome model of the *Endeavor*, Shepard's two-masted bay coaster. We also look at the society's America's Cup material. Since the first two crews were made up entirely of Deer Isle men, the Society has a nice collection of America's Cup memorabila. I ask whether there was a connection between the racing yacht *Endeavor*, contemporary with our local schooner *Endeavor* and sharing its name.

"Marnie, that's a good question."

The J boat *Endeavor* challenged and beat the *Rainbow* for the America's Cup in 1934. We can only speculate. We do not bother speculating, however, about the aircraft carrier—or the star ship—which both also shared the name with Shepard's *Enterprise*. Another appealing name they discuss is the *Livelihood*, built in 1903 at the Billings yard in Stonington, home port, Bangor; sunk in 1924.

Paul tells us he well remembers Steve Robbins of the watercolor painting. Steve was Pace's neighbor across the way. Paul recalls one day in 1989—Paul is nothing if not precise—saying to this well-regarded fisherman, "It's nice to see some color in the harbor. How is it that you came to paint your boat yellow?" Such an unusual color had earned this boat the nickname "banana boat," so it was a matter of considerable speculation.

"Well, I will tell you," Robbins had answered. "I like it."

So was there perhaps a connection between Steve Robbins's predilection for yellow and the color of his neighbor's house across the way? I ask if the Captain's home with its yellow paint was considered a fancy one for the neighborhood.

"It had paint on it, so yes."

Much laughter.

"Sorry we can't really tell you much about the house. But is there anything else you would like to know about the boats?"

More laughter.

It's pretty cold in the unheated room. The gentlemen retreat back to the archives and I head home. I wish I had recorded that encounter! I used to think it quite remarkable that my own grandmother lived before there were automobiles and died after there were airplanes. That my mother-in-law knew her grandfather through his stories of the Civil War and she herself watched the moon landing on the television and worried about the atomic bomb is almost beyond comprehension. I listened to the men at the historical society describe the end of the Great Age of Sail from their own personal experiences. My brother tells me about mariners here discussing the captains of the "internationals," the current generation of astonishingly huge luxury yachts from around the world, in our bay this past summer. I marvel at how rapidly the world changes—and how it does not.

* * *

Ken came home with fresh scallops. Hooray! There is no seafood I love more than a raw scallop, but it has to be eaten the same day it comes out of the sea. Not many boats are going out for either scallops or shrimp this year. Fuel costs and foreign competition are high and market prices for shrimp are low—if you can even find a buyer. Most of the processors went out of the business after a number of years of drastic declines of the shrimp stock. Now that shrimp populations may have recovered, is anyone going to be set up to process the catch? Dick Bridges did decide to give it another go. Carol just phoned to tell us that he has come back with some lovely ones.

Dick and Ted Ames work closely together in the fisheries alliance. The Ames family will be coming over for dinner tonight. I will cook "Chinese." I often do and I will take particular delight in steaming haddock and presenting it on a bed of seaweed. We will also have a few scallops and some of that catch of Dick Bridges' delicious little popcorn-like Maine shrimp. Dick probably knows more about Northern shrimp, which are what we have here in the Gulf of Maine, than any other fisherman alive today. He needs to know not only where the shrimp are, which varies widely depending on how cool the surface waters are since we are the southern end of their range, but also to find them when they are the right size. Our shrimp, *Pandalus borealis*, are the same species as the tiny ones the Scandinavians so cherish for their open-face sandwiches, nothing like the large farmed or Gulf shrimp.

Then, too, there is the challenge that late in the season the populations turn into females. Then they are apt to come with abdomens coated with eggs, a roe not quite up to what we like as caviar.

All week the radio has been calling it a January thaw. Ann and I have been having a wonderful time on walks together, photographing the frozen puddles that look like windows into another world. At noon our fence posts and garden gate exhale delicate plumes of vapor in the sunlight. Talk about our planet Gaia breathing! Gaia breath! When Ann goes out to photograph, the ice in her cove creaks and makes deep sounds like a whale. Gaia groans.

In the bog we saw an inch of skunk cabbage sprout and Ken reports that he has heard the chickadees' spring song. Is this what global warming is? Where is winter? The one spell of cold we had came on the day of the Christmas Bird count. After that early cold snap, the pendulum has swung the other way. Although this warm spell makes folks nervous, thinking about what it may portend, they do appreciate any days when the oil-burning furnace is not running much. We also know we can expect the bottom to drop out of the thermometers again with the next swing of the winter pendulum.

One of my favorite of all the color combinations in nature is the mix of a dusting of snow on lush moss green, a celadon delight. That is what we have today for our outing this afternoon with Ted Ames and his family. We are meeting Ted and Robin and their daughter Annie at the entrance to Crockett Cove Woods. Perhaps the preserve's most dramatic feature is a massive granite outcrop bordering the trail, boulders forming an entrance gate. Mosses and lichens festoon the rock faces, mound over old stumps, and carpet the forest floor.

The woods are almost totally silent. What are all the birds doing? Does their inconspicuousness just now mean that they are dispersed, minding their own behaviors? When Ted and his family arrive, almost the first thing Ted does is stand still, listen, and smile.

"It's the winter silence in the woods that I love," he announces.

As we head down the trail, to our right the imposing face of a house-sized granite rock is pasted with the dark scales of rock tripe—like dragon scales hung out to dry. The side of the boulder is carpeted with lichens and mosses. There is nothing of that sere winter feel of the old fields in here. Everything looks lush and vibrantly green. It would be difficult to identify the season in a photograph. Surely the winter temperatures slow the chemical reactions in plants, so it cannot be the optimum growing season for mosses and lichens. But it certainly looks as if it were.

I tell Annie about my most favorite of the field trips we have led over the years: moss and lichen walks when people flopped on their stomachs with magnifying lenses in hand.

"Grown ups or kids?" she asks skeptically. Annie is eleven years old, quite a sophisticated eleven-year old in some ways. Annie has all the budding energy of what they are calling a "tween" these days. I take it that means someone who is between being a child and being an adult. Having worked with that age group in teaching and having raised two myself, I remember clearly that you are never quite sure from moment to moment whether you are dealing with an adult or the child. I would say from her bearing and body language that Annie is not entirely sure she wants to be on this walk.

Annie is very bright. She was adopted from China, and Robin has made it a point to make Annie aware of her heritage. The three of us even enrolled in a Chinese language class last winter. Last summer Robin took Annie back to the orphanage in Anhui from which she began her journey to an American childhood.

Robin spent the years before Annie as Maine's Commissioner of the Department of Marine Resources. Before that Robin worked on the fisheries newspaper based in Stonington, so she knew the fishing community about as well as one could. Fishermen are an independent, contentious lot, so she was brave to take them on. She won their respect, though of course not their unanimous agreement on anything.

Ted was born and raised on Vinalhaven, the large island we could see from here if we were standing on the shore. He has been a fisherman all his life, as his father and grandfather before him. Listening to Ted reminds me that I regret never having tape recorded Allen Fifield's speech. Although it always took me a week or so to relearn it at the beginning of every summer, the distinctive talk of those old timers was like a sea breeze over a clam flat. Their a's were relaxed as sitting on a rock in sunshine. Their r's shimmered on the edge of nonexistence, extreme low tide, so they said no'theaster; not nor'easter. Ted and today's fishermen speak a faint echo of that, a much more accessible though still specialized language—with only occasional challenges like 'nymphs' for National Marine Fisheries Service and 'novvy' for Nova Scotia.

Robin and I have been friends for some years and gone walking together around the Island, but this is the first time I have ever seen Ted walking any distance on land. His life changed just a few months ago when out of the blue the phone rang and he heard that he had been awarded a MacArthur grant. Undoubtedly some are jealous of this unsolicited good fortune befalling one of their own, but Ted and Robin have not felt negative repercussions from the fishing community here.

"How does it feel, Ted?"

"I will say that the old knees sure appreciate it!" The physical toll of the hard work aboard any fishing boat is taking its toll on most of our fishermen friends, who are all about our age, a rather mature mid-life, to put it somewhat euphemistically. Most of the lobstermen have bad backs. I had not thought about the strain that all those years of being shock absorbers in the pounding seas might be.

Annie has disappeared ahead of us on the trail. Ted ambles slowly, admiring the groves of spruce trees.

Ted tells us about his Grandpa on Saddleback, lobstering from a peapod and then rowing the catch in to market.

"Do you know Saddleback?"

Yes, I am well familiar with that speck out on the horizon seen from the Overlook at the Barred Island Preserve.

"It's none but a small ledge," say Ted, his voice gentle with a ring of Elizabethan echoes characteristic of Island speech.

As he tells us his Saddleback story I realize that the grandfather must have known Allen Fifield, who told me of anchoring his sloop out there to go visit his friend Mariner Alley. How I love the punning soundplay of those amazing names together, both of which are still met with Down East. "The basket" I recognize from his description as the sort of boatswain's chair which they had rigged up to a boom on the northeast side. One could anchor offshore and get swung ashore.

"I have a photo of that," says Ted and I wonder if it is one I heard tell of that shows women in full skirts being hoisted ashore. I wonder, too, if the story of Mariner Alley's wife getting dunked in the water is true or apocryphal.

Ted recounts how another relative of his told the children the story of Captain Kydd, with vague references to gold coins the teller had personally stashed away somewhere, coins somehow never actually produced for inspection as far as Ted can recall. I tell him about Carolyn Olmsted's version of the story, and how the Brace tribe always referred to the story as an amusement rather than a fact. Maybe the story circulated in the other, "downstairs," circles as well. And every tale may have a grain of truth in it. Every pearl has a grain of sand.

I think once again how social stratification leads often to broken hearts. I observed when we first arrived that in self-defense the Islanders seemed to have developed a protective armor, a surface of deferential manner and reserve. Even now you may have to speak first if you are From Away.

Emily Muir was certainly someone From Away from the time she first summered here with her parents, through the brief years she lived here with her artist husband, who was quite popular with the fishermen. Through the long years of her widowhood here Emily was always perceived by the locals as a somewhat exotic figure. She was not handsome in any conventional sense, and she was not large enough to be considered inherently flamboyant. Yes, you should see her piloting her power boat around the bay. She could sure make waves. Yes, you should see her in her red sporty convertible, buzzing fearlessly around the narrow Island roads. Island youth in their pickups today have nothing on Emily.

Emily was different, however; an artist in every sense, an artist in life. When I came to the Island as a painter in those days before Haystack, people first referred to that odd artist fellow, John Marin, and then followed their observations with tales of the Muirs. Bill Muir was a sculptor, observer and carver of sensuous organic shapes in wood. The Muirs were instrumental in securing a place on the Island for Haystack Mountain Craft School.

Emily Lansingh Muir did all sorts of things: she taught herself to build those houses, she did paintings—awful bright and awful different for some tastes—and she went to the classical music concerts over at

Kniesel Hall in Blue Hill. Obviously she seemed to have money, and then there was her writing.

The writing was a tender point. Emily was so fond of her neighbors and their distinctive Island ways that she tried to capture the flavor on paper. Some of her neighbors never forgave her for that. As always when folks take issue with a piece of writing, it does not much matter whether they have read the work in question or not. Islanders love to talk about one another. If dock talk and their marine radio conversations are any measure, no one handles gossip with greater gusto than the fishermen. However, they may feel they have earned the right to talk about themselves by virtue of being born here.

In spite of the fact that Emily used fanciful *noms de plume*, some neighbors felt their privacy had been invaded, their ways held up to ridicule by an outsider. That was a sadness for Emily. I wonder if I will escape a similar fate as I lay out my own chronicles of this dear place. I have tried to be scrupulous about double-checking everything people have shared with me, and I make a point of always showing people what I have said about them before the printed page is let loose on the world. Still, it's probably a good thing I am so much of a hermit that I may not notice if folks back away after they read this.

Like many of the people who come to the Island from other lives, Emily didn't talk much about what she did on the national scene. She was the first woman on the National Commission of Fine Arts, and she was on the advisory committee of the Kennedy Center for the Performing Arts—no mean accomplishments. I think perhaps she was proudest of her efforts to build lovely homes here that fishermen could afford to buy. They didn't buy into her idea of what a house should look like, but it was a worthy attempt. The local people still aren't taking full advantage of the preserved land, but Emily's day will come. The children of today's Islanders will thank her for her foresight and generosity.

"If you think of those small clay figures Emily made of men in fishing boots and their wives in those old bibbed aprons, you realize she was a good observer," Robin was saying.

"They're quite obviously affectionate portraits, aren't they?" To the very end of her life Emily spent her failing energy speaking of her passionate commitment to the well-being of all Islanders no matter what their position on the social spectrum. Crockett Cove Woods, here for the enjoyment of all, for generations to come, is a grand testimony to that. A few days before her death, Emily called me to her bedside. She said to me, "No, I don't have a goal of getting to be 100 years old" but she almost made that! Emily said she was not competitive; she just liked to watch.

Emily put what money she had where others put only their mouth. If Emily had to sell some of her real estate in order to be able to afford putting other lands in trust, so be it. She was always outspoken, always firing off opinion pieces to the newspaper. Although she had no children of her own, Emily relentlessly made her opinions known on the school board. I remember one Fourth of July when she was going to make her usual march in the parade carrying a fervently-worded political placard. Someone trying to dissuade her expressed concern that perhaps she was getting a bit old for the hill in the heat. She snapped back that she was only eighty. No further comments.

"Marnie, please tell Ted about Emily and starting this preserve with The Nature Conservancy," Robin says, as if she were reading my thoughts. "We are working with The Conservancy in some very interesting aspects of fisheries conservation."

"Back in the days when Philip Conkling was here as a graduate student working on his master's degree, he would stay with her if he wasn't staying with us. Phil eventually went on to found Island Institute, with Emily one of the founding members. Emily gave Russ Island to Island Institute and Wreck Island to The Nature Conservancy. Emily's Crockett Cove gifts, made thirty-three years ago, total 97 acres. She made the first in 1966, and the other, at the Barbour Farm end, was January 2, 1973. We're doing a sort of anniversary celebration, aren't we?"

Emily specified that there be no hunting, no trapping, and no off-road motorized vehicles. She wanted to encourage the general public to visit in a non-consuming way. At the same time she was sensitive to the concerns of those who bought her houses on the bordering shore lands. The trails are laid in such a way that conflict is minimized; privacy of nearby owners is respected. The neighbors are de-facto stewards. Sadly, most islanders still have not visited any of the preserves, certainly not any on the opposite side of the island from where they live. Hustling to make a living does not leave you much time left over.

I bring myself back to the present moment, something for which I find nature is always helpful. The cushiony moss mats we are treading are of various shades of green, thoroughly "tweed." That is, species after species sports its particular color and texture in patches. A square yard of "fabric" will have dozens of variations.

"So, what kind of moss is this?" asks Robin, seeing Annie eyeing a particularly lush patch. Annie has rejoined us. Robin is determined that Annie reap some of the potential benefit of being with biologists. She stops to examine the mosses and asks me about how one learns to identify them.

"I like to say that on one of my walks you will easily learn how to identify six kinds of moss from your car window."

I see Annie's eyebrow raise. Annie is of the generation whose teachers in school have probably not had much of a natural history education. After the Russians sent up their Sputnik, the US went into a sort of science frenzy, but the action was all about rocket science. Rachel Carson's *Silent Spring* had the unfortunate unintended side effect of making close attention to the natural world seem less inviting, even if necessary. Environmentalism came to sound like medicine, and we would prefer to let someone else work out the dosages, thank you. Overworked, under-funded park rangers and nature center educators have often had to resort to devising simple scissors-and-crayon craft projects masquerading as nature study to entertain the busloads of school children arriving in batches of thirty or more. The kids are manageable for a short time at least, and they have something to take home. They do not have much chance to experience solitude or the spiritual aspect of communicating personally with nature.

Island Heritage Trust has just begun a program with the elementary school in which each class "adopts" a preserve. Annie Ames will just have missed it, as she has moved on to middle school this year. The trust helps recruit naturalists and volunteers to chaperone and provides teaching materials. It is amazing how challenging it is to arrange to bring a small group of children outside, beyond pavement, during a school day. That's sad but true even here in our small island school set in this jewel of the natural world.

Barbara Vickery, Director of Conservation Programs, then in charge of plant stewardship for the Maine chapter of The Nature Conservancy, put together a list of lichens and mosses for a field trip thirty years ago, and I still have that original list. The number of mosses—and the number of years—surprises even me. As I think about it, I am not even aware of any significant change in the preserve over those years.

I wish I had thought to bring hand lenses on our walk today. On our nature walks, I always remarked when I distributed hand lenses that, as one who loves plants, I find it annoying to watch someone reach out, grab a bloom, decapitate it, raise it to eye level, give it a brief inspection, and toss it away. How much better it would be, how much more considerate, to bring one's eye to the flower rather the other way round. It's easy to imagine how soon the preserve would take on a plucked look if we all grabbed up hunks of moss to examine. How little encouragement those adults had needed to enjoy flopping down on the luxuriant moss mats.

Six kinds of moss from the car window? How about that for a skill to impress your family and friends? Maybe not Annie's friends. The species I have in mind are pincushion (*Leucobryum*); hair-cap (*Polytrichum*), the spore capsules of which have what look like pixie caps; broom (*Dicranum*), which has the look of having been windswept all in one direction; feather (*Hypnum*); peat, which is what we call any of the many starry, squishy Sphagnums; and Schreber's, (*Pleurozium schreberi*), as well as little brown moss (*Dicranella*), which forms velvety tiles on our paths. Really these are the Seven Sisters, since I also like to throw in their relative, *Bazzania*, which is a liverwort. All that is before we even begin to look at the lichens: reindeer moss, lungwort, bayonets, soldiers, and others which really have no common names and are distinguished by their chemistry.

Schreber's moss is the principal species of the forest floor here. I point out that the individual plants are characterized by a red central stem which gives the entire mat a reddish cast. That's so easy to see and so straight forward that I can see Robin and Ted are now believers. I show Annie where a fringe of Schreber's trims the frosting of snow on top of a rock ledge. The similar species that does not have the distinctive red line is feather moss. Easy. Now Anne's a believer even if she knows it will not be socially useful to her to admit it.

"I always love to come to the Crockett Cove Preserve when it's raining," I say to Robin and Ted, Annie having moved out of range. "The mosses and lichens look so bright that there is no sense of disappointment however dull and gloomy the day. Looking for mosses in the snow is particularly rewarding—the oddity of seeing the lush green against the frozen white."

On the ledge we find some three-toothed Bazzania, which is not a moss but a similarly ancient plant, a liverwort. You can see, under a hand lens, the neatly jagged line of three teeth, which I take as reminders that these tiny plants have been around since the days of the dinosaur. "These liverworts can be identified from as far as you can see them by their distinctive translucent emerald color."

At the tiny remnant saucer of a bog we find pitcherplants poking up through frozen sphagnum. These are *Sarracinea purpurea* which a neighbor of the preserve years ago brought on a short transplant trip from Burntland Pond. The pitchers are being studied by the current generation of scientists like Nishi who are using new techniques to work out genetic marker studies, chemical analysis, functional differentiation, evolution in progress, evolution or extinction.

At the mere mention of that last word, Ted tries to keep anxiety or defeat from his soft, determined voice.

We kneel down looking for tiny sun dews, another insectivorous plant, between the walkway boards, and our conversation switches from issues ranging from northern range extensions accompanying global warming to species introductions. Moving the pitcher plants across the island a few miles has not been harmful, but the same cannot be said for such species as Japanese barberry, zebra mussels, green crabs, Asian crabs, and even periwinkles.

Ken remembers where there were vestiges of log corduroy put there by Francis Williams when he cut the woods for the Boston doctor who owned this land before Emily Muir, Dr. Lucy Abbot. When Dr. Abbot's daughter, Shirley Lewis, subsequently put the land up for sale, Francis thought it would be a good idea to buy it. In those days, one did not borrow money, so he'd asked Arthur Barter if he wanted to go in on it for $6,000 for the 48 acres. Since it had been cut over, Barter was not interested. In those days people thought the money was in the timber, not the land.

"Spar timber." Ted points out some especially fine trees. "That is what we used to call any good, straight old-growth wood. It would be strong and just right for boat building."

I try out my idea about land and sea parallels on Ted and Robin. "We have had some successful programs to encourage sustainable harvesting of timber. I gather that programs that have encouraged boycotting of certain fish species have not always been as well-informed as they might be. I did wonder a few years back when there seemed to be no shrimp if I ought to be eating northern shrimp, but now we seem to have more shrimp than the market knows what to do with. And we have almost no scallops at all."

"Scallop divers are mostly new to fishing. They think like miners," growls Ted. "We went from four million pounds of scallops harvested in Maine in the early 1980s to just 100,000 pounds these days. Now the bulk of the scalloping is really south of us."

I am surprised at how I bristle at that. I am turning into a real Gulf of Maine chauvinist! My dad always said apples were sweetest, best-tasting, the farther north they were grown, so Maine lobsters from our cold waters must be sweeter and our crabs and scallops tastiest.

"Just as with the fishing, I was part of the problem myself. Dragging is like clear cutting. We went from an era when we used even bed springs as a drag, and then we went to something like a 500 pound drag. When they restricted the drag size but not the weight, you saw fishermen going to drags two or three times as heavy. They fished heavier and faster. Then the divers came in and picked up the windrows of scallops that the drags had made. They also took the inaccessible large scallops. There was no brood stock for replenishing after they had picked the shoal beds clean."

"That's what we watched with such dismay off our shores the very first years we wintered here," I say. "I suspect that part of the reason we see so many fewer ducks and grebes or porpoises between us and Sellers Rock than we did at first is because of the condition of the bottom now."

Robin chimes in, "In the years when I was commissioner, we found that the scallop populations are always extremely variable. Marsden Brewer and some of the Stonington fishermen have studied how they were growing the tiny floating stage, called spat, in Japan and Canada and New Zealand. It's not all that different from the clam reseeding project. They grow the spat protected in bags, like the ones oranges come in. They have had some success getting the scallops to grow out all winter. The fishermen figure they have released about 10 million scallops, but it's a lot of work."

"And they figure they could be out lobstering and getting rich instead," Ted says. "Today's young lobster fishermen have never known what it was like in the days when a man had to fish two or three different fisheries to make a living. Crabs love to eat the larval scallops and cod used to help keep the immature crabs in check. Now we don't have the cod. Is that part of why we don't have the scallops? Marine ecosystems are very complex and we are just learning to appreciate that. When we get our lobster hatchery going, and we put out young lobster, that will be only the first step. We need these local solutions to the problems of diversifying our fisheries."

Robin adds, "And there really is no money for doing the research, just for counting the numbers."

Ken describes how he too ran his research on a shoestring all those years, funded by the National Science Foundation. "I cannot imagine trying to do such population studies now on marine ecosystems with the cost of fuel, needing a bigger boat, and finding crews. What an enterprise."

"Yet we are learning a lot from terrestrial ecology, some of it remarkably parallel," says Robin. "For instance, we are finding that there are apparently large 'mother cod' off Newfoundland that leave in migration to return to where they were born. Apparently there is some learned behavior and other cod follow them, like elephants or big horned sheep do."

Ted tells us, "My research interviewing older fishermen like my father and my uncle showed that there were two separate kinds of cod populations off the coast of Maine. One sort historically was found inshore, stayed along the coast all year, and they spawned in spring. Others were mainly further offshore and spawned in the fall, and migrated. Saying that Maine didn't have cod in winter and managing the whole area as a single population has had disastrous consequences. We find two sorts of fish may migrate and feed together for most of the year before going their separate way for spawning. If you fish them heavily anywhere you happen to find them, you risk wiping out all the subpopulations that return to specific inshore areas."

Robin adds, "The sea doesn't look like a specific place, so people got seduced into thinking of populations according to mathematical models. Our laws now mandate that National Marine Fisheries Service functions principally as an assessment organization. We manage a multi-billion dollar business with a linear, one-size-fits-all approach."

"When I was a sophomore in college," Ted says, "my brother and I were fishing south of Matinicus. I was planning to earn money for my next semester. At night we would see the horizon lit. It was the Russian fleet. The most abundant catch soon became a packing card written in Russian. Their factory ships had hunter boats they sent out to find where the fish were. They would line up ten to fifteen of these 250' trawlers. One would tow in behind the shadow of the first, with small mesh, to catch whatever had managed to escape the boat ahead. They really mollyhawked the Matinicus area. I had to scramble that year to scrape up some more scholarship money to continue my education."

We have moved down the trail to a stand of cedars. We are now on the second parcel of Emily's gift, the section eventually fronting on the Barbour Road. We come to a winding stream dark with tannins, handsomely edged with ice. The trees are still, stretching away on both sides of the trail in windless, shadowy, blue depths. We, too, stand quiet.

The panes of ice glass draw Annie. Ken and Ted compare the need for "structure" in both marine and terrestrial habitats. Nishi at Pine Hill talked most enthusiastically about developing ideas about structure in plant communities. Ken watches with interest what we learn about birds' preferences and needs for a shrub layer of a certain size, others for small trees under the canopy of mature growth.

"We have lived here long enough to appreciate the cycles of regrowth after an area has been logged," I observe. "I know where I used to be able to go to pick raspberries and where old fields have now grown up to doghair spruce deserts. Maintaining and managing for diversity is tricky."

"Kelp fronds are like tree trunks, supporting many creatures," Ted agrees. "Various sea weeds form forests. Strike the plants with a disease—like the slime molds that decimated the eel grass in the '60s—and we lose the flounder that relied on the eel grass for habitat. Or if they are heavily grazed, the plants can only achieve a certain density. Remove the grazer the way we did with sea urchin over-harvesting, and certain organisms are released, kelp in the case of the urchins. For some creatures—lobster for instance—that may be a plus. Some juvenile stages are sheltered in the kelp 'forests.' We need to think of complex systems in constant change, don't we? When I was a boy, all the islands around here had been pretty heavily logged over. Now we think of them as forest," Ted offers.

I describe Lee Fay's house in an old photograph, which shows it a small, shingled, center chimney Cape, set in cleared fields. You can see all the way to Burnt Cove Church. "Today you have to peek through spruces. If you are a great horned owl, you benefit. Lee saw one yesterday just ten feet away in the spruce tree in her yard."

"Especially since Lee has chickens, and presumably rodents that eat the feed," Ken laughs. "Snowshoe hares and deer in the woods here feast on the deciduous seedlings so that means the regrowth is likely to be skewed in favor of dense all-spruce stands. All over the Island, which was pretty heavily clear-cut by the '50s, you now have even-aged stands of mature spruces. People cut down trees now for their views without calculating which way the wind blows. They cut all they figure they can get away with without getting fined for breaking the Shorelands Ordinance. What's left, the unprotected trees, blows down, creates a mess, and breaks the power lines on every storm," he says. "Sells a lot of generators."

Ted smiles, looks around to enjoy the trees, and after a bit returns to the topic of systems. "We find that we are dealing on multiple scales interacting within ecosystems, and not only are the components linked, and constantly changing, they are systems without discrete boundaries. Once thresholds and limits have been exceeded, the changes can be irreversible."

Perhaps impatient with the two scientists engaged in theoretical discussion, Annie once again decides she wants to bolt ahead. As we watch her stride purposefully off through the trees, I think about having watched the unfolding of her entire girlhood in this small community.

The population of this island is almost totally homogeneous. I recall that Bob Williams told us that his Armenian grandfather felt obliged to change his name, Sarkis Aprahamian, to Whitman—after one of his wife's Nova Scotia forebears. Even that was considered "diverse". The nearest synagogue is in Bangor. From time to time there are a few black children in our school, usually adopted by a white couple. A few men have Asian spouses, and their children are about the extent of our diversity. Some effort has to be made when observing Martin Luther King Day to bring in a speaker who is African American. Visiting Crockett Cove Woods in January feels most appropriate, the month when we ask the people of our nation to address the issue of justice for all. More and more we are also recognizing that our morality should include issues of other species than our own. The idea fits, even though at the time it was not quite what Martin Luther King Jr. probably had in mind when he observed, "We are caught in an inescapable network of mutuality, tied in a single garment of destiny. Whatever affects one directly affects all indirectly."

Human diversity, moss diversity, diversity of fish and the other creatures of the sea; how many are the ways the lesson is writ large for us! Ignore it at our peril.

As it so often seems, when we turn and retrace our steps, the way back seems shorter than the way out. This time the trail takes us along the back side of the boulder outcrop. We notice that there are pools of water as yet unfrozen beside some of the boulders. Do the stones really retain that much heat? As we watch, the surface of the water appears to be rising and falling. When Ken comes up to take a look, I am quite sure I see the surface trembling in synchrony with his foot steps. I am reminded of those whale sounds that the ice makes on the cove over at Ann's house. What kind of inland tide is this? We stand very quiet, and still the water pulses. As near as we can figure, the wind off the ocean that we now hear soughing in the tree tops is pushing on the spruces, levering their roots back and forth under the frozen moss. The forest sighs. Gaia breath indeed.

Annie circles back, takes a quick look, pronounces it cool and is off again. Some years ago I brought Annie a book from China about the T'ang dynasty ceramic figurines in various museum collections. These beauties were a different style from what modern tastes decree as attractive. With their luxuriant black tresses swept into elaborate arrangements, and full cheeks blooming with rosy coloring, the sturdy T'ang women depicted could most suitably be called strong woman peaches. Annie looks so much like them that I hoped as a growing girl she would recognize herself.

I thought it would be good for Annie to recognize on at least some unconscious level that her own appearance is appealing though she will never be mistaken for a Paris Hilton or any of the sylphs currently in vogue. From a very early age she had asked her parents why the other children she knew here on the Island did not look quite like her. Now that her intellect is developing—she was a member of the school's Olympics of the Mind team—she also risks the loneliness most very smart young women face. Add to that what seems to be a nearly universal desire among teens and pre-teens to be cool at all times, and Annie can seem quite guarded so I was not surprised at her aloofness today in the woods.

Annie is young, and her parents are openly affectionate with her, obviously dedicated to her. They try, however, to give Annie plenty of room to be independent, to discover what pleases herself, not just what the adult world or the peer world rewards. When we arrive at the place where the path splits—one route leading over the height of the boulders and the other retracing the boggy route by which we had come—we find no Annie. Dusk is falling, and with it the temperature is rapidly dropping.

We decide to split up, Robin and Ken taking the high road, and Ted and I retracing the low road so we will know that we have not left Annie waiting for us at any point along the trail by misunderstanding. Robin and Ted are juggling an enormous load with all the pressures of developing Penobscot East Resource Center in the face of the environmental juggernaut facing fishing, facing our oceans, facing our globe. But they do not slight their parental involvement. Both parents visibly relax a bit when we see the pre-teen figure leaning against the car in the spruce shadows.

They greet their independent daughter affectionately with no hint of anxiety or reprimand. As Robin and Ted are enthusiastically thanking Ken and me for being their guides here, I walk around to Annie's side of the vehicle and turn to her, trying to draw her out.

"So what does this preserve mean to you, Annie?"

The eyebrows again. "What do you mean?" On guard, but not hostile. This is a young person accustomed to giving the correct answers, and she has enough nerve and comfort with risk to venture where the "right" answer is not obvious or even something that exists.

"Do you think preserves are a good idea? Should we let people come visit, or would it be better to let the natural areas be preserved shut away in private estates? Do you think preserves are a good way to be sure something important remains for your own children some day?" From my tone of voice, my trying not to make the questions too loaded, this most perceptive young woman can sense that I am not being patronizing, but genuinely interested in her feelings.

The T'ang beauty look comes over Annie.

"Oh, definitely, worthwhile. One day...." Her face glows with a sweetness that reminds me of both her parents. Idealism.

She knows she is one of the beads on the grand string. From T'ang to tomorrow.

* * *

Ann is sick with a terrible cold. She is hunkered down, but surviving by spending her time working on photographs for our Threehalf Press web page. We are quite thrilled with how the poems look alongside the glowing photo images on the computer screen with light coming through them. We have decided to call our works projected this way "light pages." It does not matter whether the image is produced by a CD, a DVD, on a computer monitor or on a television screen or projected in an LCD multimedia presentation. The pictures have all the hypnotic allure of color television.

Word has gotten around about the several presentations we have given: First to the land trust annual meeting, then to the Red Hat ladies, to the Parkinsons Support group, to the Methodists, the

Congregationalists, the Unitarian-Universalists, and the Community of Christ. That's a pretty complete spectrum of folks who respond to Ann's gorgeous photographs and identify with my poems. The Opera House Arts group has scheduled us to perform at the Valentine Coffee House coming up next month. Frank Gotwals has finished lobstering for the season and has his boat ashore now. He will sing and play guitar for us. His sound seems right for our flavor. Ann has been making a CD to show as trailer these next couple of weekends. What a lark. She has used some of her grass-and-snow photos to go with my six word poem, the only one of my works I know by heart:

> Wind writes
> small poems
> on grass.

It now looks as if the developers will not get the Scott's Landing property. Just when it looked as if the efforts over several years of negotiations and canvassing support had completely crumbled, Maine Coast Heritage Trust received a phone call informing them that a major donor and supporting pledges would make it possible to meet the closing for Scott's Landing scheduled for January 17th. All of the donors feel that IHT is the best owner and should manage the property, not Maine Coast. Given that this is a small teapot of an island, it is almost amusing that it is now beyond guessing who made this happen or why. Onward! A heartening amount of patience and trust and good will have gone on behind the scenes. Not all big developments have to happen on Deer Isle. Not last century; not this one. With luck and proper conservation instruments, not in the next one either.

    We just had the closing for Heritage House as well. What a week. This will certainly not seem like a long winter. Even more than usual we will need all the time there is to get ready for this summer season. Island Heritage Trust, the Historical Society, Penobscot East—everyone interested in who we are, who we were, and what is coming down the road at us—will be scurrying around. High season ahead. Onward indeed.

Life in hibernation on a winter island. Not dull. We have been hammered with the back side of a northeaster and the power on the Island has been out for two days. Lee reports that it looks from her side of the cove as if the eagles' old nest tree on Barred Island has blown down. Ken and Lee are off at an IHT board meeting to accept the final gift of Scott's Landing. Hooray!

So it looks as if it's going to be just me heading off to Barred to check on the eagles' nest tree. I check the tide table to be sure I have

plenty of time to make it over the bar and back.

The last time I went exploring at the command of state endangered species biologist Charlie Todd, it was at the end of the season to collect the remains under the eagle nest to be analyzed. I was finishing up the job when Ken decided he had just time enough to go check on a crowberry restoration project. An overused path on the far side of the island had been closed so crowberry could recover from being trampled.

I had put into the plastic bag the last bits of feather and bones and perched on the shore rocks to enjoy the sunshine. The sun dropped lower and the air cooled. I began to think about the fact that we'd gotten a late start today. The waters had already begun to lap on both sides of the bar as we'd started across the bar to the island. At high tide the water is more than six feet deep over the sand bar. One would not want to be caught on the wrong side.

Still no Ken. I began to think about what might have happened to him. If he had fallen on the rocks out here this would be a challenging rescue. That I knew all too vividly as my EMT brother had told me the public parts about a long carry out from the preserve after an accident last year.

I'd eyed the increasing waves with distaste. Even less would I like to think about Walt's trying to use his boat in a night rescue effort. Perhaps I should go check on Ken while there was still time to mount a rescue in fading daylight? On the other hand, that would mean I was not here should Ken come around the seaward side of the island in search of me. What if I had misunderstood and Ken meant we would meet at home? What if Ken had gone home and found me not there? What if he then called out a rescue effort? Cell phone coverage is nearly non-existent on this part of the island so we have yet to invest in one, but I would have appreciated a cell phone just then. Dilemma.

Eventually I'd decided to abandon my post and see if I could spot Ken from the bar. However, to my dismay, there was no bar. Now I really had a dilemma. I had no interest in spending the coming night on the island, nor in being rescued in the dark. I was not at all sure I could withstand the current or the depth if I tried to wade the bar. I'd decided to head out into the water but stop and turn back if it reached my waist or if my feet threatened to wash out from under me.

Cold! Step by step I counted my way across. Deeper. Deeper. But my belt stayed dry, just. I made it all the way across. I'd made the jog home in record time. Cold and wet, I arrived to find Ken somewhat baffled by my absence.

"I called you and you didn't answer. I thought you'd gone home so I came home," he said.

And then what? Shivering though I was, I was by then really steaming. Only later could I contemplate that I had now joined the ranks of those around here who have been caught somewhere by the tide. It is a not inconsiderable number. It is surprising that I do not know of any fatalities. The most dramatic incident I suppose was when Bob Williams rescued a scallop diver from a ledge where he had taken refuge after his boat floated away. Fortunately Bob spotted the empty boat and figured out what that might mean. He went looking in the right spot at the right time. This is a pretty place, where the granite meets the sea. Not a place you would ever want to take lightly, nor turn your back on.

I find it now quite lovely to step onto the sand bar with no other footprints marking the way. On the sand is a scattering of razor clam shells, large blue mussel shells and something like a dozen huge clam shells. Are these quahogs? They are surely something unlike any I have seen before. Each shell is still a joined pair. The shells have a hoary, ancient look, with what appear to be growth rings. Sequoias of the bivalve world? Old growth clams? The insides are quite fresh looking, but empty of any trace of live animal. Most mysterious. They seem to have been gnawed on their narrow ends. What could that be?

I round the island and lean into the teeth of the wind. A few long-tail ducks yodel, blissfully unconcerned by the chop. Ah, yes, here on the windward side of the island there is now a gap, as if a tooth had been extracted. The eagles' tree has been toppled. I notice for the first time that the tree just windward—a mature spruce—had some time back been sawed off about waist high. Who did that? Could it have been back when the young eaglet got hanged in the tree top? I thought that was further to the east, but they did cut a tree then. How ironic if the eagle-trapping tree which had served as a windscreen now claims the nest site as well.

Looking at the uprooted stump of the toppled tree I am struck by how shallow the roots were, how they just formed a cap over the granite ledge. There is the nest, a saucer almost six feet across. What a crude weaving job of sticks, each a bit bigger around than my thumb, perhaps two feet long, none as large around as my forearm. The stick network frames a view of Scraggy Island.

Will you look at that—there is a soft lining to the nest! Spilled out and frozen stiff, but nevertheless, there is a saucer of what look to be fine grasses and wood fern fronds. There are several duck carcasses, some crow feathers and a lobster claw along with some long bones scattered in the nesting material. I pick up the lobster claw to examine how it was cracked open—a rough hacking job. Which is the bigger wonder, that the eagle can evidently crack a lobster or that it can catch one? I wonder what the fishermen would say about that!

There is now nothing to keep the wind from tearing into the small clearing that forms the middle of Barred Island. As I look around at the withered fern fronds, I catch sight of crab claws, some empty sea urchin shells, and an occasional lobster claw or carapace. On one mossy stump there is a whole table setting of seafood refuse. Alongside are piles that look like otter scat. Otters have my vote for producing the loveliest of scats. Theirs is rainbow-colored, with bits of blue mussels, green urchins, and red crabs. More looking, more droppings. This whole hidden area is an otter restroom. Why is it that I am amused and delighted with the idea of otters using this refuge as a toilet, but I still remember with revulsion that human visitors used to fill this glade with toilet paper and worse?

Why is it that I think the lobstermen would happily share a few lobsters with the bald eagles, but I am not so sure how they would feel about sharing with otters? I never hear fishermen mention seeing otters, just the occasional mink. I do know how they feel about seals and the fact that seals are protected under the Marine Mammal Act. Are otters considered marine mammals? No, although they are mammals, and ours spend at least some of their time in the sea.

In the mud I can read where otters have scraped what looks like a small drinking hole. On one side is the glistening, slippery scrape; on the other two very fresh looking tracks. The footprints are larger than a dog or a coyote, but smaller than a bear. Impressive. The prints have been made since yesterday morning's rain. I feel I am being watched. Not fair; I have never ever actually seen an otter.

I pick my way through the spruces to the outer perimeter of the island, just about where sits a boulder that is measeled with red marks. This is a rather unglamorous but highly accurate way of saying that this rock is filled with garnet crystals. It was a favorite of Carolyn Olmsted. It is as if the boulder is the jewel and the island is the setting which she presented to the people of her beloved home-town island.

I find most appealing the idea that the otters have both a front door on the bay and, across the island, a back door facing the land. As I turn around and head home I realize that I read the path differently now. I see and register that I am seeing urchins, cracked mussel shells, crab bits, lobster claws, and rainbow piles of fecal material every so often. In the past we have wondered how crows could get quite so many shells so far above the tide. The dense canopy of spruces seems to point to some creature other than sea gulls dropping the bits.

At every promontory along the path—everywhere there is a lovely sea view—there is a toilet spot. Scraped bare, crowberry mat scuffed up, little brown moss tiles scattered, these spots are quite deliberately fashioned. Do they serve as territory advertisements for otters? I think with some amusement, irony really, of those rusting iron spikes, territory markers spaced out along this granite shore by the Olmsted firm, back about 1899, when a planned subdivision idea had been envisioned. The signs say this is otter territory now.

Skiing with Symbols

The birdbath wears a quite outlandish hat
and there's a foot of snow in the lawn chair's lap.
One black crow cawed by some time ago
but the only sound in this white world
is the hiss of skis and the creak of poles.

Passing into the temporary twilight
of the old logging road, I nod to weighted
spruce spires aproned low with white,
tracks of red squirrel, out before the fox,
and the crater whence the grouse exploded
from its powdered bivouac.

The slender wrist of willow
which the buck likes to rub
arches pinioned down by snow.

Surely that is asking it too much to bear
so I shake my sister loose, interfere
by beating birch tops free
with a rush of satisfaction that
clears the air like an apt apology.

How I am enlarged by wonder at these
ordinary incarnations of divine.
I feel my smiling face aflame
as I return, rejoin the cats who watch
from the windowsill without a word.

January Dusk

In the shadowing dark
no path promises to lead me home;
the antlered birches step aside,
hooves barely clicking in the quiet,
white rock unfolds hind legs,
moves off when I glance aside.

Ice shutters bog eyes which since noon
have been staring at the sun.
On owl wings the winter bat sky flies.
Shape-shifters all, shamans on the journey
on behalf of others,
risking night because we look away.

February — **Barred Island Preserve** — 12

This afternoon we are being hit with a bona fide blizzard. Snow is coming down fast. On our side of the Island, the lee, there is not much wind in the treetops, but the bay is seething with gun-metal-green waves from the north. An occasional gust lets me know that we may shortly be in for a big blow. A good day not to be a bird. How on earth did the Paleo-people ever manage northeasters?

The news is full of tales of New England and East Coast paralysis due to the storm. Last night we were scheduled for this first big snowstorm of the year. When we headed down to the Opera House for our pre-Valentine's Day coffee house performance, the nearly-full moon gleamed in a glittering cold, clear sky. With local musicians singing and playing their stuff, we presented a show of my poems and Ann's photos, our Island Valentine. By the time the show was over and we were headed home, there was a wondrous huge ring shimmering around the moon. This morning dawned ominous: grey and chill and damp. I am glad that the weather held off for the coffee house. The crowd was really pleased with being out, being together, being on an island, in spite of the considerable cold.

I have seen satellite images of winter cyclones. They look like a giant chambered nautilus on its side, poised out there over the whole of the Atlantic Ocean, with the mollusk's aperture, door, facing the Carolinas and the whole swirl over the back of the shell aimed right at Maine. That's a portrait of a northeaster, or as the fishermen here say it, no'th-east-ah.

While I work at the computer now, snug indoors, watching out the window as I write, I am treated to that especially *sumi-e* look of new snow painted with ink black of spruces. Ann phones to tell me she has just come in from photographing falling snow. She used to photograph snowflakes as a kid. She sounds delighted. I will work a little more and venture out myself. I love the sound of snow.

Reviewing my notes, I see that it was on February 4, just a year after we first met each other at the Chinese New Year's dinner, that Ann and I tracked the otters into the bog that lies on our back boundary with The Nature Conservancy's Barred Island Preserve. Under the canopy of alders and hidden behind a barricade of uprooted wind-thrown spruce stumps, we found the unmistakable signs of another grand toilet. It appears that the otters are in some sort of residence at Barred Island. We found their fresh tracks again yesterday.

I send Judy Hill an e-mail to tell her that the home insulation crew showed up at Heritage House just in time to get some of the work done before the latest temperature drop. Judy had come over for a lunch of seafood chowder last week and we discussed how to begin a "green retrofit" of Heritage House. We feel a responsibility to renovate the charming old house in a way that is also environmentally responsible. Heritage House can be a place to see some of the new eco-friendly building products of the past decade. Judy is especially eager to see the historical society's good work integrated with that of the land trust.

Island Heritage Trust and the Historical Society cooperated last summer on setting up Lee Fay's timeline garden at the Sellers house. The Trust bought very nice interpretive signs for the charming little gardens that Lee has created representing different time periods. It's fascinating to look at how fashions and practices in gardening have changed on the Island over the last century.

There is quite a variation in how sophisticated people are in their knowledge of natural history. In an era when many people equate "ecology" with "recycling" they can be forgiven that. It interests me that Frederick Law Olmsted so specifically referred to plant species as the palette with which he worked. Landscape is a form of art. At the end of his life when Olmsted accepted his last commission for landscaping the Biltmore estate of the Vanderbilts, the way he was working was certainly interesting. Much has appeared in print about Olmsted recently, quotes which show that Olmsted had come to see great value in native species for his palette. When we visited the Lenocis in Asheville we got further insights into Olmsted's development as a botanist and ecologist. His work was evolving into an early form of restoration ecology. He was exploring the relationship of landscaping to forestry.

We chose to deal with an area of extensive blow-down on our property around a unique and supremely handsome boulder outcrop in a way which pays tribute to Olmsted and this sensitivity to native species. The boulders form a dome reminiscent of Yosemite's Half Dome, only in miniature, Deer Isle-size. We cleared the debris and replanted with a few showy native plants, which have promise for landscapers. Just as Heritage House can be a place to check out some "green" retrofitting ideas, so this Boulder Garden is a place where landscapers can come to see what particularly decorative native species look like, green in several senses of the word.

We were surprised to read that Mary Olmsted had written in her diary that while waiting for their new home to be finished, she and Frederick had camped at those same Half Dome-like boulders. Mary wrote that they were reminded of Yosemite, where they had found great happiness when Frederick had been manager of the mine at Mariposa, essentially the forerunner of Yosemite National Park. Olmsted would no doubt approve of our land trust's efforts both to preserve natural beauty and to make the enjoyment of it available to all. FLO Jr's only child, Charlotte, was mother of the current owner of The Binnacle, Stephen Gill. Stephen, himself a generous supporter of IHT, takes pleasure in the fact that both Margaret and Carol had planned protection for Barred Island and had discussed it with him as eventual heir to their property. No wonder then that when Charles Bradford of the Maine Chapter of The Nature Conservancy came to give a presentation at the Stonington Methodist church, I heard Carolyn take him aside and say essentially, "I liked what you said and I want to talk to you about giving you my island." Land protection decisions are such a string of beads.

When it stops snowing—and before the next melt—I will take Ann on a loop through our prospective conservation easement and down the length of the preserve trail as well. Both Ann and I read the technical weather discussions on the Web. This winter a persistent upper atmosphere pattern over Hudson Bay and Labrador has been sending us cold air and bringing up great pendulum swings of warm moist air from the south. We've been reeling with the effects of one storm after another.

Either the coast gets hit with snow as the storms track down east, or the northern part of the low sends most of the snow off to the "County" where Ann was born and raised and they get the back side of the snow circle.

Not infrequently Ann and the peninsula get snow, while we down here on the Island get rain. This winter we seem to be getting snow, then some ice glaze, then more snow—or not. In Siberia they have been having record cold. In Montana buttercups have bloomed on a record early date in the Bitterroot Mountains. Last month was perhaps the warmest January on record here. Are we seeing natural weather fluctuations or the ominous foretaste of global warming?

The wind shakes the house and shrieks. There goes the power. Out.

* * *

The phone rings. "Marnie, this is Linda at the bank. When Ken was in the other day, he said you were looking to see otters. I just saw two of them at the Mill Pond dam." Talk about a small town!

Ann and I have been planning to spend the day at Barred Island Preserve, photographing the otter tracks we hope will be apparent at Barred Island after the new snow. We agree to meet at the Mill Dam. When I arrive, I recognize the car of a friend pulled over. When I get out of my car, wearing camera and binoculars, she rolls down her car window and without any introduction says, "They were just out on the ice, two of them. They'll be back," and with that she drives off.

They will be back? I hope so. I have never ever seen an otter, only tracks. There is no sign of otter. I think of how one finds elk or big horn sheep in the Rockies along the TransCanada highway. Stop where the other cars are. Five minutes crawl by. In the Serengeti you find lions by where the Land Rovers are. Five more minutes. No Ann. What if the otters have come and gone by the time Ann arrives? Ann's car pulls up.

Two otters pop up. Otters! I can scarcely believe it. They have the winsome face of seals. One has great whiskers—oh, that is a crab in its mouth. They have the curve of a harbor porpoise when they dive—and what looks like the tail of a rat goes into the water last! Other cars pull over. We are joined by other otter fans. The otters come over and give us a periscope look—curious, quite like a harbor seal. The otters seem not to mind our presence at all.

"Listen to that crab crunch," I say.

"And their snuffling breathing," adds Ann.

The otters are, of course, wet when they emerge. They seem to flow onto the ice and their fur gleams smooth in the sunlight. Not the least bedraggled looking. Grace epitomized. Again and again one slides off the ice shelf—and then the other—and both disappear into the water, only to reappear a minute later following each other. Enchanting.

After a ten minute romp, the pair disappears once more beneath the ice. Reluctantly Ann and I climb into our cars and head for our morning assignment. Now that the snow has settled a bit, Ann and I are going to check Barred Island again. The bar will not be long exposed so we have to stick to a schedule. Somewhat.

"Yesterday I skied to the bar to see if the otters had been out, but apparently they were still snuggled in somewhere," I say, getting out the skis and snowshoes. Ann tucks her camera inside her parka to keep it warm.

"The full moon reflecting on the water this morning at dawn was lovely," I rattle on. "Moonwake. The rising sun turns a window across the bay in Camden into a flaming red reflection for just a minute or two. When the setting moon casts a silver path on the bay and the hills are decorated with snow frosting, it's quite a sight."

I am grateful to see that today there is just sufficient snow to use our snowshoes. That's because the trail has been extremely icy lately. The spruces shade the trail so deeply that the sun scarcely shines on it to melt the trampled snow after a freeze. There are just enough contours, rocky ledges, bare roots, and raw boulder faces that the going had been quite treacherous the past couple of weeks.

"Did you hear that the official closing on the Scott's Landing property has actually come to pass?" I ask as we head off. "The terrain there is much kinder for the less nimble. I expect people will love it for its family friendliness. Not only will folks of all ages go there to pick blueberries and admire the flaming red wood lilies—without picking them I hope—but you'll be able to go there for winter walks. When we get snow, there's a good chance the cross country skiing will be passable."

Ann and I had discussed whether snowshoes, cross country skis, or hiking boots would be best for today's expedition. We'd loaded all three into the car, knowing that once we started out, no doubt we'd decide we made the wrong choice. We both keep our skis on our front porch so we can seize whatever moment presents itself. The private lanes leading to the unoccupied houses of the summer people offer the best skiing, but you have to be prompt! Putting a snowplow on the pickup truck is a good way to make extra money, so they're out plowing almost as soon as the second flake lies upon the first.

The parking lot here for Barred Island Preserve is small, sized right for about eight vehicles. The lot sits on the very narrow sliver of land that TNC owns here. It was designed by then-landscape architecture graduate school students Tom and Sarah Crowell—our son and his wife—to provide sufficient visibility for safety, with enough natural vegetation screening that it does not seem an eyesore. A screen of trees separates the lot from the main road. There's enough room to pull in and pull out, but parking a recreational vehicle would not seem like a good idea. There's also the question of the carrying capacity of the preserve. The small island and the small sand bar simply cannot offer too many people at once the kind of experience that they are hoping for.

The parking lot pattern has subsequently been repeated at other Island preserves. In this case, the site was determined by its being the only spot both flat enough to accommodate cars and also located in a safe spot for entering and exiting the lot. There was surprisingly little land to choose from. Much of what today's visitor sees along the wooded road is privately owned. Our perception of wilderness these days is largely an illusion. This small parking lot is too close to a cabin visitors never see, in the opinion of its owner, the nearest neighbor. He now hears visitors' car doors slam. The neighbor knows, however, that he could well have been cursed with worse neighbors, more high density development. He does appreciate that the protected mile-long strip of land makes Barred Island accessible to those not fortunate enough to own a boat.

A line of grouse tracks crossing the head of the trail immediately draws Ann's attention. She squirms into position to get the light just right to try to capture the feathery quality of the edges of the track. Ruffed grouse have remarkable winter-adapted, all-natural, scaly, built-in snowshoes on their feet.

There is a sign at the entrance to the trail asking dog owners to leave their pets at home, but we frequently see dog tracks on the sand bar. Not only that, we not infrequently meet owners with their dogs. I once had a college professor stand in front of the no-dogs sign with his own dog on a leash, happily telling me how his dog was different, no trouble at all. When I explained to him that ground nesting birds react to any member of the wolf clan, he was completely contrite. Dog owners have no idea just how many people visit the preserves these days. What a caloric cost there is for the animals which live here to react again and again to party after party of visitors. The trust tries to offer the resident animals some sanctuary.

People still hunt with packs of dogs here. Up until a year ago one particular Islander and his son insisted on bringing their hounds to the Barred Island Preserve. "It's traditional," he probably thought.

Eventually it came out that the family for whom he was winter caretaker expressed to him that they felt it more important to be good neighbors to the preserve, and they completely supported the preserve policy. Coming from an employer, this evidently carried some weight, as we have not heard those dogs nor met them in our yard lately.

Sunlight lines the gentle snow swells with blue shadows from the tree trunks. A scatter of spruce needles crosshatches the snow. Ann is in paradise.

"Did you call spruce needles sprills when you were growing up in The County?" I ask as she photographs.

"No, we called them spills."

"Did that apply to spruce or to pine?"

"Just spruce. All the pines were logged off long ago for the King's Navy."

The drifts look decidedly like sugar frosting spread over the boulders. The blue shadows etch an exotic calligraphy of complex lines.

"Slant light," says Ann happily behind her camera. To look into the snow shadows at the base of the boulders Ann flops down, not unlike my summer moss-watching team. She has made a funny snow angel. Ann says she wishes we had skis so we could schuss down a slight slope on the trail. I would not dare it.

"In some places yesterday there was not enough snow to ski on, but in other places it was perfect." I say. "The sound of skis on a powdered track is what I like best. The word 'susurration' sounds right for the waves in the background, but even that's much too loud for what I mean. Whisper 'hush' and then turn down the volume, and you've got it about right."

"Why of course," Ann smiles, "that would be how my friend, the poet, hears the snow." As we brush through a stand of juniper she can't refrain from exhaling, "Ah, can't you just taste that spicey aroma of the juniper berries?"

Tracks crisscrossing the trail are those of the red squirrels. Before snow season one can see sizeable middens of spruce cone scales at most of the higher spots in the preserve. They use these favored spots as lookouts while they tear apart the cones to get at the seeds. The smaller tracks emerging and lacing from tree base to tree base are those of the deer mouse, the cute ones, the ones with large, winsome looking eyes, the ones that move into empty cottages in winter and leave their calling cards. Locals quite logically call them house mice, but they are a different species. So too are the ones which tunnel out in the grasses a different species. Those mice are called meadow voles. They were the principal species that Ken was studying on the islands. I always thought they looked as if they had tobacco-stained teeth. They were quite pugnacious little thugs. Quite unfair characterization on my part, I admit.

One winter I did a little experiment of my own with these mouse tunnels. I spotted the quarter-sized holes at intervals throughout a meadow where we were skiing. Carefully I chopped a slab of snow crust with my mittened hand and laid the chunk softly on top of the hole like a hatch cover. Next morning I returned to see that mice had reopened every single hatch. I tunneled inside a few to see what was going on. I found there at each hole a chamber stained with yellow of urine. At other places were piles of brown droppings. The mice clearly liked a bathroom with a view. Now I'm sorry I bothered them.

The mice should see the bathroom views our otters choose! Ann and I maintain the fiction that we are just out to see what we can see, but we are both reeling from seeing the otters. She tells me that she read a report of an eagle having trouble carrying off an otter. Our otters may benefit from the protection of the Barred Island eagles. In the several years since the island has been largely off-limits due to eagle nesting, the otter signs around here have proliferated. When she phoned from the bank, Linda said otters were often reported in the Mill Pond in the village when she was a girl. We now see otter tracks on the preserve shore here, but that may be simply because we are here to look.

"It's like living with leopards," I say to Ann. I explain that in Kenya, we saw signs aplenty that there were leopards in close proximity with villages and our field camps, but only rarely did we see a leopard. In the parks where the guides took the tourists, the leopards seem to have acclimated to the park scenario and the guides radioed one another as to where the leopards could easily be seen.

"The guides never could get it through their heads that I spoke Kiswahili and could understand their conversations. 'Ah, yes, I think I have spotted the leopard up ahead in that tree. We are very lucky...'

they would say in an elaborate act. My brother does almost the same thing with his parties. 'Ah, yes, I think I have found some seals over there on those ledges.' Since the seals have quite traditional spots where they haul out, he's pretty certain of finding seals there. I don't think he ever pretends to have discovered the Barred Island eagles, but in just a few years he and most everyone else have gone from muttering that the eagles are a nuisance and interfere with recreation enjoyment, to saying they are very worried about whether or not the pair will reestablish their nest on Barred."

Ann and I climb somewhat clumsily up a swelling granite outcrop and find deer have been here first. They have pawed away the snow just like caribou. It looks as if they are eating the lichen popularly known as reindeer moss. Okay, so they are deer, not reindeer. And the plant in question is lichen, not really a moss. Reindeer lichen is a better name. The pale clumps of a true moss we find where the deer have trampled away the snow are pin cushion moss. Their distinctive silvery mounds protruding where snow is windswept are definitely a car window species. Up here where the wind has scoured the ledges bare we find what look to be owl pellets.

"I heard great horned owls hooting the other night," says Ann.

"The owls are probably courting. A friend says he had one attack him the other day when he went out to put his chickens back in the coop for the night. The owl was on a duck it had killed. When he tried to drive it off, the owl dived-bombed him. He said the owl came right at his face." I demonstrate ducking and covering my head. "He covered his eyes, but the bird dug at his scalp. He grabbed the owl by the leg. The bird was too strong for him and it flew away, but not before inflicting real scalp wounds on poor man."

I found owl pellets on the crowberry along the shore the other day. The tiny foot bones of what was perhaps a shrew looked almost like miniatures from a science fiction drama, some sort of other planet's creature with almost embryonic flippers. The tiny tooth of a meadow vole among the hairs in the pellet looked like a cow molar in miniature, with wavy parallel ridges. According to Ken, that makes them easy to identify.

Barred owls, too, know that in spite of appearances, it is spring. If Ann and I came back here at night with a owl recording, they would answer us with their characteristic four hoots. "Who cooks for you?" Ann imitates. I tell her about the doves in Africa which say the same thing. As women with good husbands who are learning to take a turn at cooking, we both chuckle. Ann, who loves puns more than anyone else I know, can't resist adding, "What a hoot!"

We detour onto the private property of Goose Cove Lodge so I can show Ann a special spot overlooking the cove and tell her what I call the Goose Cove Love Story. We settle ourselves on the colorful granite of a pair of benches situated under majestic spruces.

"This is the spot where Elli Pavloff most especially loved to come, to commune with her God, and honor the spirit of the place. George Pavloff, a quiet, contemplative and caring man, was director of a girls' high school when he met a vivacious woman named Eleanor who was applying for the job of art teacher. The two became friends for ten years, and after George left the priesthood, they married. This man who had grown up in an orphanage was utterly swept away by her love. Two more outwardly different but inwardly identically passionate people could hardly be imagined.

"They embarked on the grand adventure of innkeeping after a year-long search. George and Elli named their new venture the Pilgrim's Inn. Any traveler is a pilgrim if they but recognize the journey for what it may be. Elli, however, came to feel the sunset power of the western side of the Island as well. When the nature-oriented lodge at the end of the dead end road on Goose Cove came on the market, they bought that too. For two hectic years George and Elli and capable managers ran both inns simultaneously—until Jean and Dud Hendrick came to the Island to take up the dream of running an inn and took on the Pilgrim's Inn.

"Elli was in love with Goose Cove. She felt she had found her spiritual home in this spot where we are sitting. Elli was in every way substantial. She was outgoing and caring and demonstrative and made an ideal hostess for the hospitality business on which they were embarked. George found splitting and hauling wood to feed more than a dozen woodstoves at Pilgrim's Inn more than enough woods work, so he would never own a chain saw. He would probably have been content to stay 'in town,' a remark I have to make with a smile, Deer Isle village being what it is."

Ann smiles. "The first time I brought Charlie back to Maine, we stayed at Goose Cove Lodge. Our stay was magical. We hiked the Barred Island trail by moonlight as Elli had encouraged. I remember that in the morning fog we kayaked in absolute awe. The fog was so thick we could only hear, not see, the boats of the fishermen pulling their traps. We laughed, calling the lobster boats 'sea tractors,' since we were both farm raised. We were just getting used to the idea that these fishermen were going to be our new neighbors."

I think that the fishermen would not have been pleased had they known kayaks were out there in the fog waiting to be mowed down. Ann and I look out over the gentle waters of the cove, drinking in the beauty.

"Ah, beads and string," she says softly. "I feel I have come full circle now."

Chickadees calling everywhere demand our attention. For several weeks now they have been making their spring courting songs, a whistled "fee beee." I especially enjoy the fact that no matter how engrossed I may be with the treadmill of everyday affairs, these tiny birds are sure to be around to remind me that it's almost Valentine's Day and I should be thinking about making appropriate appreciative gestures to those I love.

"The birds know we're telling love stories," I laugh. "George had left the guest-greeting to Elli. Private to the point of being described as having a Mona Lisa smile, George kept himself—and his delicate but incisive wit—very much in the background. Together George and Elli raised an independent-minded daughter, Elena, and ran the business with all the usual challenges. Then Elli found out she had ovarian cancer, which was to prove quickly deadly.

"Elli rallied her friends to come and say goodbye. In her hospital bed in the upstairs apartment of the Lodge, Elli said in her characteristically loving, adventurous, and spiritually committed way, 'I am on the glory train.' She died in June of 1990. George later told their friends, 'She ran through the door to embrace the Christ who had enchanted her from early childhood.' George did eventually remarry. The lovely Linden, whom he met a year or so after Elli's passing, became George's wife.

"One of Elli's dreams was to share her beloved cove and forest with the economically disadvantaged. The Pavloffs toyed with the idea of developing affordable housing on Stinson Point. The State of Maine in its anti-sprawl zeal these days would be quick to point out that people would be better served if a soil map were consulted so proper septage could be chosen, so proper roads in and out could be laid out to service the new community, and so the existing old village could be supported rather than bled to death by the consequences of unplanned growth. Perhaps most importantly, new families could be encouraged to locate within walking distance of grocery stores, schools, and other social amenities.

"When Elli died, George took realistic stock of the situation. He owned a very valuable piece of real estate. Its true highest value might be to the soul rather than to the pocket book. He decided that he would be able to provide sufficiently for his daughter's needs, so he gave nearly fifty acres of beautiful coastal Maine to The Nature Conservancy that all might enjoy Barred Island in perpetuity. As The Conservancy changed its emphasis to larger bioregions, it, in turn, delegated management to our local land trust, a very satisfactory direction.

"Widower, all alone in the spotlight, George decided the lodge business was not for him. He sold the business after a careful vetting of prospective buyers and moved to Portland. There he does volunteer work as a religious minister in the Cumberland County Jail. George also works for the Catholic Bishop of Maine as canon lawyer on his marriage tribunal. George still returns for visits. Talented daughter Elena is making her way in the world of advertising quite happily in New York City. Every Christmas George sends the latest chapter in the children's book he is writing. No surprise that the book is a sensitive examination of the complicated choices facing youngsters in today's world.

"Subsequent lodge owners for a time sought to turn the once simple family-style accommodations into a luxury retirement condo village. That did not go over well with the community. George said he prayed to Elli to use her influence Up There to see that did not happen. Understandably the hospitality business is a tough one, but coastal Maine still seems to provide opportunities for some in that business.

"What the customers are buying is in no small way the ambience. Our preserves provide that for all the Island visitors, from near or far. In addition, preserves fulfill a niche both in their ecological function and in their aesthetic and psychological contribution. A mere 3 % of our Island— no matter how you calculate it, for the Island of Deer Isle or for the Town of Deer Isle—makes a contribution of inestimable value. The western edge of the Island every spring is host to a veritable wave of migrating warblers. Every fall a similarly amazing concentration of hawks comes funneling down our ridges to gather before the hawks head off over the bay on their way south. What a subtle but crucial part of a global net of beads and strings!"

Ann and I fall silent in our own spiritual moment.

Tracks leading down the long slope appear to be those of coyotes. Coyotes may be fairly recent arrivals on the Island. We read their tracks and find their scats. Occasionally someone reports hearing them "sing." That's a sound I love. Like the call of the loon, it is enough to make you shiver. I champion coyotes—which is somewhat out of fashion in the state of Maine—but even I admit to respecting their dramatically wolfish appearance. And we keep our cats indoors.

A single line of dainty tracks is unmistakably that of a fox. Like a coyote, the fox puts its hind foot in the same print that the forepaw makes. The fox too is no slouch at making crazy sounds. The foxes help us keep our resolve never to let our two house cats outdoors. How could any ornithologist in good conscience add cats to the list of challenges facing song birds today? Here on the Island, foxes cycle from boom to bust as mange periodically hits. In the good times, folks commonly report seeing them. Nothing in the world is cuter than fox kits. For some years we had a fox who asserted its ownership of the land to which we held a mere deed. In the late afternoons it would curl up on the lichens and blueberry mat just outside our window and go to sleep in the sun for an hour or so. Then it was off again on its rounds. More than once it trotted up on our deck to peer in the bedroom window.

I am always most uncomfortable at our national parks when something like a ground squirrel comes up and demands a handout. Other folks in the parking lot seem to think it's cute. They rummage around for some junk food. That makes me wince too. Coexisting with wildlife takes thought. Even the trails that we may cut into the heart of some of our preserves can serve as high speed access routes for house cats and raccoons. Penetrating into what were once safe retreats for such species as hermit thrushes, they make short work of the shy singers. Preserve managers now try to restrict trails to perimeters.

We are taking advantage of an old-fashioned trail. Naturalist Ralph Waldron, who built Goose Cove Lodge, laid out the first trail network. One of those trails, the one leading over to Crockett Cove, was named the "Wolfe Trail" in honor of his friend who joined in purchasing the land of Stinson Point, most of which ultimately became Goose Cove Lodge property. Dr. Wolfe's daughter, Ronnie, and her family still own and cherish that point of land between Goose Cove and Crockett Cove.

Walking the trails of the old Goose Cove Lodge trail system, I often thought Dr. Waldron had planned a detour to every plant of interest, or else he was trying to maximize the time people could spend on trails. The only map available in the early days was hopelessly inaccurate and confusing, adding to the labyrinth-like quality of the experience. Guests were constantly getting lost and ending up at our house. We could never adequately direct them back through the maze. There was nothing for it but to take them back ourselves.

When a complete Gazeteer of Maine was first published, it erroneously showed a road to Barred Island going through our back yard, which meant even more disappointed visitors. When The Conservancy acquired the land access, they closed all the side branches of trail and devised one long relatively straightforward route. That strategy has been quite satisfactory. I should speak for myself. Now people end up in Lenocis' driveway instead of ours, I suppose. Dr. Waldron's grandchildren own cottages down on the point and they report visitors quite obligingly polite about observing preserve boundary signs.

    The trail on which Ann and I make our way cuts right down the entire length of the preserve. At least the streamlined version of the trail is not a motor highway cutting the preserve in two. Often species refuse to cross such a barrier or get killed by traffic if they do try. Shades of our night at Settlement Quarry with the salamanders! I've seen cat tracks—the domestic sort—only occasionally in the woods around here, and not in the preserve yet, but I suppose given the ring of houses surrounding the woods, creeping down the point, someday more cats are inevitable. We have seen feral cat tracks in the most amazing spots.

    Ann and I skirt the cove, pausing to admire the view of Mark Island Light, Scraggy Island beyond, and make a quick survey for loons. There's one—and another—and we scan the sky for any signs of eagle.

    "Charlie Todd says we may see eagles carrying sticks for new nests. They fly straight to the site that they have picked. Lee has been seeing them hanging around Barred, so they may be planning to rebuild here."

    The sand bar itself is just emerging. We have timed it so we catch the last of what I call the "zipper phenomenon." This is one of my favorite of all natural phenomena around here. As the tide comes or goes, waves cover or uncover the bar in a sequence that zips or unzips the path. Ann and I observe that waiting for a break in the waves as the tide goes out enough to let us onto the bar is quite like the hummingbirds famous for flying through a ventilating fan into a local nursery's greenhouse: doable if you time everything just right. Since we are on our way onto the island rather than off, we cannot miss.

    The wet sand is littered with clam shells bigger than the palm of my hand, what I now think are surf clams which dwell in fairly deep water. I've decided they were probably nearly exposed by the recent "moon tide." Since they don't bury themselves very deep in the sand, they might have been fairly vulnerable to predators. From the looks of the clambake, clearly something has been harvesting them. I pick one up and show Ann, explaining how Richard Penfold of Stonington Sea Products, a prize-winning artisan seafood craftsman, taught me how to deal with the oysters now harvested from the bay.

"Richard was brought here from England to oversee the salmon smoking. He really loves sea food. It's fun to talk with him about his craft. First he says that you should store oysters domed side down so they can rest in their own juices. To open an oyster, you insert an oyster knife—or any stout blade slimmer than most screwdrivers—at the oyster's hinge place. That means you rock the blade tip until you can find the sweet spot, the groove between upper and lower shell. A slight twist, and it opens enough that you can then slide in the blade and sever the adductor muscle, after which the oyster opens fairly easily."

Ann doesn't seem convinced that it is easy. We inspect a surf clam's hinge place, but it is at the far end from where the gnaw marks are. What can an otter use for a knife having neither teeth nor claws that seem as long as a screwdriver? But the teeth of these river otters must be long enough and strong enough! California sea otters manage to pry abalones off the rocks and crack them on their chests. We see that many of the shells of mussels and surf clams here on the beach are cracked in addition to being opened. Do otters somehow vacuum-suck out the contents? Amazing. I wedge a big clam shell pair into my pocket to show Richard.

"The Barred Island eagles had seemed to be managing well enough until their nest tree blew down," I observe. "They seem to be adjusting to the fact that we humans live here too. All winter people have been reporting seeing eagles. Several eagles seem to fly daily from Burnt Cove, over Crockett Cove Woods and the cove itself, past our house, and on up the island."

Ann has an eagle nest near her home on the Bagaduce River. She has her camera ready, but just now we see none of what look like flying diving boards. We do see signs of otters. There are several tummy slide marks down the little island's sloping granite and into the sea. Water slides! I show Ann the urine stains and bloody-looking patches in the toileting area, and we follow clear tracks leading right across

Barred Island, all the way from the ocean-facing entrance under the spruces across to where the trail emerges from the trees at the land-facing entrance. The tracks are obviously fresh. Since I was checking down here yesterday and saw none, we know these tracks were made last night or early this morning. Were the Barred otters on their way to the Mill Pond? We like to think the otters who claim this place are the same otters we just saw. I enjoy sharing the joys of discovery of this private otter lair with Ann. Although most of the tracks and otter signs are not photogenic, Ann is properly intrigued.

"It is becoming apparent that we are interviewing otters for their special insight into the place," I say, only half joking. "The river otter makes a great symbol, icon, mascot for the preserves. A land mammal, the river otter is associated with fresh water, and here we find it using the marine environment of our bay. Talk about the ecological importance of interfaces!"

The bar would give us several more hours on the island, but now the sun is paling and the temperature is dropping, so we retrace our steps. We began our pilgrimage around Deer Isle in March because that is when Basho and Sora set out on theirs. Now with February, the year has gone round a complete cycle. Is February a beginning or an end? The days now definitely give the feeling that the dark season is behind us. I know that today would have been a day when the maple sap ran, if one had sugar maples. I do miss them here on the Island.

A duck heads in, low over our heads, wings whistling—a golden-eye, the "whistler." The western light of late afternoon spangles the wet shore pebbles. Because it is an especially low tide, wavelets run along a lower "bench" at the edge of the bar with a soft hiss. How these outings deliver!

Ann and I head back along the shore, leaving the preserve. We inspect Lenocis' empty house as we plod along their driveway. I explain to Ann that Lenocis chose to situate their home right next to the old road which runs from Barred Island to Felsted. We pointed out to the Lenocis before they built that as owners of the land along the way, our property came with a legal right of way to the island. They are pleased to have the steward of the preserve watching out for them as well, and we are not likely to choose that direct route during the summer when they are in residence. Neighborly cooperation is still something to be cherished. We cooperated with them in siting their septic system. That meant the woods between us was not further subdivided by road and clearing, preserving a larger block of habitat undisturbed.

I recount to Ann the story of meeting the Lenocis in the woods here when they were first looking at the property. For much of his career, Bill managed his firm's southern headquarters in Asheville, North Carolina. In addition to raising their three strapping sons, June served on the board of the Asheville land trust. Bill likes to tease me about how less than subtle I was about what qualities I thought Deer Isle was expecting in would-be residents. He knew "green" when he saw it!

Lenocis have more than met my hopes. To begin with, they discovered that a kiosk in the Bangor Airport was advertising for sale the land next to what they were purchasing. A little checking revealed that The Nature Conservancy's property line actually ran across the north shoulder of the overlook knoll. The knoll is a key part of the preserve since it overlooks Barred Island and the entire sea view. A house lot inserted there would also have overlooked the windows of any home the Lenocis might build. They let the owner know that trying to squeeze another lot out of the site would put the sale of the prime house lot in jeopardy.

Ken and I had unsuccessfully tried to interest the previous land owner in making a donation to The Nature Conservancy. "I don't do charity" had been the initial response. On the other hand, eventually the seller calculated what the tax would be on the hefty capital gain he would be making on the sale of the one lot. A donation which the IRS probably would recognize as a charitable contribution became quite an appealing prospect.

I consider this another story where everyone wins. The preserve got a donation that guarantees the integrity of its holdings. The donor received some sweetening from the Internal Revenue Service. The town gets tax revenue from the lovely home the Lenocis built in the same shingle Cottage style as Felsted, just down the shore. The Island got a couple who are both generous and interested in supporting the community. People like the Lenocis do not send children to the school system and do not make much demand on town services. The influx of retired couples like them is not in itself sufficient to keep the community vital and flourishing, but this is much preferable to large scale development of gated communities of disinterested folks.

Bill and June are generous about contributing to local needs. They know well the importance of a well-endowed local health center, June having faced several trials of her own. They are also keen supporters of cultural opportunities for our young people. June was formerly very involved with the symphony in Asheville and now enjoys the Kneisel Hall summer festival concerts here. The Lenocis give to the community as well as partake in its pleasures, a pattern of commitment which makes them welcome additions to the Island even though they divide their time, spending part of the year in warmer climates. I, however, do not wish I were anywhere else, not even somewhere else for winter. Ann says she could not agree more.

Ann and I follow the trail along the shore to what we call the Old Man of the Bay. Now that New Hampshire has lost its Old Man of the Mountain on Crawford Notch, our small version here on the shore looking west seems a lonely hermit. This Old Man has snow on his nose. The rocks along the shore glisten with gold and creamy stalactite-like ice coatings, frozen runoff from land. Here the runoff is probably not carrying invisible toxic runoff. This area faces a deep underwater channel, what I call the Sellers Trench. I don't think fishermen are quite ready to set aside an area as a marine preserve here, but what a candidate! Here where the Barred Island Preserve offers protection from overdevelopment, the interface between terrestrial and marine habitats might make the idea effective.

The shadows of rusted iron rods along the shore attract Ann. I remind her of our first journey along this shore by boat when I pointed out that these were drilled and inserted at intervals from here to Felsted in an Olmsted development scheme which did not come to fruition. "According to Stephen Gill, the Olmsted brothers' firm—FLO Junior and John Olmsted—was ultimately responsible for some 160,000 projects, including 650 parks and park systems, an outstanding contribution to our country's landscape architecture."

While Ann photographs, I add "I'm just as glad that this particular development did not happen. The Lenocis joined us in putting a conservation easement on this stretch of shore and Ken and I are now completing the gift to IHT of another easement on 28 acres of our woods and our half of a small bog."

This whole neighborhood is a relatively unsettled strip of coast, with the two preserves—Barred and Crockett Cove Woods—and several conservation easements protecting nearby islands. Yes, the otters and the eagles do seem to have a knack for choosing protected lands. It helps that most people here take pride in seeing our national symbol soar overhead. They grudgingly or proudly seem to have concluded that it is well worth the slight inconvenience of sharing Barred Island.

We come upon more otter tracks in the vegetation and bare scrapes just above the pink granite shore rocks. Last year I followed tracks of two otters from Barred Island all along this shore. They laced in and out the trees, scooted along the shore, and followed my tracks right up to the house. Ken had tried a ski run or two down our slope. The otters agreed with him and did a slide run there. They came onto the deck. They peeked in the compost pile and inspected the birdbath. Then they took off down our driveway and headed down the road. I could see where they turned into the bog. The otters think they own what was the Olmsted estate.

Our new conservation easement will include much of the forested back-land which was once Olmsted's estate here. The acreage contains the only pool of drinking water for the preserve. What we call the Black Lagoon functions as a vernal pool, supplying the preserve with a full complement of salamanders and wood frogs. The wooded area provides a habitat patch of a much more useful size than the narrow strip which is actual preserve. And the otters evidently want the bog.

Ann stops to photograph the snow-laden bent willow branch across the path. I explain that this little tree was a favorite buck rub before it broke off. Why they prefer these small willows, I have no idea. Two summers ago we found large tracks of a moose pressed clearly in the damp sphagnum moss here on the remnants of what June Lenoci calls the Mossy Way. This path, uncut for fifty years, remains clear through the woods. It has a very romantic, Victorian post card look about it. Once it may have carried buckboards on picnic outings for Frederick Law Olmsted and his family and friends. Then in the fifties it was the principal logging road when the area was cut for spruce pulp. Here and there you can still find enormous old yellow birch trees, and all along the way younger birches sprout in odd shapes, recovering from wounds of the logging days.

We puzzle over fox and coyote scat. "Once I found a bear scat pile by the bog, and cat scratches on spruce trunk back in there. Elli Pavloff once saw a bobcat in these woods."

"That would be fun to see."

Distinctive prints of snowshoe hares appear across our path. There can easily be six feet between hops. The furry prints of their natural snowshoe feet are amazingly huge. They could be mistaken for coyote tracks especially after a warm day since all tracks look larger when they melt out. One unaccustomed to the winter woods might be forgiven for unease.

"What sort of fierce predator is out here? You want me to believe it is only the Easter Bunny? Come on. This year Easter comes very early. Snowshoe hares will probably still be white. They are the only species of rabbit we have here."

I'd love to spot a hare just now so Ann could photograph it. Last fall I was surprised on one of my rambles to spot a white quartz rock where I had not known one. Of course, when I looked again, the "rock" was hopping away. The snowshoe hares come to the small square of grass that we keep, a token lawn where we play croquet on summer evenings. We have to clap our hands at them to keep them anything like respectful. They too think they own the place, which they do.

I realize that wildlife watches us far more expertly than we humans watch wildlife. "Once when we were sitting out enjoying the winter sunshine with a mug of steaming tea, a chickadee flew to Ken's jacket collar and plucked off a hair, presumably for its nest building. Islanders are convinced that wildlife is tamer on this side of the bridge."

"Brigadoon!" Ann laughs.

When I was first married and moved to the woods of Vermont, I tamed the chickadees. They would come to my hand to eat sunflower seeds. We have a photograph of me holding up binoculars and a chickadee sitting on the glasses peering into them back at me. When a hunter came to the house and told me how surprised he'd been that the chickadees were chasing him, I decided perhaps I had been unwise. We still feed the birds, but we no longer tame them or allow them to become too comfortable with us.

For a while we fed the crows and ravens scraps we got from the butcher. Ken was particularly interested in watching their behavior. We had to give it up, however as the sea gulls caught on. A neighbor was feeding the gulls, and they had become quite acculturated. They always knew when we had food out and they were quite the pests. Maine doesn't need overwhelming numbers of "garbage gulls" again. Gull numbers on the coast have dwindled back to more reasonable numbers now that open dumps are no longer permitted. No bird is more lovely than a back-lit white-winged adult herring gull soaring over the sea. But in moderation, please. We humans make such messes when we put our thumbs on the scale of nature's balance, intentionally or not.

"Several folks on the Island are feeding mallards these days, and Brad Allen of the Department of Inland Fisheries and Wildlife tells us that mallards are getting very plentiful. He says hybridization with black ducks is a big issue, especially where black ducks are getting more rare— as in the Mississippi Flyway. Genetically the two species are extremely similar. The department does not recommend feeding of course. They also find that hunters selectively take mallards whenever possible, but they certainly take their share of black ducks and the department has the band recoveries to prove it. The challenge is to see what percentage of the population is being taken by hunters and to be sure that is within allowable limits for adult mortality of a long-lived species. Confounding the black duck decline is the fact that black-backed gulls now eat more than 90% of the ducklings in the bay. Compared with 20 years ago, even the eider populations are now much reduced. Black ducks don't need humans to make matters worse. Birders always express their worries at our annual Christmas Bird counts."

As we crunch along the shore trail back to my house, I describe to Ann our lunch date with Judy Hill the other day, our seafood chowder. "Ken confessed to her that when he and a student came up one spring vacation to do some carpentry work on the Thistle, our little house on the Pressey Village cutoff road, before the little boys and I took up summer residence, they stopped over to see Clark and Marjorie Hill, Judy's parents. As luck or hope would have it, the two young men were just in time to be invited to share a supper of fish chowder. Marjorie Hill was well acquainted with the prodigious appetites of young men, having served Francis Williams mid-day meals as he logged the woods next door, the lands which eventually became Shore Acres Preserve.

"It was Francis who put in the corduroy on the road Ken remembered in Crockett Cove Woods, once the family property of the Williams. It was Francis who lumbered the woods from Felsted to Barred Island for Arthur Barter. It is interesting how the cycles of tree growth and regrowth, and the economics of timber harvest determine the fate of development or preservation of natural areas. Areas that Ken once censused as blow-downs are now marked on his maps as grow-ups.

"As young teenagers, Judy told us, she and her sister Lib and a friend from the French Camp bicycled over to see what was then the Mott Cottage, next door to our lot. To their embarrassment they encountered a party, ladies having luncheon on the lawn. The hostess said to us, 'Can I help you?'

"How often I've used just this line on the folks who come exploring down our lane and end up in our laps. Sometimes they actually are lost.

"Judy said to us, laughing, 'A fabulous fib just flashed into my head and I said, 'Oh, our parents are considering buying this place. We have come to see if we would like it.' We were shown all around, inside and out. Salt water plumbing and all."

"We had heard tales that there had been a system next door to pipe salt water into the house. We had presumed it was for the bath tub, to take advantage of putative healthful effects of salt water bathing."

Gleefully I explained to Ann that some years ago when Ken and Tom and I spent a week in a nature photography seminar sponsored by Cornell University on the Isle of Shoals, we discovered that the toilets were operated with salt water. When you flushed the toilet in the middle of the night, the bowl would glow. This was because the phytoplankton in the water were triggered by turbulence into bioluminescence, light produced by living creatures. It is thought that perhaps phytoplankton have evolved using a chemical reaction similar to that in glow sticks, as a sort of motion-detecting device. When predatory tiny crustaceans called copepods come after the plankton, they find that the "security light" turns on, exposing them instead to their predators. Ken thought I had developed a severe case of diarrhea the night I first observed the phenomenon. Flush! Flush! Flush!

I wonder who it was here on the Island that Reeds and Motts socialized with in those early Gatsby-esque days. Flamboyant display of wealth was not at all the behavior of the restrained Old New Englanders of Dunham's Point. And even less was that the style of Arthur Barter, the man who literally owned most of the Island real estate. Daily he went to work at his hardware store in grey Dickey work clothes.

I smile to think of Judy and her sister and friend brazening their way into a house tour. Inspecting big new houses in off season or under construction is still an Island favorite sport. The big house next door stood empty when we first came to take up residence here. Then a couple from Texas bought the place. He rode a big, loud motorcycle to get his mail—two miles down the road—at the tiny Sunset Post Office, which was far smaller than his garage. Locals were amazed when they paid good money to have their already large dining room enlarged to accommodate a larger table, or was it a larger painting? Any way, it was a larger something. And they put in a Texas-scale ranch gate over the end of the driveway. They could be thought of as just a bit ahead of time, ahead of the era of multimillion dollar mansions and egos. The story goes that the Texan quarreled with Neville Hardy, the head selectman, about his tax assessment.

"Who says this place is worth a million dollars?"

"You did, when you bought it."

"And that," they say, "is why those Texans moved off the Island, went back up the coast, nearer Portland." Well, that's how they like to tell it.

The return trip seems to take Ann and me half the time of the way out. Isn't that always how it seems? Nowhere on this 12 mile by 12 mile island can you go for a very long hike. Our natural areas are all very moderate, both in size and in character. They are nonetheless valuable for that.

Ann now has lots of pictures. Did you see this, Ann? How about this? Did you capture this? Ann no longer has to keep putting on a tactful smile at such queries. She no longer asks me "What's this?" when I share some further nugget of information which fascinates me. Of course Ann has seen "this." She always does. She is always interested in what interests me. That's why we are so happy to work together.

We have a nicely packed track to clomp along on. We snowshoe in silence. Neither of us feels the need to voice how refreshed our outing has made us feel. You could read it on our faces. Humble pleasure, yes; small, but grand.

We fall eventually into discussion about the challenges of collaborating, another serendipitous example of how we often find ourselves thinking the same things at the same time. As a psychologist Ann speaks often about appropriate boundaries. I tend to think of Unitarian Universalist one-ness, or even Zen none-ness. But coming from our opposite directions, we have discovered, Ann and I, that we particularly enjoy and appreciate working together. Her pictures are a distinctive way of seeing things; my voice suits our projects. Why, we ask ourselves, do we need both—the verbal and the visual? Words add depth, another layer of meaning to photographs. I have been teased that my poems sometimes read like a biology lesson. I agree. My poems often refer to scenes from nature that are now, however, unfamiliar to many. Ann's photos make these images more available, more understandable.

We live now in an age of movies' ascendant over books. Ann and I enjoyed experimenting making a trailer of our poems and photos to be shown in the Opera House the weeks before our appearance in the Valentine coffee house, but it felt mildly like consorting with the enemy, making that tiny little movie. Ann and I agree that verbal and visual are properly regarded as a draw. We aim for a perfectly equal partnership. When we go out, Ann always has a pencil and paper in her camera case. She writes poems. I often have a camera around my neck. I take pictures. We find, however, that we consistently choose her photos and my words for this project. Ours has been a companionable pilgrimage.

Ann says, "I think of pilgrimages as journeys undertaken toward a spiritual goal of discovery, awareness, perspective, depth of understanding. The goal would include a spiritual growth that would benefit others, if only by the changed individuals being in the world."

"People go on pilgrimages for a lot of reasons," I suggest.

And Ann adds "Including the fun of going on a guided group tour to a place where they can dress up in an exotic identity and wear it for their own social enhancement, whether it is really a good fit or not." More seriously she adds, "Ordinarily I don't do group tours or guided travel. Usually for me it's pretty much a solo trip."

I recognize that feeling. Our collaboration is for both of us a bit of an exception. Like the other valuable relationships in our life, we find this one takes considerable care and attention.

"It feels like a duty and a privilege, having worshipped the things of our natural earth since my beginning." continues Ann. "Safeguarding the net."

We press our snowshoes atop more snowshoe hare tracks. It's cold now. Our breath comes in visible clouds. Clouds of living being. Clouds of being. I exist somewhat in a cloud of being, both in the dimension of time and of space. My grandparents and my parents loved me with as much reality as anyone now. When I am gone, there will be some reality of me in the minds of my own children and grandchildren and any surviving peers. On this very day, I am somewhat in the minds of people I know in quite disparate places around the globe. What I regard as my physical body is a cloud of living entities: white blood cells roaming around my capillaries, neurons stretching and knitting here and there, uninvited bacteria and viruses and even some which might more accurately be regarded as cultivated, welcomed, if not invited. Bone marrow is creating cells of me even as skin is sloughing off cells of me. Oxygen and carbon dioxide molecules are constantly in a state of becoming me, becoming not me.

I can only think of *me* as a description of a system, a cloud of being, over time and space. Various religions around the world have quite lovely metaphors for this thinking, often involving the term "soul," a wheel of recurrent being, or a jeweled net wherein each node reflects all others, or a precious father-son relationship, fractal in nature and extending to all generations. Not being trained in religion I cannot venture there. Since I cannot even think of this grand system of systems in very precise language, I certainly cannot speak it, write it.

But I feel it. I have only to look at certain of Ann's photographs to have all the emotions and the envelope brought keenly to my awareness. Her images bid me pay attention to the shape of shadow across what I may have casually taken for reality. I have only to watch a bird fly across the sunset in autumn, or watch an ant climb up a fern on a spring morning to feel keenly the essence of being alive.

I did not ask for or earn the privilege of existing. I feel a sense of duty, a need to give thanks for the privilege, a responsibility to preserve the options for others, to honor and safeguard the net. Stewardship commanded by a higher power? Generosity? Altruism? Self preservation? Selfish survival of the genes?

One of the beauties of a net, a self-regulating system, is that responsibility is shared. I as a lonely individual do not feel I have to answer precisely the grand questions of life. I live in a world now that has a long history of religions and legions of philosophers. We can pool our thinking. I live with the gifts of many artists, both verbally and visually talented. I look at the paintings, the photos, and make the poems which express something of the feeling. We write the essays which explore something of what makes the experience.

I have come to feel a satisfying kinship with the people I have encountered on this pilgrimage. I feel a close connection likewise with the natural areas and all the creatures I recognize living there. Beads on the strings that make the net.

Profound Cold

Like a clattering Chinese bird toy
whirled on a string
crossbills circle the spruce tops,
red and merry and utterly without
foreboding

but just before dark, great rolls
of cloud rear up across the bay,
threatening snow squalls
which never come.

Dawn shrieks in the rattling trees;
my huddled bones know
I will wake to see
Dead Men Walking

the bright bay—
pale skeins
of frozen fog—
indifferent beauty,
deadly silent universe.

AFTERWORD

Farewell, I say. From here, we go our separate ways. I will not be coming back over the bridge with you, but will go back to my hermitage, to telling my own beads for whatever length of string is allotted to me. The strings of 108 devotional beads of Buddhists known as *mala* are offered these days for sale at temples throughout China. In Japan today one presumably accumulates merit as well as collecting a variety of special miniature items as the pilgrim does the round of these spiritually significant sites. Basho doesn't tell us that he and Sora collected anything other than poems and paintings on their round of temples.

Ann and I have finished our round of special places, collecting words and photographs. Look at what we have here. Our preserves are an amazing gift to the island. What poetry they speak to us. Hiking all our preserves is not as grand an enterprise as peak bagging, climbing all 46 of the High Peaks in the Adirondacks or all 284 of the Munro peaks in the Scottish Highlands. But, visiting natural areas is a worthy and attainable goal wherever we are. The really significant thing is to look around at our protected islands and conserved lands and historic sites, and to realize that any place on the globe is a bead on the string of the jeweled net.

And you? Farewell and all good wishes go with you—and yours. We are all quite familiar with signs and brochures in this country asking the visitor to take nothing but photographs and leave nothing but footprints. By now you may realize that it may not be quite that simple. First you find yourself giving your heart to a place. Gradually you find yourself becoming another bead in the necklace of those who make a lasting contribution to the welfare of the world for generations to come. Be warned: be welcome.

I read our metaphor of beads and string whenever I look at a map of our part of Penobscot Bay with its generous spangle of islands. It comes naturally to think of a special place, a flower, a sight or an experience in the natural world as a gem. We have come to recognize that Place and Time string together various people who are certainly gems of being. I have also recognized that we who love this place are linked, even as we sort ourselves into strands that favor birds or trees or sea creatures. Perhaps we sort ourselves by primary interests such as recreation, natural history or cultural history. We may sort ourselves by whether we think in terms such as the Gulf of Maine, the State of Maine, Penobscot Bay, or Deer Isle, our Island.

Many have a rather unfortunate habit of thinking that the play begins when we ourselves come onto the stage. I therefore feel obliged to point out that when I string the memory beads of land conservation here, I find the string worth retelling is very long. This is, after all, the country of the New England town commons, the state of Governor Percival Baxter who set aside Mt. Katahdin. My personal recall begins with the early days of the Maine chapter of The Nature Conservancy, which was formed in 1956 and was, for some years, essentially the only land protection game in town.

I remember when Maine Coast Heritage Trust was a new idea. That was 1970. When we first asked about joining a Deer Isle effort with theirs, Maine Coast Heritage Trust told us to be patient. As the land trust idea matured, we would build sufficient numbers, amass sufficient energy as it were, for the tasks that would confront us. We watched and learned from Blue Hill Heritage Trust, first on the peninsula. Their first acquisition was probably a gift of land along Camp Stream courtesy of the Crowells.

Over time we came together on this side of the bridge as well, an awesome and varied string of people united by a common love of place. And what energy! In 1987 our Island Heritage Trust was formed. Early stalwarts who should not be forgotten include some who acted as paid staff—Stephanie Levy, who pioneered taking nature activities into our schools—and others like genial early president Rowan Wakefield who did far more than anyone can be paid to do. His petite wife Barbara was one of the Pressey village Presseys. Indefatigable volunteer Ruth Harris returned to the island of her Small forbears and created an invaluable data base for the Trust—a data base which she and Rowan generously made available to both the Memorial Ambulance Corps and the fledgling Island Medical Center. Jean Shepard Welch, Trust secretary, who only recently retired from the Trust board, lent her gentle spirit for many years. Lloyd Capen was an Islander who returned after a career as elementary school principal in Massachusetts. He settled in to raise apples here, hardly an undemanding retirement, with all his volunteer activities. Pilgrim's Innkeeper Dud Hendrick somehow found time for the trust, especially if it meant flying over properties in his plane. Cherie Mason served the Conservation Commission as well as the Trust before turning her attention to radio station WERU and MERI, the Marine Environmental Research Institute. The mark of retired architect Don Reiman can be seen all over the island—in such buildings as the Chase Emerson Library addition, in the Deer Isle Congregational Church sanctuary renovation, and in various preserve kiosks. Far too many to catalog here, the list goes on, rising and falling like the tides, celebrating successes, weathering storms.

What motivated these people you are joining, those who worked to have these preserves set aside, and those who so loyally provide stewardship for our preserves with their time and their money? The list is not a portfolio of millionaires or billionaires. More than one of these good people at one time felt forced to do something like selling some of their beloved land to pay the bills, and perhaps that helped them come to the realization that something formal had to be done before our Island all gets sold away.

There is no way to give a complete answer explaining why we do things. However, several threads seem to connect the stories here. Those most interested in social justice quickly point out how the natural areas benefit those who don't have their own access to the healing natural spaces. The biologist is apt to consider first the plants and animals which need refuge and provide stability for our biosphere. The people born here who have seen change sweep over the Island with amazing and alarming and ever-increasing pace may want a sanctuary that has at least the appearance of stability, a place that stays looking the same, with continuing access to what they emotionally perceive as theirs. The person who has most recently come over the bridge gets accused of the same desire: close the gate now that I am here because the Island is just right and should be kept that way.

All of these ideals have a worthy component, and none can be realized completely in our world today. The window of opportunity may have lasted just fifty years. That is the approximate post-war span of years when we felt buoyantly optimistic. We saw the development of various mechanisms to take care of preserved lands—land trusts, conservancies, and town and state park-like entities. Government at all levels rewarded land protection with at least some tax incentives. One did not make a profit by philanthropy, but at least the gift was acknowledged. Today our coastal real estate tax situation has grown so onerous and complicated, the price of real estate has risen so high, and the number of large tracts has shrunk so dramatically that perhaps the window of opportunity here has indeed closed. Is this the end of the story?

Post 9/11, the island has seen noticeable numbers of summer people opting to stay here beyond their vacation, urgently instructing builders to add insulation and make other improvements to their homes so they could take up residence. The "pig in the python" or "bump in the boa" that represents the Boomer Generation is now retiring. Where to? We are on the map. New people are constantly showing up to join our community. We now have "weekenders" from the small but nearby cities of Bangor and Ellsworth coming in to buy second homes. Even the geocachers have found us!

I am sure that Islanders will continue to welcome newcomers who wish to become part of our community. We do have some notion of diversity. Islanders have always been surprisingly cosmopolitan in their own low key way. Island men captained fishing boats, formed the crew of the America's Cup defenders and of many sailing yachts of the wealthy. Deer Isle men served round the world in the wars and the merchant marine. We watched another sort of general opening to outsiders when significant numbers of Islanders became snowbirds, themselves seasonal "people from away" somewhere else.

I have flown in a plane over the beaches of Florida north of Miami where I spent all my childhood winters, and seen only a solid line of high rises. I have visited the island of Hong Kong, about the size of Deer Isle, now packed with gleaming new towers in almost incomprehensible density. I am not predicting that Deer Isle will be paved over in such degree, but I do suspect the years of setting aside large natural areas here on Deer Isle are coming to an end.

Ecologists call islands "depauperate," that is, having few species in comparison with similar areas on the mainland. That makes island populations especially vulnerable to perturbations and especially interesting to scientists who are trying to figure out what is the significance of islands of habitat on the mainland. For most of the years I have walked around this island, people who live here would tell you that, for good and ill, what makes this place different is that there aren't too many people. The 1939 opening of the bridge was viewed as hugely significant. Everything from the arrival of skunks to the arrival of New Yorkers has been attributed to that.

You don't need much of a backpack or provisions to hike around this necklace of island natural areas. We will certainly need more science and more political experimentation to keep coping with changing challenges headed our way. We are all, as a nation, as a globe, waking up after years of the illusion of endless resources. We see the dawning of the new age of options. Is this a new era or merely a precious instant? Who knows?

I am aware that it has been both a blessing and a burden to have lived to see two ways from this mountain that is an island: back to the past and forward to the future. Just as I graduated from high school in Haddonfield, New Jersey, the peach orchards out by the traffic circle became a gleam in a developer's eye: Cherry Hill, one of the oft-cited landmarks marking the beginning of the "mall-ing" of America. In Maine the process has been slower, but sprawl is trying to spread even to our island doorstep.

We are realizing that food locally produced might be better for us than relying totally on our newly global food system. So too, a complex of "middling" local preserves—under a hundred acres—close by wherever you may live, might be a good thing. Deer Isle shows that there seems to be a role for preserves sized somewhere between national parks and small urban refuge pocket parks. Can that happen elsewhere? You, dear Reader, may still have some opportunities wherever you live. It may be possible if you and other ordinary folk like you, like us, put heads together—and then pocketbooks.

In *Greener Pastures*, my first book, I claimed that any pasture is worth greening. The book, about living in an old farmhouse on the edge of the Adirondacks, shares stories of the place and the lives of my neighbors from that time in my life. A reporter once asked our son David, "What's it like having your mother write a book about you?" "Oh," he answered, "we do all the stuff; she just writes it down." How true. This book is in a very real sense dedicated to those who do all the stuff. Here on the Island, there are many good people of strong values and stout hearts. Only some of them have the means to make significant donations of land for the public good. Only some have both the inclination and the land suitable for voluntary land protection agreements, i.e. conservation easements. Still others make their contributions in other ways. All have in common a commitment to acting according to their principles. They take small steps to deal with whatever confronts them.

These days Maine Coast Heritage Trust acts as a sort of elder sister to all the state land trusts bound together by their Maine Land Trust Network. With a national association, LTA, Land Trust Alliance, as a resource also, land trusts in general now have a broad base of experience and sufficient track record to be more understood. We have seen a past half century of the door swinging open to provide options for ordinary people, citizens of modest income who wanted to conserve land for future generations. Yes, perhaps we are also seeing the door swing shut on that era of individual citizen-based ecological philanthropy. There is so much pressure to develop every square inch!

We have just red squirrels and river otters, not gorillas or tigers or pandas. There are no spectacular redwoods here, rather red spruce and rhodora. We don't find penguins or quetzals here, just warblers and eiders. We are mostly pretty ordinary folks, natives and summer people alike. What we did here over that past half century did not require permission of a king or cooperation of a corporation. It was just a local effort, or rather a sweet series of independent and local efforts. That is precisely the story.

I say we were all ordinary, but that may or may not be so. The firm, gentle, constant glow of commitment that shines through these stories will guide us, lantern-like, as we confront issues affecting us today and our children tomorrow. It is what will guide landowners of the present and future as we explore using such tools as conservation easements to preserve our natural landscape in functioning ecological units. It will illuminate our struggle to find appropriate measures to deal with whatever the next challenges are.

Many of the people who live on the Island now have been all around the world, not unlike the days when the sailing ships took Islanders globe-circling. Having seen the rest, we choose to drop anchor here. Like them, we are conscious that we are all islands. I'm an island. Ann is an island, you are an island—and none of us are. We are all in the same sea with its tides and calms and storms. That is what this pilgrimage is about, what these narratives and photographs and poems are saying. But the essence of the experience, like the precise sound of a breaking wave, is beyond expressing in words or pictures. It's up to you to make that in your own heart.

The end of the story is never quite THE END.

Island Heritage Trust has now moved its headquarters to Heritage House. The floors in this handsome old house have been refinished, including the elegant parquet in the north parlor that is now the trust office. Plaster has been repaired and walls have fresh paint. The barn is now an insulated multi-purpose room with gallery lighting.

Judy Hill died in the spring of 2007. Just weeks before her death, Judy sent us a bunch of red tulips. The florist also made surprise visits to the trust office and to a number of Judy's friends on the Island. To the end, the aggressive brain tumor which attacked her physical brain failed to conquer her agile mind. Judy had asked that there be no service, but come spring you can see the blooms of red tulips planted in front of Heritage House and at the gate in the stone wall by her friends from both the trust and the historical society.

Maine Coast Heritage Trust repeated an increasingly successful practice that land trusts are using to deal with astronomically high land values. They sold a house lot at the upper edge of Scott's Landing meadow. The arrangement includes various protective covenants. The proud new owners of the lot are pleased to have been able to purchase such a fine place and not incidentally help the trusts. Revenue from the sale provides IHT with a stewardship endowment and completes successful preserve negotiations, to the delight of conservation buyers and donors. Another win-win.

A successful archeological field school led by Steve Cox at Scott's Landing found artifacts from periods spanning at least four thousand years. In addition to various tools, there were shell beads. Two pieces of worked bone are particularly interesting. One is decorated with diagonal bands and dots, and the other appears to represent the head of a fish. Apparently people gravitated to this lovely spot called "where the fish weirs are" and made art to wear, to use, to admire, and to enrich the spirit long before Haystack. Long may that continue.

Penobscot East Resource Center thrives and is actively helping fin fishermen pursue the strategy of local management, which has served the lobstermen so well. Penobscot East is forming a permit bank to buy up federal groundfish permits with a history of landings and days at sea so they can be held for communities in perpetuity. This permit bank will be called the Eastern Maine Sustainable Fisheries Trust. Our fishermen are learning that they have to work together if they are to become a force for maintaining any of the marine resource diversity. So essential. Decline of various stocks exceed the normal season to season fluctuation. Even lobster landings were down last year.

On the other hand, Deer Isle and Stonington clammers are now seeing an amazing resurgence of the flats thanks to the conservation and management efforts of the joint Shellfish Commission. According to Virginia Olsen, chairman, our Island harvesters recently brought $846,000.00 back into the Island economy. Add an economic spin-off of .07% and that number becomes $905,220.00.00 for the 2007 season.

The Opera House Arts dance production at Settlement Quarry, Quarryography, was a huge success. Rick Weed with his excavator partnering with the dance troupe enthralled audiences for three glorious days, four sold-out performances at the quarry.

Burnt Cove Church, still functioning for weddings and funerals, is actively being restored with the objective of making it available as a community resource. The efforts of Bob Williams, his son John, and Bob's wife Diane, are now pleasantly augmented. A board of trustees has been formed to lend a hand overseeing the judicious care of this jewel of a building. Bill Whitman, the cousin who recently bought Emily Muir's place, has added new energy to the endeavor. This Beads and String pilgrimage is indeed a story about interconnections.

Felsted was sold to Richard Spear of Cincinnati, Ohio. Rick and his wife Lisa had owned a house on Vinalhaven for fifteen years, but it was love at first sight when they saw Felsted starring on screen. Now they and their eight children and four grandsons come to their beloved Maine whenever they can. From their camping trailer David and Georgia Pashley supervised the building of their energy-efficient solar house next door.

Goose Cove Lodge was sold at a bankruptcy auction. We watch with great interest and hope that its future development will be sensitive to principles of responsible land use.

The Deer Isle-Stonington Historical Society has embarked on its expansion plan, using the land which Judy Hill's gift made available. With more space to work with, the society happily accepted the gift of the last of our Maine Indian baskets, and that has prompted others to come forth with gifts of old Indian baskets connected with the Island. David Pashley made a gift of the lobster pot buoys which washed up on the Felsted beach over some forty years. A wall-full of the colorful buoys and old bottle toggles now hangs on display. The fanciful bird and animal wood carvings by George Hardy, now displayed in Heritage House, seem to be having a similar magnet effect.

Hoorah for our heritage.

AUTHOR

Marnie Reed Crowell is a poet, biologist, and natural history writer whose publications include **Great Blue—The Odyssey of a Great Blue Heron** (Times Books) and **Greener Pastures** (Funk & Wagnalls) and Quick Keys for the Island Conservation Commissions. Marnie has written for public radio and television. Recently she was commissioned to write a poem for an opening ceremony of the Penobscot Narrows Bridge. Her articles have appeared in such magazines as *DownEast*, *Natural History*, *Redbook*, and *Readers Digest*. Marnie lives on Deer Isle.

PHOTOGRAPHER

Ann Flewelling has studied photography and related arts at The Southeastern School of Photographic Arts, The Maine Photographic Workshops, and Haystack Mountain School of Crafts. Her work is exhibited in area galleries. In 2008 Ann's photography was included in the "My Favorite Maine" show juried by Carl Little as well as the Maine Photography Show juried by Joyce Tenneson. A practicing clinical psychologist and a native Mainer, Ann makes her home along the Bagaduce River.

THREEHALF PRESS is a small independent press located in Sunset, Maine. It is dedicated to publishing artistic work that speaks on behalf of our natural environment. We invite you to view our works on line at www.threehalfpress.com.

A poem is a picture you hear,
a photograph is a poem you see.